STEP UP 成长 with CHINESE

TEXTBOOK 3

顾问： **张黎**
Consultant **Li Zhang**

美国教育专家 American Educators:

编者： **陈少元** **陶洁琳** **竹露茜** **谭大立** **高思畅**
Writers **Carol Chen-Lin** **Janice Dowd** **Lucy Chu Lee** **Dali Tan** **Sichang Gao**

北京语言大学 Beijing Language & Culture University:

陈丽霞 **张兰欣** **徐式婧** **王宏蕊**
Lixia Chen **Lanxin Zhang** **Shijing Xu** **Hongrui Wang**

CENGAGE Learning®

Australia • Brazil • Mexico • Singapore • United Kingdom • United States

CENGAGE
Learning

Step Up with Chinese Textbook 3

Publishing Director: Roy Lee

Editorial Manager, CLT: Zhao Lan

Associate Development Editor: Titus Teo

Senior Product Manager: Joyce Tan

Regional Manager, Production & Rights:
Pauline Lim

Senior Production Executive: Cindy Chai

Creative Manager: Melvin Chong

Compositor: Sok Ling Ong

For product information and technology assistance, contact us at
Cengage Learning Asia Customer Support, 65-6410-1200

For permission to use material from this text or product,
submit all requests online at
www.cengageasia.com/permissions
Further permissions questions can be emailed to
asia.permissionrequest@cengage.com

ISBN-13: 978-981-4455-19-0
ISBN-10: 981-4455-19-9

Cengage Learning Asia Pte Ltd
151 Lorong Chuan
#02-08 New Tech Park
Singapore 556741

Cengage Learning is a leading provider of customized learning solutions with office locations around the globe, including Singapore, the United Kingdom, Australia, Mexico, Brazil, and Japan. Locate your local office at **www.cengage.com/global**

Cengage Learning products are represented in Canada by
Nelson Education, Ltd.

For information on our Chinese language teaching products, visit
www.cengagechinese.com

To learn more about Cengage Learning Solutions, visit
www.cengageasia.com

Printed in Singapore
Print Number: 01   Print Year: 2015

Welcome to Step Up with Chinese!

Step Up with Chinese is an innovative, standards-based Chinese textbook series for high school students with little or no Chinese background. Highly learner-friendly and task-centered, *Step Up* develops all four language skills while incorporating the principles of ACTFL Five C's — Communication, Cultures, Connections, Comparisons, and Communities. Students will learn all the necessary material to engage others in meaningful communication and gain a better understanding of the Chinese culture

> "The instructional framework is EXCELLENT! It is nicely aligned with the National Standards." – *Jianhua Bai, Kenyon College*

This series consists of three volumes covering three years of instruction. Each volume includes a Textbook and a Workbook. Each textbook offers ten themed lessons that are structured around key communicative goals. The textbook features a clear, step-by-step approach to help students progress from small "steps" of language usage towards larger communicative goals. Instead of the traditional text-and-vocabulary grammar centered approach, each lesson is broken down into small chunks of patterns to learn and practice.

Students will get plenty of practice on new vocabulary and grammar. The activities have been carefully designed so that students develop confidence with the new material before moving to the next step. Each step builds upon previously learned vocabulary and sentence patterns in a systematic way. The integration section at the end of each chapter gives students the opportunity to synthesize and apply what they have learned in more challenging, authentic tasks, further reinforcing their interpretive, interpersonal and presentational skills.

> "I like the way this textbook organizes each chapter. The step-by-step approach makes each task very clear." – *Lihua Li, Berkeley Preparatory School*

The authors have interweaved a variety of cultural content, Chinese culture vis-a-vis Western culture, throughout the program — in the visuals, practice activities, readings, writing activities, cultural snippets and *Fun Time* section of each chapter, to foster students' cultural awareness from a global point of view. The program also reinforces language learning by making connections to students' prior knowledge, their personal experiences and other content areas that are relevant to them.

Step Up with Chinese provides ample support for students to gain a positive learning experience and to become a lifelong learner of Chinese.

> "This is a very up-to-date book that is very appropriate for high school students in the States. The students can really relate to a lot of scenes in the book and see their own lives in the book instead of just knowing someone else's life in China." – *Jie Lei, George C. Marshall High School*

Textbook

The Textbook contains information and activities that the student need for in-class use and self-study. Each textbook contains 10 lessons structured around key communicative goals, and covers topics of high interest and relevance to high school students. Each lesson opens with a clear learning agenda, and a warm-up activity to introduce the subject matter. Each lesson has several main communicative goals which are broken down into smaller steps to learn and practice. Each step comprises a vocabulary list, a grammar section with usage examples and explanation, related cultural snippets, and activities for grammar and language practice. Following the last step is an integration section offering more challenging, authentic activities that require students to synthesize and apply what they have learned; and a *Fun Time* section with theme-related, enjoyable material such as songs, poems and rhymes to extend learning. The lesson ends with a complete list of vocabulary and sentence patterns, and a self-assessment checklist.

Textbook 3 of the series introduces an American teenager, Ding Qiang (丁强), who has the opportunity to travel and live with a host family in China. Through Ding Qiang's eyes, students will get various glimpses into his life in China and his interactions with various members of his host family. Ding Qiang's experiences will cover many aspects of Chinese life (for example, traveling, academic life, shopping, entertainment, and festivals). He will learn about Chinese practices, products, and perspectives from conversations with different family members and friends of the family. Textbook 3 is characterized by longer texts in the form of dialogs, blog entries, and reading passages. These texts are intended to encourage students to enhance their reading comprehension and gain stronger literacy skills. The new sentences structures are interwoven into the texts to reinforce learning and to improve the students' communicative abilities.

"The text provides a lot of different ways for students to practice their reading, with ample pictures to maintain interest and mitigate character reading fatigue, always a challenge for younger learners of Chinese." – Adam Ross, Lakeside Upper School

Workbook

The Workbook offers a wide variety of exercise to give students ample practice of what they have learned in each lesson. There is a good balance of listening, speaking, reading and writing activities to keep students engaged in their learning process. Also included in the Workbook are two review test sets—one mid-term review and one final-term review. The Workbook audio program may be accessed from the companion website.

"Excellent! The workbook is one of the first I have reviewed that appears not to waste students' time. Each activity was based on a scenario, encouraged development of a new skill, or give students specific practice for subsequent class interaction." – Leslie Zimring, Summit School District

Companion Website http://stepup.cengageasia.com

The companion website is open to all students and no registration is required. Students can access the *Pinyin* pronunciation guide, complete text and workbook audio program, lesson-by-lesson interactive vocabulary flashcards and extra online practice activities. Instructors may register to download the complimentary instructors' resources including teaching suggestions, audio scripts and answer keys.

　　《成长》是一套具有开拓性的、专供初学者使用的中学中文教材。本教材的教学理念和目标是根据美国外语教学委员会 (ACTFL) 的国家语言教学标准 (5C) 制订的："沟通和交际能力 (Communication)"、"文化理解和体验能力 (Cultures)"、"与其他学科贯连的能力 (Connections)"、"语言、文化比较能力 (Comparisons)"和"在多元文化社区中学以致用的能力 (Communities)"。

　　《成长》分三级。每级有十个单元，可以在一个学年内完成。教材所应用的教学方法是循序渐进的，能帮助学生从最基本、简单的表达，慢慢提升到更长、更复杂的表达。和传统教材以"生词－课文－语法"为中心的教学方法不同，《成长》每一个单元的内容根据交际目标分解成几个大步骤，每个大步骤下面又有几个小步骤，这样既能降低初学者的学习难度，又能让学生打好基础、不断巩固所学。每一单元都经过了精心设计，同时融合了人际交往的三种模式 (语言沟通、理解诠释、表达演示)。

　　教材还在课文和活动中融入了许多中国传统与现代的文化内容，让学生可以更深入地了解中国、中国人、中国文化和中国习俗。课本里也安排了许多美国人熟悉的人物和场景，能够激发学生对用中文解释自己的本土文化产生兴趣。为了强化语言学习的效果，编者还在语言教学和其他学科之间设置了许多有意义的联系。

　　《成长》每一级教材都有课本和练习册。课本每单元开篇清楚列明学习目标，并通过热身活动导入正题。每个单元有几个主要教学步骤和交际目标。每个步骤都有一个生词表、语法解释、相关文化知识和练习。在主要步骤之后，设有综合练习和趣味活动，让学生能够延伸学习。单元末还列出该单元所介绍的所有生词和句型，以及一个自我评估表。课本附录则包括中英生词索引、主要句型表和中国地图。

　　第三级课本以美国学生丁强到北京留学一年的故事为主线，让学生通过他在中国所接触的人事物，学习关于旅游、教育、购物、娱乐、节日、中国艺术等丰富的内容。课本以对话、博文及阅读篇章的形式介绍不同课题、语言点和生词，借此提升学生的阅读及沟通交际能力。

　　练习册包括形式多样的练习题。听力练习通过录音片段训练学生的听力理解能力。情景活动培养学生在沟通交际和演示交际方面的口语表达能力。多样化的阅读篇章有助于培养学生的阅读理解能力。在书写能力方面，学生会练习以正确的笔顺书写生字词，并用中文回答各种形式的问题，例如简单的填充题以及更具挑战性的自由题。

　　教材还配有专门的学习网站 (http://stepup.cengageasia.com)，提供汉语拼音总表、互动式词卡、课本和练习册录音 (mp3)、额外的网上练习以及教师辅助资源 (包括教师手册、课本和练习册录音稿和参考答案等等)。

　　《成长》可让学生积极、有效地学习中文，掌握应用中文的技能，并培养他们终身学习中文的兴趣。

STEP UP 成长 with CHINESE 3

CONTENTS

VI

VII

STEP UP with CHINESE 3 成长

交际目标 Communicative Goals	主要步骤 Main Steps	核心词汇 Core Vocabulary	语言点 Language Focus

1 ◆ My journey to China   我的中国行

◆ 描述地方 Describing places	**Step 1** **到中国旅游** Visiting China	1. 机场入境 Airport arrivals	1. 谁会来机场接你? 王叔叔会来接机。
◆ 表达对交通状况的看法 Stating one's opinions on traffic conditions	**Step 2** **从一个地方到另一个** **地方** Traveling from Place to Place	2. 旅游观光 Sightseeing	2. 天安门广场非常大。 故宫十分壮观。
◆ 叙述出游行程的顺序 Expressing the sequence of travel		3. 程度副词 Degree adverbs	3. 如果不是有事,还是不要 在早晚高峰出行。
◆ 表达对交通工具的选择 Stating one's preference on modes of transportation	**Step 3** **出游住宿** Places to Stay	4. 交通状况 Traffic conditions	4. 对他来说,他早已经习惯 北京的交通状况了。
◆ 描述行程和地点 Describing a route and relative locations		5. 北京和上海的名胜地 Places in Beijing and Shanghai	5. 从月坛朝西走是玉渊潭 公园。
			6. 我一到上海就去旅店办 入住手续。

2 ◆ My host family in China   我的寄宿家庭

◆ 谈论家庭生活 Conversing with others about family life	**Step 1** **成为家庭的一员** Becoming Part of the Family	1. 中文亲属称谓 Chinese kinship terms	1. 丁强,你好! 你来啦!快进来!
◆ 描述不同时段所发生的事 Explaining events that occurred in different time frames	**Step 2** **家庭聚会** Gathering the Family Together	2. 社区服务 Community service	2. 我没吃过北京烤鸭。 大家一边吃着饭,一边 讨论北京生活的趣事。 我在那里买了很多衣服。
◆ 陈述物品的概数 Stating an approximate quantity of items		3. 欢庆春节的相关词语 Chinese New Year celebrations	3. 你还会见到我好几个亲 戚。
◆ 比较人们做某事的能力 Comparing how well people do an activity	**Step 3** **参与社区活动** Being a Part of the Neighborhood		4. 每个周末,大家再忙也 要和亲人聚在一起吃饭。
◆ 表达对社区服务的看法 Stating one's opinions on community service			5. 我们有的会去敬老院陪 老人聊天,有的会去农村 给"留守儿童"补课。
			6. 这里的活动比那里的多。

SCOPE AND SEQUENCE

文化知识 Cultural Knowledge	贯连和比较 Connections and Comparisons	任务和实践 Tasks and Community Applications

1

| 1. 中国各地区
Geographical regions of China

2. 北京的名胜古迹
Attractions in Beijing

3. 上海的景点及磁悬浮列车
Attractions in Shanghai and the Shanghai Maglev Train | 地理 Geography:
• 中国大陆的地理地区划分
Different geographical regions in mainland China

看地图 Map Reading:
• 北京和上海地图上的著名地标
The relative locations of famous landmarks on the maps of Beijing and Shanghai

音乐 Music:
• 《我家住在北京城》
A song on Beijing city | 1. 两人一组：看登机牌，然后根据牌上的信息进行问答。
Pair work: Read a boarding pass and ask and answer questions on information on the pass.

2. 写一篇博文，谈谈家乡的交通状况。
Write a blog entry about the traffic in your hometown.

3. 给家人安排一个中国十日游。搜集相关资料，然后制订一个详尽的行程表。
Organize a 10-day trip to China for your family. Research the information and create a detailed itinerary with information on the cities and the sites within those cities. |

30

| 1. 在家或外出用餐
Eating at home or in a restaurant

2. 中文敬称
Chinese honorific titles

3. 客套话
Polite expressions

4. 中国的庙会
Chinese temple fairs | 数学 Mathematics:
• 学生参与不同社区活动的图表
Bar graph and pie chart of students doing different community work

家政 Home Economics:
• 炸酱面的食谱
The recipe of a famous Beijing food — Zhajiangmian

比较 Comparison:
• 各国关于拜访他人的习俗
Customs in different countries on visiting someone's house | 1. 根据阅读篇章，做一份家谱。
Draw a family tree based on the description in the reading passage.

2. 小组活动：讨论不同的社区活动，并谈谈自己参与社区活动的经历。
Group work: Discuss different types of community work and state whether you have done it before.

3. 制作一张给华人移民提供服务的宣传单，其中包括教育服务或保健信息等服务。
Create a brochure about the services for Chinese immigrants who are moving to your community. You may focus on educational services, health information, or any other possible services that are available in your community. |

交际目标 Communicative Goals	主要步骤 Main Steps	核心词汇 Core Vocabulary	语言点 Language Focus

3 ◆ My learning experience　　我的学习经验

◆ 描述课外活动 Describing after school activities ◆ 谈论学业压力及考试 Conversing about homework pressures and examinations ◆ 谈论焦虑与期望 Conversing about worries and expectations ◆ 比较作业量和大学入学考试 Comparing the homework load and college entrance examinations	Step 1 参与中国的学习生活 Participating in Academic Life in China Step 2 培养技能 Developing Skills Step 3 面对期望与应付压力 Meeting Expectations and Dealing with Pressure	1. 表动作频率 Adverbs of frequency 2. 和学业相关的词语 Studies-related vocabulary 3. 和压力相关的词语 Stress-related vocabulary	1. 我看你的功课太多了，常常周末也在做作业。 2. 只有考到好成绩，才能进入理想的大学。 3. 学生每天不是在学校上课，就是去上课外补习班。 4. 每天即使没有钢琴课，我也会在家练习。 5. 这个星期的作业很多，你做得完吗？ 6. 由于学生不想辜负父母和老师的期望，所以每天早起晚睡，努力学习。

4 ◆ Shopping in Chinese markets　　在中国市场购物

◆ 谈论商品与服务的价格 Conversing about the prices of goods and services ◆ 讲价 Bargaining to get the best deals ◆ 讨论在商场购物和网上购物的优缺点 Discussing advantages and disadvantages of in-store and online shopping ◆ 描述一次购物体验 Describing a shopping experience ◆ 描述讲价策略与步骤 Describing bargaining strategies and procedures	Step 1 购物和讲价 Shopping and Bargaining Step 2 购买物品 Purchasing New Articles Step 3 了解消费主义 Understanding Consumerism	1. 人民币 Chinese currency 2. 讲价 Bargaining 3. 中国特色产品 Chinese specialty products 4. 和购物相关的词语 Shopping-related vocabulary	1. 这双蓝色的运动鞋多少钱？原价 400 块。现在我们有促销。 2. 50 块太贵了！25 块卖不卖？ 3. 我想看看这件蓝色的上衣。 4. 只要学会讨价还价，就能买到价廉物美的商品。 5. 网购除了节省时间以外，东西也比较便宜。 6. 我一共花了 300 元。什么打折我就买什么。

1. 科举制
The imperial examination

2. 中国的辅导班
Private tutoring in China

3. 中国的评分制
Chinese grading system

教育 Education:
- 中国、美国以及其他国家的教育制度

  The education system in China, the United States, and other countries.

比较 Comparison:
- 四个国家（日本、韩国、中国和美国）的家长对孩子的期望

  Parents' expectations for children's success in four different countries (Japan, Korea, China, and the United States)

1. 调查：找出同学们从最常做到最不常做的活动，然后向全班汇报调查结果。

   Survey: Find out the activities that classmates do, from most frequent to least frequent. Present the results orally to the class.

2. 给寄宿家庭写一则电邮，谈谈你参加的数学营以及它的高强度时间表。

   Write an email to your host family about a math camp you are attending and its intense class schedule.

3. 两人一组：讨论中国和美国教育制度的优缺点。

   Pair work: With a partner, discuss the strengths and weaknesses of the education system in China and the United States.

1. 讲价的技巧与步骤
Bargaining skills and procedures

2. 中国丝绸
Chinese silk

3. 中国消费主义
Chinese consumerism

4. 中国特产
Chinese specialty products

文字游戏 Word Game:
- 字谜

  Chinese riddles

比较 Comparison:
- 在中国和自身文化里所使用的讲价策略

  Bargaining strategies used in China and in your own culture

1. 跟一位同学描述你经历过的一次愉快的购物体验，形容一下给你留下深刻印象的商品或服务。

   Tell a classmate about a pleasant retail experience that you had, describing the goods or services that left an impression on you.

2. 情景演练：和另一位同学扮演一个讲价的情景，一个当店主，另一个当顾客。

   Role play: With a partner, role play a bargaining scenario in which one is a shop owner and the other is a customer.

3. 为学校杂志的中国交流特辑写一篇题为"如何在中国购买衣物时讲价"的文章。

   Write an entry on the topic "How to bargain while shopping for clothes in China" for the special column of your school Chinese magazine.

交际目标 Communicative Goals	主要步骤 Main Steps	核心词汇 Core Vocabulary	语言点 Language Focus

5 Maintaining health and fitness — 健康与运动

交际目标	主要步骤	核心词汇	语言点
◆ 描述如何过健康的生活 Explaining how to create a healthy lifestyle ◆ 劝告他人不要做某事 Advising someone not to do something ◆ 利用助动词表示能力、许可与必要性 Expressing ability, permission, and necessity ◆ 表达活动的次数与时间长短 Describing frequency and duration of activities	**Step 1** 谈论健康课题 Discussing Health Issues **Step 2** 通过运动强身健体 Keeping Fit Through Exercise **Step 3** 分析替代疗法和健身 Analyzing Alternative Treatment and Fitness	1. 各种运动 Different types of exercises 2. 健康与保健 Health and fitness 3. 替代疗法 Alternative medicine and therapy	1. 我们都叫你别熬夜了，你就是不听。 2. 睡眠不但可以消除疲劳，而且可以提高人体的抵抗力。 3. 我在美国每周健身三四次。 4. 我已经报名参加今年的北京铁人三项比赛了。 5. 既然丁强喜欢喝汤，以后我就多做一些有营养的汤给你喝。 6. 看到自己被朋友们超越了，我会再出去走一圈。

6 Meeting the challenges of modern life — 面对现代生活的挑战

交际目标	主要步骤	核心词汇	语言点
◆ 表达积极的生活态度 Describing a positive attitude ◆ 解释如何与他人相处 Explaining how to get along with others ◆ 分析以及描述如何化解冲突 Analyzing and resolving conflicts ◆ 利用反问句强调某事 Emphasizing a point using rhetorical questions ◆ 进一步说明某事 Making clarifications	**Step 1** 面对现代生活的压力 Experiencing the Pressures of Modern Life **Step 2** 培养积极的心态 Developing a Positive Mindset **Step 3** 寻找解决方法 Finding Solutions	1. 现代生活的压力 Pressures of modern life 2. 正面的思想 Positive thinking 3. 冲突与解决方法 Conflicts and solutions	1. 我们好像永远都在跟时间赛跑，做什么事都离不开一个"快"字。 2. 功课这么多，这个周末恐怕哪儿都不去也应付不过来。 3. 不管失败多少次，他都不会放弃。 4. 难道你没看见我们在忙吗？ 5. 我不是身体不舒服，而是心里不舒服。 6. 父母越管孩子，孩子越想反抗。

文化知识
Cultural Knowledge

贯连和比较
Connections and Comparisons

任务和实践
Tasks and Community Applications

123

1. 五行说
   The Five Elements Theory

2. 中国武术
   Chinese martial arts —
   Wushu

3. 中国大妈跳广场舞
   Square dancing by *damas*

4. 李时珍
   The medicine of
   Li Shizhen

5. 手部按摩
   Relaxation with hand
   massage

健康 Health:
- 瑜伽的不同姿势
  Different yoga postures

比较 Comparison:
- 五行说与体液学说
  The Theory of Five Elements and the Theory
  of Humors

1. 根据不同学生的健康问题，制订每日半小时
   的健身计划，帮助他们修建肌肉。
   Study the various profiles of students with different
   physical conditions and write up a half hour daily
   workout to help students rebuild their muscles.

2. 访问一位同学，了解他/她参与各项运动的
   情况。
   Interview one of your classmates to determine his/her
   involvement in different physical activities.

3. 设计一份传单或者小册子，介绍自己开办
   的一家新健身中心，说明所提供的服务以
   及收费。
   Create a flyer or brochure to advertise your new
   fitness center, including information on the types of
   services that will be provided and their prices.

1. 中国著名企业家：
   马云
   Famous Chinese
   entrepreneur — Jack Ma

2. 社交媒体：微信
   The social media of
   WeChat

3. 中国文化中关于
   和谐的思想
   Harmony in Chinese
   culture

压力管理 Stress Management:
- 如何消除压力
  Ways to eliminate stress

正面的思想 Positive Thinking:
- 关于从失败中学习以及拥有积极态度
  的故事
  Inspirational stories on learning from failure
  and having a positive attitude

冲突管理 Conflict Management:
- 如何化解冲突
  Ways to resolve conflicts

1. 调查：问同学们他们在生活中最离不开的
   事物是什么。
   Survey: Find out from your classmates what is the
   most important thing that they cannot live without in
   modern life.

2. 情景演练：一个同学遭遇挫折，另一个同
   学鼓励他/她不要灰心，继续努力。
   Role play: With a partner, act out a scenario in which
   one of you encountered a setback (lost a competition,
   failed a test, etc.) and another tries to encourage him/
   her not to be affected and to continue to press on.

3. 制作一个海报，提供如何化解冲突的建议。
   Create a poster that provides suggestions as to how
   people can resolve conflicts.

交际目标 Communicative Goals	主要步骤 Main Steps	核心词汇 Core Vocabulary	语言点 Language Focus

7　My favorite Chinese entertainment　中国的娱乐

交际目标 Communicative Goals	主要步骤 Main Steps	核心词汇 Core Vocabulary	语言点 Language Focus
◆ 谈论中国的电视、音乐和电影 Talking about TV shows, concerts, and movies in China ◆ 描述名人 Describing famous celebrities ◆ 劝告他人并解释后果 Giving advice to someone and explaining consequences ◆ 表达对电影的喜好 Expressing movie preferences	Step 1 观看中文电视节目 Viewing Chinese TV Entertainment Step 2 听中文音乐 Listening to Chinese Music Step 3 看中文电影 Going to Chinese Movies	1. 中文电视节目 Chinese TV programs 2. 歌曲和音乐 Songs and music 3. 和电影相关的词语 Movie-related vocabulary	1. 只要愿意认真地唱歌，普通人也能成为明星。 2. 这些综艺节目都很受欢迎，连孩子都成了它们的粉丝。 3. 她的歌听起来旋律很优美。 4. 第一次听这首歌，我就被它吸引住了。 5. 尽管是一年多以前看的，印象还是很深刻。 6. 李阿姨不让子明常看好莱坞电影，以免分心影响功课。

8　Celebrations in China　一起来庆祝

交际目标 Communicative Goals	主要步骤 Main Steps	核心词汇 Core Vocabulary	语言点 Language Focus
◆ 谈论生日、中国节日及婚礼 Conversing with others about birthday celebrations, Chinese festivals, and weddings ◆ 描述传统节日及其庆祝方式 Describing traditional festivals and their celebrations ◆ 比较生日、婚礼及其他节庆的异同 Comparing similarities and differences in birthdays, weddings, and other celebrations ◆ 邀请与回复 Extending invitations and responding to invitations in culturally appropriate ways	Step 1 庆祝生日 Observing Birthdays Step 2 欢庆中国传统节日 Enjoying Major Traditional Chinese Festivals Step 3 经历人生重要里程碑 Experiencing Milestones in Life	1. 庆祝生日 Birthday celebrations 2. 中国传统节日 Traditional Chinese festivals 3. 婚礼与习俗 Weddings and customs	1. 今天学校为三月过生日的同学办了一个集体生日会。 2. 王叔叔一家人请丁强吃饭。他们送了他一把吉他。 3. 中国人把农历五月初五定为端午节。 4. 春节时，人们把家里打扫得干干净净。 5. 我想请你参加我的婚礼。 谢谢你的邀请，我一定出席。 6. 无论将来怎么样，我们都有信心去微笑面对。

文化知识 Cultural Knowledge	贯连和比较 Connections and Comparisons	任务和实践 Tasks and Community Applications
		178
1. 李安和张艺谋 Famous Chinese movie directors — Ang Lee and Zhang Yimou 2. 王菲和周杰伦 Famous Chinese pop singers — Faye Wong and Jay Chou 3. 卡拉OK Karaoke 4. 新歌唱组合：TFBoys The new Chinese singing group: TFBoys	音乐 Music: • 中文歌曲欣赏 Chinese song appreciation 比较 Comparison: • 中国和美国的真人实境秀 TV reality shows in China and the United States	1. 调查：问同学喜欢哪些类型的电影，然后向全班汇报调查结果。 Survey: Find out what types of movies your classmates like. Record your findings and present them to the class. 2. 情景演练：劝告一个沉迷于追星的朋友，建议他/她好好安排与利用时间。 Role play: With a partner, act out a scenario in which one of you is the person who has spent too much time on the life of a singer and the other is the person offering advice on how to manage and balance time wisely. 3. 制作简报，介绍你最喜欢的歌星或影星。 Make a set of presentation slides introducing your favorite singer or movie star.
		206
1. 中国传统节日 Chinese traditional holidays and festivals 2. 中国节日中物品的象征意义 Symbolic meanings of items used in Chinese festivals 3. 敬老 Chinese respect for the aged 4. 过寿与婚礼 Chinese birthdays and wedding celebrations 5. 送礼 The Chinese practice of gift-giving	庆祝 Celebration: • 生日、节日、婚礼、毕业典礼 Birthdays, festivals, weddings, and graduations 比较 Comparison: • 中国和美国的婚礼和生日习俗 Wedding and birthday customs in China and the United States	1. 两人一组：向同学描述一次为他人办庆祝会的经历。 Pair work: Tell a partner about an experience in which you organized a celebration for someone. 2. 邀请同学参加生日会，让他们回复是否会参加。 Invite your classmates to your birthday celebration and have them respond by indicating whether or not they will attend. 3. 根据一首关于母爱的中文诗，写一篇关于母爱/父爱的文章，并把这首中文诗和另一篇美国名人的相关作品进行比较。 Write an article on maternal/paternal love by making references to a Chinese poem on maternal love and comparing the Chinese poem with another poem/article by a famous American.

交际目标 Communicative Goals	主要步骤 Main Steps	核心词汇 Core Vocabulary	语言点 Language Focus

9 ❖ Chinese cultural treasures — 中国文化珍宝

交际目标 Communicative Goals	主要步骤 Main Steps	核心词汇 Core Vocabulary	语言点 Language Focus
◆ 介绍中国画家和书法家 Describing Chinese painters and calligraphers ◆ 比较不同艺术作品的特点 Comparing and contrasting different art works ◆ 按时间顺序连接事件 Sequencing events in a timeline ◆ 表达因果关系 Demonstrating consequential ideas	Step 1 中国国画 Chinese Paintings Step 2 中国书法 Chinese Calligraphy Step 3 中国表演艺术 Chinese Performing Arts	1. 描述绘画作品 Describing paintings 2. 中国书法 Chinese calligraphy 3. 京剧 Peking opera	1. 国画既是中国的国粹，也是世界的珍宝。 2. 徐悲鸿的马虽然细节上不如素描那么具体，但是马的生命力却体现得非常到位。 3. 凡是学书法的人，都要有"文房四宝"。 4. 为了把字练好，王羲之每天都练习书法。 5. 就算是中国人，也不一定听得懂京剧。 6. 梅兰芳能把花旦的角色演得很好，因此非常有名。

10 ❖ The changing society in China — 变化中的中国社会

交际目标 Communicative Goals	主要步骤 Main Steps	核心词汇 Core Vocabulary	语言点 Language Focus
◆ 谈论新科技给生活带来的改变 Discussing changing lifestyles because of new technology ◆ 表达和分析对城市问题的解决方案的看法 Stating and analyzing opinions on solutions to problems in urban life ◆ 描述以前与现在的经历 Describing one's past and current experiences ◆ 表达自己目前的决定与未来的理想 Expressing and explaining one's current decisions and aspirations for the future	Step 1 使用新科技 Using Modern Technology Step 2 体验中国的生活变化 Experiencing Lifestyle Changes in China Step 3 实现我的中国梦 Realizing my Chinese Dream	1. 数码时代 The digital age 2. 环境问题 Environmental issues 3. 城市问题 Urban issues	1. 有的人宁可在家里和朋友网上聊天，也不愿意出门和朋友面对面交流。 2. 面对面有面对面的优点，而微信聊天则有微信聊天的好处。 3. 大家再不正视环境污染问题，我们的健康就会受到很大的影响。 4. 北京必须改变现状，要不然交通拥挤问题会更加严重。 5. 自从来到中国，我就越来越喜欢这里的风土人情了。 6. 我希望将来可以在北京工作。

文化知识 Cultural Knowledge	贯连和比较 Connections and Comparisons	任务和实践 Tasks and Community Applications

1. 北京798艺术区 Beijing 798 Art Zone 2. 印章与篆刻 Seals and seal engraving 3. 中国著名小说家与 剧作家：老舍 Famous Chinese novelist and dramatist — Lao She 4. 中国国画 Chinese paintings 5. 中国书法 Chinese calligraphy 6. 中国表演艺术 Chinese performing arts 7. 清明上河图 Famous Chinese Painting — *Along the River During the Qingming Festival*	艺术 The Arts: • 国画、书法、相声和京剧 Painting, calligraphy, crosstalk, and Peking opera 比较 Comparison: • 弗雷德里克和徐悲鸿的画作 Horse paintings by Frederic Remington and Xu Beihong	1. 比较两幅关于马的画作，然后写两段文字，说明两幅画的异同。 Compare and contrast horse paintings and write two paragraphs about what you see in the paintings and how they are similar and different. 2. 搜集一位自己感兴趣的中国艺术家的资料，然后向全班介绍他/她的作品和成就。 Research a Chinese artist that you are interested in and introduce him/her to the class by describing his/her works and major accomplishments. 3. 为一家新开的中国博物馆的其中一个展区制作一个虚拟游览，介绍国画、书法或京剧。 Create a virtual tour of one wing of a new Chinese museum, showcasing painting, calligraphy, or Chinese opera.

1. 中国的数字化原生 世代 China's digital natives 2. 中国政府如何应付污 染问题 The Chinese government's response to pollution 3. 中国的公共电话 Public telephones in China 4. 中国的地铁系统 The Chinese subway system 5. 中国未来的发展 China's future developments	科技 Technology: • 数码时代的生活 Life in the digital age 地理 Geography: • 环境与城市问题 Environmental and urban issues in China 数学 Mathematics: • 中国各城市与各省的数码公民 Statistics of digital citizens across cities and provinces in China 比较 Comparison: • 中国梦和美国梦 The Chinese dream and the American dream	1. 调查：问至少五个同学他们对科技、互联网以及社交媒体在现代生活中的角色有什么看法。 Interview: Survey at least five of your classmates to find out their views on the role of technology, the Internet, and social media in modern life. Report your findings to the class. 2. 情景演练：一个同学沉迷于互联网或科技产品，另一个同学劝告他/她不要再沉迷下去了。 Role play: Act out a scenario with a partner in which one of you is the friend who is addicted to the Internet or a technological gadget and another of you tries to warn him/her by highlighting the consequences if he/she continues to indulge in this practice. 3. 根据两篇毕业演讲词，写一篇博文/网志，谈谈学到了什么，以及演讲词里的建议如何指引学习、工作与未来的生活。 Write a blog entry to explain what you have learned from two commencement speeches and how the advice from the two speeches will help to guide you in your study, work, and future life.

XVII

Temple of Heaven, Beijing

My journey to China

我的中国行

COMMUNICATIVE GOALS

- Describing places
- Stating one's opinions on traffic conditions
- Expressing the sequence of travel
- Stating one's preference on modes of transportation
- Describing a route and relative locations

Cultural Knowledge

- Geographical regions of China
- Attractions in Beijing
- Attractions in Shanghai and the Shanghai Maglev Train

The story: John and some of his classmates have begun their journey to China on a student exchange program. His Chinese teacher had given him a Chinese name, 丁强, which he will use in China. John will study in a local school in Beijing for a year and will live with a Chinese host family, the Wangs. We will join him in this exciting adventure of learning and discovery.

John has just arrived in Beijing Capital International Airport (北京首都国际机场 Běijīng Shǒudū Guójì Jīchǎng) and is required to fill out an arrival card. Passengers can choose to fill out the card in either Chinese or English. John has filled out the card in Chinese. In pairs, use the information on the arrival card to answer the questions on the next page in Chinese.

0000012345

外国人入境卡 Arrival Card

姓 Family name	Dinh	名 Given name	John
国籍 Nationality	美国	护照号码 Passport no.	123456789

男 Male [X]　女 Female [ ]

在华住址 Address in China	北京市西城区南大街 28 号 12 楼 1035 室

入境事由（只能填写一项）Purpose of visit (one only):

出生日期 Date of birth	年 Year 1998	月 Month 12	日 Day 08

签证号码 Visa no.	F2965520

签证签发地 Place of visa issuance	纽约

航班号 Flight no.	UA7620

Purpose		
会议/商务 Conference/Business [ ]	访问 Visit [ ]	观光/休闲 Sightseeing/leisure [ ]
探亲访友 Visiting friends or relatives [ ]	就业 Employment [ ]	学习 Study [X]
返回常住地 Returning home [ ]	定居 Settling down [ ]	其他 Others [ ]

以上申明真实准确 I hereby declare that the information given above is true and accurate.

SAMPLE

签名 Signature: *John Dinh*

Beijing Capital International Airport

这个人是谁？

他是哪国人？

他今年多大？

他是怎么来中国的？

他来中国做什么？

他在哪儿得到签证？

qiānzhèng
visa

他到中国以后住哪儿？

STEP 1

VISITING CHINA

A. Arriving in China

谁会来机场接你？

王叔叔会来接机。

B. Exploring famous sites

天安门广场非常大。

故宫十分壮观。

STEP 2

TRAVELING FROM PLACE TO PLACE

A. Describing modes of transportation

如果不是有事，还是不要在早晚
高峰出行。

B. Talking about traffic conditions

对他来说，他早已经习惯北京的
交通状况了。

STEP 3

PLACES TO STAY

A. Explaining locations

从月坛朝西走是玉渊潭公园。

B. Describing my itinerary

我一到上海就去旅店办入住手续。

VISITING CHINA

A Arriving in China

丁强 is talking with one of his classmates, 张安, as they get off the plane.

Questions with interrogative pronouns

张安：谁会来机场接你？	Who
丁强：王叔叔会来接机。	
张安：他怎么接你去他家？	How
丁强：他会开车接我去他家。	
张安：办理入境手续需要什么证件？	What
丁强：需要护照、签证和入境卡。	
张安：边检在哪儿？	Where
丁强：往前走，向右拐。	
张安：昨天马克的班机是什么时候到达的？	When
丁强：他的班机延误了一个小时，九点差一刻才到。	
张安：他的班机为什么延误？	Why
丁强：因为天气不好，所以延误了。	

Pinyin	Simplified	Traditional	English
jīchǎng	机场 n.	機場	airport
jiējī	接机 v.	接機	pick up at the airport
bànlǐ	办理 v.	辦理	handle
rùjìng	入境 n.		arrivals
shǒuxù	手续 n.	手續	procedure
zhèngjiàn	证件 n.	證件	documents
hùzhào	护照 n.	護照	passport
qiānzhèng	签证 n.	簽證	visa
rùjìngkǎ	入境卡 n.		arrival card
biānjiǎn	边检 n.	邊檢	immigration control
bānjī	班机 n.	班機	flight
dàodá	到达 v.	到達	arrive, reach
yánwù	延误 v.	延誤	delay

↑→ 🧳🧍 边检
← 🧳🧳 行李提取处
↑ 🏠 免税店
→ 🚻 卫生间

张安：行李提取处离这里远吗？

丁强：不远，你看，向左拐就到了。

张安：我们的行李在二号转盘还是
　　　三号转盘？

丁强：在三号转盘。

张安：免税店的东西贵不贵？

丁强：我觉得应该不贵。

张安：我想去看看，你要不要
　　　一起去？

丁强：王叔叔可能在外面等着我，
　　　所以我不去了。

张安：好。这里有没有行李车？

丁强：有，就在那边。

xínglǐ tíqǔ chù 行李提取处 n.	行李提取處	baggage claim
zhuǎnpán 转盘 n.	轉盤	carousel (for luggage)
miǎnshuìdiàn 免税店 n.	免税店	duty free shop
xínglǐ chē 行李车 n.	行李車	luggage cart

LANGUAGE FOCUS: REVIEW

You have learned the five Wh- question words (谁, 什么, 在哪儿, 什么时候, 为什么) and H-questions (怎么, 几, 多少) and also have learned how to use them in Chinese. Review these question words and other ways to form questions in Chinese: placing 吗 at the end of the sentence, using 还是 for choice-type questions, or using the pattern "Adj + 不 + Adj," "V + 不 + V," or "V + 没 + V" to form affirmative-negative questions. Read the examples below and try to figure out the meaning. Question words are marked in red.

Examples:
❶ 王叔叔是谁？
❷ 免税店里有什么东西？
❸ 行李提取处在哪儿？
❹ 他的班机什么时候到达？
❺ 班机为什么延误了？
❻ 怎么办理入境手续？
❼ 今天几月几号？

❽ 你有多少件行李？
❾ 请问这是你的行李吗？
❿ 你喜欢坐飞机还是坐火车？
⓫ 这里的边检快不快？
⓬ 你要不要行李推车？
⓭ 你有没有入境卡？

1. Study the following schedule for incoming flights into Beijing and answer the questions in Chinese.

	Present time:	07:40	
hángbānhào 航班号 Flight number	chūfādì 出发地 From	yùjì 预计 Scheduled time	zhuàngtài 状态 Status
UA7617	洛杉矶 (LAX)	06:30	到达
AF128	巴黎 (CDG)	06:45	到达
SQ800	新加坡 (SIN)	06:50	到达
BA39	伦敦 (LHR)	07:05	延误
BR716	台北 (TPE)	07:12	延误
CA108	香港 (HKG)	07:18	到达

❶ 哪几个班机延误了？

❷ 哪几个班机到达了？

❸ 从台北来的班机延误了多久？

❹ 六点三刻到达的那个航班是从哪儿来的？

⑤ gàoshìpái
告示牌上的班机是不是都到达了？
board

2. Read the following dialog and decide if the following statements are true (对) or false (错).

丁强在机场边检办理入境手续。

工作人员：先生，您好！

丁 强：您好！

工作人员：您从哪里来？

丁 强：美国华盛顿。

工作人员：您做什么工作？

丁 强：我是学生。

工作人员：您来中国做什么？

丁 强：我来中国学习和旅游。

工作人员：在中国多久？

丁 强：一年。

工作人员：好，这是您的护照，欢迎您来中国！

丁 强：谢谢，再见。

❶ 丁强是从美国芝加哥来的。 对 / 错　　❹ 他打算在中国住半年。 对 / 错

❷ 他是学生。 对 / 错　　❺ 他在办理入境手续。 对 / 错

❸ 他来中国学习和工作。 对 / 错

3. Read the boarding pass. With a partner, ask and answer questions on who the pass holder is, where she is from, where she is traveling to, the travel date, the boarding time and gate, and if she travels often. Feel free to use your imagination to elaborate on the traveling information.

谁　哪儿　多久　什么　几　吗

Example: 她叫什么名字？她叫李红。

登 机 牌 BOARDING PASS					登 机 牌 BOARDING PASS
航班 FLIGHT **3U 8872**	日期 DATE **20 JUN**	舱位 CLASS **R**	序号 SERIAL NO. **010**	座位号 SEAT NO. **12D**	航班 FLIGHT **3U 8872**
目的地 TO **CHENGDU**		出发地 FROM **TAIYUAN**	登机口 GATE **G12**	登机时间 BDT **2100**	日期 DATE **20 JUN**
姓名 NAME **LI HONG** **李红**		身份识别 ID NO. **NI234567891234987600**			目的地 TO **CHENGDU**
		票号 TKT NO.			座位号 **12D**
					常旅客 FQT **ETKT**
登机口于起飞前10分钟关闭 GATES CLOSE 10 MINUTES BEFORE DEPARTURE TIME					

Blog

在北京的第一个周末，我去了几个地方。前门大街很<u>热闹</u>，天安门广场非常大。后来我买了门票去了故宫。故宫<u>十分</u><u>壮观</u>，地方也<u>特别</u>大，我在里头走了一<u>整</u>天。<u>最后</u>我买了一些<u>纪念品</u>，打算送给朋友。

Qiánmén Dàjiē 前门大街 *p.n.*	前門大街	Qianmen Street
rènao 热闹 *adj.*	熱鬧	bustling, lively
Tiān'ānmén Guǎngchǎng 天安门广场 *p.n.*	天安門廣場	Tiananmen Square
ménpiào 门票 *n.*	門票	admission ticket
Gùgōng 故宫 *p.n.*	故宮	Forbidden City
shífēn 十分 *adv.*		especially
zhuàngguān 壮观 *adj.*	壯觀	magnificent
tèbié 特别 *adv.*		particularly
zhěng 整 *adj.*		whole, entire
zuìhòu 最后 *n.*		final, last
jìniànpǐn 纪念品 *n.*	紀念品	souvenir

EXTENDED VOCABULARY

Sightseeing

游览 v.	遊覽	yóulǎn	sightsee
旅客 n.		lǚkè	traveler
风景 n.	風景	fēngjǐng	scenery

Degree adverbs

真 adv.		zhēn	truly
多 adv.		duō	much, so

Describing places or sceneries

优美 adj.	優美	yōuměi	fine, graceful, beautiful	古老 adj.		gǔlǎo	ancient
秀丽 adj.	秀麗	xiùlì	beautiful, pretty	庄严 adj.	莊嚴	zhuāngyán	solemn
迷人 adj.		mírén	mesmerizing	美丽 adj.	美麗	měilì	beautiful
雄伟 adj.	雄偉	xióngwěi	grand				

LANGUAGE FOCUS

When describing people, places, and things, there are a number of adverbs that you can use to intensify your description. We have already learned how to use 很, 太, and 非常. In this lesson we introduce words for truly (真), so (多), especially (十分), and particularly (特别). These words are adverbs because they can modify an adjective and they indicate the degree of intensity. Read the following sentences and observe the placement and meaning of these adverbs.

Examples:

❶ 长城真壮观！ (Chángchéng)

❷ 你看，故宫多雄伟啊！ (Gùgōng)

❸ 颐和园真是太迷人了！ (Yíhéyuán)

❹ 这里的风景美极了！

❺ 这条街人很多，十分热闹！

❻ 这个地方的交通特别方便！

1. Refer to the pictures in Cultural Highlights on page 10 and describe them in full sentences using an appropriate adjective and an adverb of degree (真, 多, 十分, or 特别).

   For example, for the first picture of the Great Wall, you can say: 长城特别壮观。

2. With a partner, make a sentence stating a place you have been to and when, and another sentence describing that place using an appropriate degree adverb.

   Example: 我上个月去了加拿大。那里的风景十分优美。

Different Regions in Mainland China

Mainland China can be divided into the following geographical regions. There are provinces and cities that belong to each of these regions. Locate these regions on a map of China.

❶ 华北 Huáběi, North China

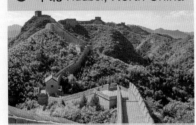

The Great Wall (长城), Beijing

- 北京 Běijīng
- 天津 Tiānjīn
- 河北 Héběi
- 山西 Shānxī
- 内蒙古 Nèiménggǔ

❷ 东北 Dōngběi, Northeast

Sea view of Dalian (大连), Liaoning

- 辽宁 Liáoníng
- 吉林 Jílín
- 黑龙江 Hēilóngjiāng

❸ 西北 Xīběi, Northwest

Ancient tower on the city wall of Xi'an (西安), Shaanxi

- 陕西 Shǎnxī
- 甘肃 Gānsù
- 青海 Qīnghǎi
- 宁夏 Níngxià
- 新疆 Xīnjiāng

❹ 华东 Huádōng, East China

Pudong (浦东), Shanghai

- 上海 Shànghǎi
- 江苏 Jiāngsū
- 浙江 Zhèjiāng
- 安徽 Ānhuī
- 福建 Fújiàn
- 江西 Jiāngxī
- 山东 Shāndōng

❺ 华中 Huázhōng, Central China

Longmen Grottoes in Luoyang (洛阳), Henan

- 河南 Hénán
- 湖北 Húběi
- 湖南 Húnán

❻ 华南 Huánán, South China

City view of Guangzhou (广州), Guangdong

- 广东 Guǎngdōng
- 广西 Guǎngxī
- 海南 Hǎinán

❼ 西南 Xīnán, Southwest

People's Square, Chongqing

- 重庆 Chóngqìng
- 云南 Yúnnán
- 四川 Sìchuān
- 西藏 Xīzàng
- 贵州 Guìzhōu

❽ 特别行政区 Tèbié xíngzhèngqū, Special Administrative Regions

Victoria Harbor, Hong Kong

- 香港 Xiānggǎng
- 澳门 Àomén

TRAVELING FROM PLACE TO PLACE

丁强 blogs about his experience on getting around in Beijing.

A Describing modes of transportation

北京是一个大<u>都市</u>，每个工作日早上从7点到9点，北京的几条<u>主干道</u>都会非常<u>拥堵</u>。

所以，我觉得坐地铁最好。可是，在<u>早晚高峰</u>，地铁也非常<u>拥挤</u>，地铁上<u>满满</u>的都是人。虽然地铁很拥挤，在早晚高峰坐地铁还是要比开车快一些。

除了早晚高峰，北京的地铁、公交车在<u>其他</u>时候并不拥挤，有很多<u>座位</u>，所以，如果不是有事，<u>还是</u>不要在早晚高峰出行。

dūshì 都市 n.		city
zhǔgàndào 主干道 n.		main road
yōngdǔ 拥堵 adj.	擁堵	congested
zǎowǎn gāofēng 早晚高峰 phr.		morning and evening rush hours
yōngjǐ 拥挤 adj.	擁擠	crowded
mǎnmǎn 满满 adj.	滿滿	full
qítā 其他 pron.		other
zuòwèi 座位 n.		seat
háishi 还是 adv.	還是	had better

LANGUAGE FOCUS

DECISION MAKING EXPRESSION

You have already learned how to use 还是 (or) to form a choice-type question. In this section, we will show you another way to use 还是. When you want to choose among various options that you have already mentioned, use the word 还是 to state what your preference is and that you are "better off" following your stated preference. You should also give a reason for your decision.

Example: A: 我们可以搭公交车、地铁或者火车去。

B: 可能会堵车，我们还是搭火车吧。

In these sentences, there are three possible modes of transportation and speaker B decides to choose the last option.

1. Complete the dialogs using sentences containing 还是.

    Example: A: 你送什么礼物给你的接待家庭？你可以送糖果、香水或者茶叶。

                B: <u>还是送茶叶比较合适。</u>

❶ A: 去哪儿旅游近一点儿？上海、西安还是香港？

    B: _____

❷ A: 我们可以打车回家，也可以坐地铁。

    B: _____

❸ A: 上海的火车站太挤了！巴士站没有这么多人。

    B: _____

❹ A: 我想要喝可乐，我不喜欢喝温水。

    B: 你生病了，_____

❺ A: 好冷啊，我们快点打车回家吧！

    B: 现在是晚高峰，会堵车，我们 _____

❻ A: 你能告诉我怎么坐地铁去颐和园吗？
        gàosu / tell

    B: 太远了，我的中文不太好，_____

❼ A: 你今晚想吃中国菜还是意大利菜？

    B: 我昨天刚吃过意大利菜，_____
         gāng / just

❽ A: 妈，我去学校了。

    B: 好像要下雨了，_____
    hǎoxiàng / looks like

2. Read the following paragraph and select the most appropriate sentences to fill in the blanks from the choices listed below. Be sure to write out your answers in Chinese.

今天我和子明一起去子明的表姐家玩，子明的表姐是一个画家，我非常期待见到她。出发的时候正好是下午6点，是北京的晚高峰，我和子明商量怎么去他表姐家，子明说："❶_____"。

于是，我们坐地铁去了表姐家。舅妈准备晚饭时问我们："你们想吃炒菜还是面条？"我想吃炒菜，可是子明想吃面条，我们两个想了半天，❷_____。

晚饭后，我们一起等表姐回来。等了一个多小时，表姐还没回来，子明的舅舅说："❸_____
_____。"我们看表，已经快10点了，子明说："❹_____。"

从表姐家出来已经很晚了，我问子明："回去是打车还是坐地铁呢？"子明说："❺_____"我想了想，为了省钱，❻_____。

a. 还是决定吃面条。

b. 这么晚了。她可能去朋友家住了。你们还是回去吧。

c. 路上很堵。我们还是坐地铁好。

d. 还是你决定吧！

e. 我们还是走吧！

f. 我们还是坐地铁吧，打车太贵了！

每天早上，王叔叔都会开车送我们上学。<u>对他来说</u>，他早<u>已经</u>习惯北京的<u>交通状况</u>了，可是对我来说，每分钟只走 100 米真是太<u>难受</u>了！王叔叔说，北京有这么多的人开车，交通拥堵<u>并</u>不<u>奇怪</u>。

duì...lái shuō 对……来说	對……來說	as for (person)
yǐjīng 已经 adv.	已經	already
xíguàn 习惯 v.	習慣	get used to
jiāotōng zhuàngkuàng 交通状况 phr.	交通狀況	traffic conditions
nánshòu 难受 adj.	難受	unbearable
bìng 并 adv.	並	actually
qíguài 奇怪 adj.		strange

LANGUAGE FOCUS

To express your personal opinion, use the expression 对我来说. If you are talking about someone else's opinion, simply replace 我 with the person's name or another personal pronoun.

The translation for this is "as far as I am concerned…" or "as for me…"

Examples: 对我来说，学习中文十分有趣。
对他来说，去中国旅游很贵。

The Shanghai Maglev Train

The **Shanghai Maglev Train** (上海磁悬浮列车, Shànghǎi Cíxuánfú Lièchē) is a magnetic levitation train, or *maglev* line, that operates in Shanghai, China. Construction of the Chinese maglev line began on March 1, 2001, and commercial service began on January 1, 2004. The top operational speed of this train is 431 km/h

or 268 mph, thus making it the world's fastest train in regular commercial service since its opening in April 2004. The train line connects Shanghai Pudong International Airport and the outskirts of the central Pudong region where passengers can change to the Shanghai Metro to continue their trip into the city center.

1. Describe each of the pictures by using the adjective given below and the expression 对……来说.

Example:

Answer: 对我来说，挤公交车非常痛苦。
tòngkǔ
painful

痛苦

 好吃

 有意思

 好听

 有趣

 方便

 无聊

 难

 便宜

2. Based on Ding Qing's two blog entries in Step 2, answer the following questions.

❶ 北京的早高峰是什么时候？

❷ 丁强觉得北京的交通怎么样？

❸ 王叔叔对北京的交通有什么看法？

❹ 丁强对坐地铁的看法怎么样？

❺ 丁强对在北京出行的建议是什么？
jiànyì
suggestion

3. Using Ding Qing's blog as a model, write your own short blog about traffic in your hometown. Be sure to use the expression 对我来说 (as for me) at least once in your blog.

PLACES TO STAY

A Explaining locations

Blog

　　我在北京住在月坛 附近，我家就在月坛公园的南面，月坛南街上。月坛一带 属于北京的市中心。从月坛朝西走是玉渊潭公园，每年四五月份，北京人都喜欢来玉渊潭公园看樱花，玉渊潭公园的樱花特别美。

fùjìn 附近 n.		nearby
yídài 一带 n.	一帶	area
shǔyú 属于 v.	屬於	belongs to
cháo 朝 prep.		towards, to
yīnghuā 樱花 n.	櫻花	cherry blossom

沿着月坛南街往东走，就到了西单，再往东就是中南海。西单有很多百货商厦，来北京的游客一般都会去西单购物。

从月坛往北走就就是著名的医院；月坛的东北方向有中国地质博物馆，月坛的西南方向还有一个有名的军事博物馆。

yánzhe 沿着 prep.	沿著	along
bǎihuò shāngshà 百货商厦 phr.	百货商厦	shopping mall
yìbān 一般 adv.		normally
zhùmíng 著名 adj.		famous
fāngxiàng 方向 n.		direction

EXTENDED VOCABULARY

Places in Beijing

月坛 p.n.	月壇	Yuètán	Temple of the Moon
玉渊潭 p.n.	玉淵潭	Yùyuāntán	Yu Yuan Tan Park
西单 p.n.	西單	Xīdān	Xidan (a major commerical area in Beijing)
中南海 p.n.		Zhōngnánhǎi	Zhongnanhai (an imperial garden in Beijing)
中国地质博物馆 p.n.	中國地質博物館	Zhōngguó Dìzhì Bówùguǎn	Geological Museum of China
军事博物馆 p.n.	軍事博物館	Jūnshì Bówùguǎn	Military Museum

LANGUAGE FOCUS

The prepositions 朝, 向, and 往 all refer to going "toward" a direction or place, and must be placed before the direction word and the verb. For example, 朝东走, 朝那里去, 向左走, 向右看, 往前跑, and 往后开.

The preposition 沿着 refers to going along a certain path.

Look at the following sentences and determine their meanings.

❶ 沿着长安大街往前开五分钟就到了。

❷ 师傅，麻烦车再往前开一下。

❸ 我们可以从这个街口朝东走。

❹ 他沿着黄浦江边往前跑。

❺ 他和朋友朝和平饭店走去。

❻ 沿着这条街一直走就是地铁站。

❼ 从月坛公园朝东走，就是故宫。

❽ 要是你往南看，就可以看到人民广场。

Attractions in Beijing

As the capital of China, Beijing is a populous city with many places of great historical and cultural interest. Here are some of the city's most popular attractions:

Gùgōng
故宫 *p.n.*
Forbidden City

Tiān'ānmén Guǎngchǎng
天安门广场 *p.n.*
Tiananmen Square

Yíhéyuán
颐和园 *p.n.*
Summer Palace

Wángfújǐng
王府井 *p.n.*
Wangfujing *(famous shopping street in Beijing)*

Bādálǐng Chángchéng
八达岭长城 *p.n.*
Badaling Great Wall

Tiāntán
天坛 *p.n.*
Temple of Heaven

Yuánmíngyuán
圆明园 *p.n.*
Old Summer Palace

Běihǎi Gōngyuán
北海公园 *p.n.*
Beihai Park

Àotǐ Zhōngxīn
奥体中心 *p.n.*
Olympic Sports Center

Běijīng Dàxué
北京大学 *p.n.*
Peking University

Qiánmén Dàzhālán
前门大栅栏 *p.n.*
Qianmen Dazhalan
(famous commercial street)

hútong
胡同 *n.*
hutong
(traditional alleys in Beijing)

Yōnghé Gōng
雍和宫 *p.n.*
Yonghe Temple

Dìtán
地坛 *p.n.*
Temple of Earth

Jǐngshān Gōngyuán
景山公园 *p.n.*
Jingshan Park

Míng Shísān Líng
明十三陵 *p.n.*
Ming Dynasty Tombs

1. Look at the map below and answer the following questions in complete sentences. Use the words 朝, 向, and 往 in your response.

❶ 天安门附近有什么景点？

❷ 北京北边一带有什么景点？

❸ 世纪坛在哪个地方的旁边？

❹ 从天安门往北走会到达什么地方？

❺ 从颐和园到奥体中心怎么走？

❻ 我住在朝阳公园附近，想去北京世界公园，怎么走呢？

❼ 圆明园在颐和园的什么位置？

❽ 地坛向南是什么景点？

❾ 沿着天安门—世纪坛往西可以到达什么地方？

❿ 从奥运村开车到八达岭应该往哪个方向开？

2. Below is a map of the city center of Shanghai. There are seven famous tourist attractions marked by yellow stars in the map. Provide directions to these attractions by using the following words or expressions: 在……东边, 附近, 一带, 沿着, 旁边, 往, or 朝. The first one has been done for you.

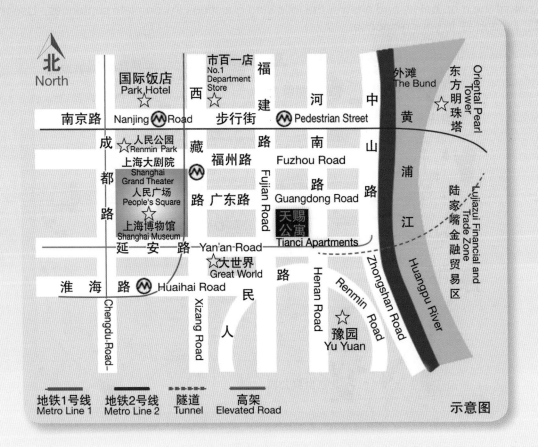

Example:

沿着南京路往东走，你可以看到市百一店在国际饭店对面。

B Describing my itinerary

丁强，你周末去哪儿玩了？
7 Apr, 2015 6:30 pm

我周末去上海了！
7 Apr, 2015 6:32 pm

哦！你一个人去吗？
7 Apr, 2015 6:34 pm

不是，我和两个朋友一起去。
7 Apr, 2015 6:37 pm

你在上海住哪儿？
7 Apr, 2015 6:38 pm

我住在一家青年旅店，在南京路一带，地点很好。我一到上海就去旅店办了入住手续。
7 Apr, 2015 6:41 pm

南京路很热闹，住那里应该很方便。
7 Apr, 2015 6:43 pm

是，旅店附近有很多商店，一走出旅店就是南京路。
7 Apr, 2015 6:46 pm

你参观了哪些热门景点？
7 Apr, 2015 6:48 pm

外滩、东方明珠塔、豫园、朱家角我都去了。
7 Apr, 2015 6:50 pm

你最喜欢哪个景点？
7 Apr, 2015 6:51 pm

我最喜欢外滩，那里的风景真是太迷人了！
7 Apr, 2015 6:53 pm

qīngnián lǚdiàn 青年旅店 n.		youth hotel/hostel
Nánjīng Lù 南京路 p.n.		Nanjing Road
dìdiǎn 地点 n.	地點	location
yī...jiù... 一…就…		once...then..., as soon as
rùzhù shǒuxù 入住手续 phr.	入住手續	check in at the hotel
rèmén jǐngdiǎn 热门景点 phr.	熱門景點	popular tourist attraction
Wàitān 外滩 p.n.	外灘	the Bund
Dōngfāng Míngzhū Tǎ 东方明珠塔 p.n.	東方明珠塔	Oriental Pearl TV Tower
Yùyuán 豫园 p.n.	豫園	Yu Garden
Zhūjiājiǎo 朱家角 p.n.		Zhujiajiao *(an ancient town in Shanghai)*

Use the expression 一…就… to show that one action immediately follows another. This forms a pattern of two events in quick succession, the first preceded by 一 and the second preceded by 就. Often the expression 一…就… is translated as "as soon as" or "immediately after."

Examples: ❶ 他一到学校就去图书馆借书。

❷ 我一回到家就玩电脑游戏。

1. Match the texts in the left column with the correct ones in the right column so that they form complete sentences. These sentences relate to actions that take place while traveling. The first one has been done for you as an example.

❶ 你一下飞机

a. 乘客就可以使用手机。
chéngkè
passengers

❷ 他一到达机场

b. 就去边检办理入境手续。

❸ 我们一过了安检
ānjiǎn
security check

c. 就坐下系上安全带
jì ānquándài
fasten seat belt

❹ 他一找到座位

d. 就应该去办理乘机手续。
chéngjī
board a plane

❺ 飞机一降落
jiàngluò
land

e. 就去登机口准备登机。
dēngjīkǒu
boarding gate

❻ 一拿到托运行李
tuōyùn xínglǐ
checked in luggage

f. 导游就去买门票。

❼ 一到了旅游景点入口处

g. 我就给接待家庭打电话。
jiēdài jiātíng
host family

❽ 他一看到导游回来

h. 就看到火车站在街对面。

❾ 他们一从酒店走出来

i. 就问他纪念品商店在哪里。

❿ 我一到火车站

j. 就去三号月台。
yuètái
platform

2. Read the dialog and decide if the following statements are true (T) or false (F).

芳芳：我们住的宾馆地点真好。一走出去就是王府井。

bīnguǎn / hotel

玛丽：是啊，我最喜欢购物，住在这里真方便！

芳芳：明天你打算去哪里？

玛丽：我在宾馆前台看到一个北京一日游的广告，早上去

qiántái / front desk, guǎnggào / advertisement
八达岭长城，下午去十三陵，还提供午餐，只需
要180元，看起来不错。

yuán / yuan, RMB

芳芳：哦，但是我不太喜欢跟团，一到景点就要跟着导游

gēntuán / join a tour group
走，自由活动的时间很少，太没意思了！

zìyóu / free, huódòng / activity

玛丽：你说得对。那么我们就自己安排行程吧。

ānpái / plan, xíngchéng / itinerary

芳芳：好，先吃晚饭，回来再讨论。

❶ 芳芳和玛丽的宾馆在王府井一带，地点很好。　　（　　）
❷ 玛丽建议明天参加北京一日游，去长城和故宫。　（　　）
❸ 北京一日游不提供午餐。　　　　　　　　　　　（　　）
❹ 芳芳比较喜欢自由活动，不喜欢跟团。　　　　　（　　）
❺ 她们最后还是觉得参加北京一日游比较好。　　　（　　）

Step Up!

1. Look at the following advertisement for a day tour in Beijing. After you read the information about the tour, use the map of Beijing to label where you will go and what time you will be there.

行程安排

8:00	集合出发；前往皇家园林——颐和园
9:00	到达颐和园(游览约2.5小时)；佛香阁、石舫、十七孔桥等都是颐和园里著名的建筑。
11:30	到餐馆用餐。
13:00	前往天坛(游览时间约1.5小时)；世界上最大的古代祭天建筑群，被列为"世界文化遗产"之一。
14:30	游览北京故宫三大殿(游览时间约3.5小时)：太和殿、中和殿、保和殿；历经了明、清两个朝代二十四位皇帝，有五百多年的历史。
18:00	行程结束。

皇家	huángjiā	imperial
佛香阁	Fóxiāngshān	Tower of Buddhist Incense
石舫	Shífǎng	the Marble Boat
十七孔桥	Shíqī Kǒngqiáo	the 17-Arch Bridge
建筑	jiànzhù	architecture
世界	shìjiè	world

古代	gǔdài	ancient
祭天	jìtiān	heaven worship
列	liè	list
世界文化遗产	shìjiè wénhuà yíchǎn	World Heritage Site
太和殿	Tàihédiàn	Hall of Supreme Harmony
中和殿	Zhōnghédiàn	Hall of Central Harmony
保和殿	Bǎohédiàn	Hall of Preserving Harmony
历经	lìjīng	experience
朝代	cháodài	dynasty
皇帝	huángdì	emperor
结束	jiéshù	end

2. Imagine that you are about to graduate from high school, and your family has decided to take a 10-day trip to China to celebrate your graduation. They want you to organize their trip for them. In the group will be your maternal grandparents, your parents, your older sister and her husband, and your younger brother. Since this is their first time to China, you must decide on the itinerary and create a detailed plan with information on the cities and the sites within those cities. Research the information and create a written plan to present to your family.

3. With a partner in the class, compare your itineraries and decide which one is preferable. Ask each other questions about why you chose the places you did, why you decided to stay as long as you did, and other factors that influenced your decision. With your partner, write up a new itinerary that incorporates material from both itineraries and present it to the class along with your reasons for planning in this way.

Fun Time!

Most people are proud of their hometowns or the places they live. Many people from Beijing are proud of places and sites in the city. Read the lyrics to the following song about Beijing and discover what Beijingers like about their city. You can also listen to the song online.

For more fun, in a small group, make up a song in Chinese about your hometown that reflects the things you are most proud of. You can use the melody to a song that you know or make up your own music.

我家住在北京城

我家住在北京城，过了前门再往东。

建国门前大高楼，我家住在十八层。
　　　　　　　　　　　　　céng
　　　　　　　　　　　　　level

清晨能听到北京站的钟，夜晚能看到五光十色的灯。
chén
morning　　wēifēng
大饭店好威风，出租汽车忙不停。
　　　　impressive

我爱北京，我爱北京，我在这里生，我在这里长。

我爱北京，我爱北京，我在这里生，我在这里长。

　　　　　zìháo
我骄傲，我自豪。我骄傲，我自豪。
　　　　　proud
我家住在北京城。

　　　　　míng　　　　　　　　　　cǎopíng
花儿开，鸟儿鸣。街心公园绿草坪。
　　　　　chirp　　　　　　　　　　field
lìjiāoqiáo
东西南北立交桥。四通八达南进城。
overpass

要买东西你去王府井。要玩得开心你去康乐宫。

颐和园景山公园还有八达岭。

我爱北京，我爱北京，我在这里生，我在这里长。

我爱北京，我爱北京，我在这里生，我在这里长。

我骄傲，我自豪。我骄傲，我自豪。

我家住在北京城。

I have learned...

Verbs

接机	接機	jiējī	pick up at the airport	游览	遊覽	yóulǎn	sightsee
办理	辦理	bànlǐ	handle	习惯	習慣	xíguàn	get used to
到达	到達	dàodá	arrive, reach	属于	屬於	shǔyú	belongs to
延误	延誤	yánwù	delay				

Nouns

机场	機場	jīchǎng	airport	最后		zuìhòu	final, last
入境		rùjìng	arrivals	纪念品	紀念品	jìniànpǐn	souvenir
手续	手續	shǒuxù	procedure	旅客		lǚkè	traveler
证件	證件	zhèngjiàn	documents	风景	風景	fēngjǐng	scenery
护照	護照	hùzhào	passport	都市		dūshì	city
签证	簽證	qiānzhèng	visa	主干道		zhǔgàndào	main road
入境卡		rùjìngkǎ	arrival card	座位		zuòwèi	seat
边检	邊檢	biānjiǎn	immigration control	附近		fùjìn	nearby
班机	班機	bānjī	flight	一带	一帶	yídài	area
行李提取处	行李提取處	xínglǐ tíqǔ chù	baggage claim	樱花	櫻花	yīnghuā	cherry blossom
转盘	轉盤	zhuǎnpán	carousel *(for luggage)*	方向		fāngxiàng	direction
免税店	免稅店	miǎnshuìdiàn	duty free shop	青年旅店		qīngnián lǚdiàn	youth hotel/hostel
行李车	行李車	xínglǐ chē	luggage cart	地点	地點	dìdiǎn	location
门票	門票	ménpiào	admission ticket				

Adjectives

热闹	熱鬧	rènao	bustling, lively	庄严	莊嚴	zhuāngyán	solemn
壮观	壯觀	zhuàngguān	magnificent	美丽	美麗	měilì	beautiful
整		zhěng	whole, entire	拥堵	擁堵	yōngdǔ	congested
优美	優美	yōuměi	fine, graceful, beautiful	拥挤	擁擠	yōngjǐ	crowded
秀丽	秀麗	xiùlì	beautiful, pretty	满满	滿滿	mǎnmǎn	full
迷人		mírén	mesmerizing	难受	難受	nánshòu	unbearable
雄伟	雄偉	xióngwěi	grand	奇怪		qíguài	strange
古老		gǔlǎo	ancient	著名		zhùmíng	famous

I have learned...

Adverbs

十分		shífēn	especially	还是	還是	háishi	had better
特别		tèbié	particularly	已经	已經	yǐjīng	already
真		zhēn	truly	并	並	bìng	actually
多		duō	much, so	一般		yìbān	normally

Prepositions

朝		cháo	towards, to
沿着	沿著	yánzhe	along

Pronoun

其他		qítā	other

Phrases

早晚高峰		zǎowǎn gāofēng	morning and evening rush hours
交通状况	交通狀況	jiāotōng zhuàngkuàng	traffic conditions
百货商厦	百貨商廈	bǎihuò shāngshà	shopping mall
入住手续	入住手續	rùzhù shǒuxù	check in at the hotel
热门景点	熱門景點	rèmén jǐngdiǎn	popular tourist attraction

Constructions

对……来说	對……來說	duì…lái shuō	as for (person)
一…就…		yī…jiù…	once…then…, as soon as

Proper nouns

前门大街	前門大街	Qiánmén Dàjiē	Qianmen Street	中国地质博物馆	中國地質博物館	Zhōngguó Dìzhì Bówùguǎn	Geological Museum of China
天安门广场	天安門廣場	Tiān'ānmén Guǎngchǎng	Tiananmen Square	军事博物馆	軍事博物館	Jūnshì Bówùguǎn	Military Museum
故宫	故宮	Gùgōng	Forbidden City	南京路		Nánjīng Lù	Nanjing Road
月坛	月壇	Yuètán	Temple of the Moon	外滩	外灘	Wàitān	the Bund
玉渊潭	玉淵潭	Yùyuāntán	Yu Yuan Tan Park	东方明珠塔	東方明珠塔	Dōngfāng Míngzhū Tǎ	Oriental Pearl TV Tower
中南海		Zhōngnánhǎi	Zhongnanhai (an imperial garden in Beijing)	豫园	豫園	Yùyuán	Yu Garden
西单	西單	Xīdān	Xidan (a major commercial area in Beijing)	朱家角		Zhūjiājiǎo	Zhujiajiao (an ancient town in Shanghai)

SENTENCE PATTERNS

谁会来机场接你？王叔叔会来接机。

天安门广场非常大。故宫十分壮观。

如果不是有事，还是不要在早晚高峰出行。

对他来说，他早已经习惯北京的交通状况了。

从月坛朝西走是玉渊潭公园。

我一到上海就去旅店办入住手续。

I can do!

Interpretive Communication

❑ I can understand when people give me directions on how to get to some places.

❑ I can read a boarding pass and understand where to go.

❑ I can read a Chinese map and locate important places.

Interpersonal Communication

❑ I can discuss places to go with a friend and express my preferences.

❑ I can support my opinions and thoughts with details.

❑ I can come to a consensus with a partner on places to visit in China.

Presentational Communication

❑ I can present a plan of places to visit in China.

❑ I can give directions on how to get to somewhere using a map.

❑ I can state information in a logical sequence.

❑ I can describe places using adverbs of degree.

❑ I can develop a detailed itinerary to follow when visiting China.

❑ I can explain the steps to take when planning a trip to China.

❑ I can state my opinion in written form and defend it.

❑ I can compose a blog about my travels.

Cultural Knowledge

❑ I can describe the various geographical regions of China.

❑ I can briefly talk about the features of the Shanghai Maglev Train.

❑ I can state famous landmarks in Beijing and other Chinese cities.

My host family in China

我的寄宿家庭

COMMUNICATIVE GOALS

- Conversing with others about family life
- Explaining events that occurred in different time frames
- Stating an approximate quantity of items
- Comparing how well people do an activity
- Stating one's opinions on community service

Cultural Knowledge

- Eating at home or in a restaurant
- Chinese honorific titles
- Polite expressions
- Chinese temple fairs

Get ready...

Read the list of customs and check off those customs that you practice when you go to someone else's house for a visit. Write an **A** if you do it in the United States or in your culture and a **B** if you think people do it in China. If you think it is done in both countries, write **A & B**. If you think it is not done in either country, write a **C** before the number.

zhǔrén dài kèrén
① 主人带客人参观主人的家。
host bring guest

② 主人问客人需不需要洗手。

tuō   huàn
③ 一进门，先脱鞋，换上主人给的拖鞋。
remove   change

qīnwěn
④ 进门时亲吻主人／女主人。
kiss

hùxiāng jūgōng
⑤ 进门时向主人和客人互相鞠躬。
each other bow

⑥ 主人接过你的外套，帮你挂起来。

wòshǒu
⑦ 与新认识的朋友握手。
shake hands

⑧ 主人请客人去客厅吃一些点心。

jìng   héshílǐ
⑨ 进门时向主人敬合十礼。
greet with putting palms together

⑩ 进门问好，问主人需不需要换鞋。

lǐwù
⑪ 为主人准备一份礼物，比如鲜花、
gift
糖果，并双手送给他。

zhāodài
⑫ 主人倒茶招待客人。
serve

After you have completed your checklist, compare your answers with a classmate's and briefly discuss why you matched the country and cultural practice.

STEP 1

BECOMING PART OF THE FAMILY

A. Making people feel welcome

丁强，你好！

你来啦！快进来！

D. Settling into my new home

我没吃过北京烤鸭。大家一边吃着饭，一边讨论北京生活的趣事。我在那里买了很多衣服。

STEP 2

GATHERING THE FAMILY TOGETHER

A. Meeting the extended family

你还会见到我好几个亲戚。

B. Bonding with the family

每个周末，大家再忙也要和亲人聚在一起吃饭。

STEP 3

BEING A PART OF THE NEIGHBORHOOD

A. Exploring different activities

我们有的会去敬老院陪老人聊天，有的会去农村给"留守儿童"补课。

B. Comparing happenings in the community

这里的活动比那里的多。

BECOMING PART OF THE FAMILY

A Making people feel welcome

丁强从机场和王叔叔一起回家，李阿姨（王叔叔的太太）和他们的孩子王子明在家里等着他们。

（咚！咚！咚！敲门声）

李阿姨：来了，来了！子明，快去开门。

（子明开门）

丁强：你好！我是丁强。

子明：噢！丁强你好！你来啦！快进来！

李阿姨：丁强，你好！我是子明的妈妈，
李阿姨。

丁强：李阿姨，您好！

李阿姨：先换拖鞋吧。

丁强：谢谢！

李阿姨：不客气，你来客厅坐吧！我让子明
把你的行李搬到房里去。

丁强：好的。

李阿姨：你喝点什么？茶？果汁？

丁强：我喝茶就好。对了，我带了一些
礼物来送你们。

（礼物递给王叔叔）

王叔叔：哎呀！你太客气了！带什么礼物啊！

丁强：只是小小心意，希望你们会喜欢。

王叔叔：谢谢！

李阿姨：来，喝茶。

丁强：谢谢。

李阿姨：坐了十几个小时的飞机，累不累？

丁强：还好，想到我将要在北京生活一年，
我就特别高兴！

qiāomén 敲门 phr.	敲門	knock on the door
jìnlai 进来 v.	進來	come in
huàn 换 v.	換	change
kèqi 客气 adj.	客氣	courtesy
dài 带 v.	帶	bring
lǐwù 礼物 n.	禮物	gift
dìgěi 递给 phr.	遞給	to pass on
xīnyì 心意 n.		regards

王叔叔：哈哈，希望你会喜欢这个地方。
　　　　今晚我们<u>出去</u>吃一顿，<u>为</u>你<u>接风</u>！

（子明从卧室<u>出来</u>）
　子明：丁强，你的行李我<u>拿进</u>房间了。
　　　　以后我们两人会睡同一间卧室，
　　　　希望你会习惯。
　丁强：没问题，我在美国也是和弟弟睡
　　　　同一间房。我可以<u>进去</u>看看吗？
　子明：当然可以！来，往这儿走。

chūqu 出去 v.		go out
wèi 为 prep.	為	for
jiēfēng 接风 phr.	接風	give a welcome dinner
chūlai 出来 v.	出來	come out
ná 拿 v.		take out
jìnqu 进去 v.	進去	go in

LANGUAGE FOCUS

The use of the verbs 进来, 出来, 进去, and 出去 have the meaning of coming toward or going from a place. The difference depends on where the speaker is in relation to the listener and what the speaker wants the listener to do. If the speaker wants the listener to come toward the speaker, and the listener is not close to the speaker, then he/she uses the verb 进来 (come in/enter); if the listener is close to the speaker and the speaker wants the listener to move away from him/her, he/she uses the verb 出去 (go out/leave).

However, if the speaker and the listener are apart and the intent of the speaker is for the listener to leave a space and come closer to the speaker (as in leaving a room to approach the speaker), then he/she will say, "出来" (come out); whereas, when they are in the same space and the speaker wants the listener to enter a place before he/she does (as in entering a room), then use the verb 进去.

These verbs can also function as complements of direction by placing them after a main verb, such as 拿, 带, and 放, to indicate the direction of the action from the speaker's position:

　拿进来 *(toward the speaker)*
　take in

　带出来 *(toward the speaker)*
　bring out

　放进去 *(away from the speaker)*
　put in

　拿出去 *(away from the speaker)*
　take out

One of Confucius' famous analects is "有朋自远方来，不亦乐乎" (yǒu péng zì yuǎnfāng lái, bú yì lè hū). It means that Chinese people are happy to welcome friends from far away. It is used on many occasions to show an appreciation for China's warm hospitality.

1. Look at the following pictures and create a sentence that explains what you see. Follow the example.

Example:

把蛋糕放进去。

2. Read the dialog from Step 1A and answer the questions in Chinese.

❶ 丁强一到王叔叔家，李阿姨给了他什么？

❷ 子明帮丁强做了什么？

❸ 丁强会在北京住多久？

❹ 丁强和王叔叔一家人晚上会在哪里吃饭？

❺ 丁强介意和子明同睡一个房吗？为什么？
jièyì
mind

Blog

　　在寄宿家庭的生活非常有趣、舒服。他们都对我很好。

　　李阿姨每天都为我们准备好吃的饭菜，她担心我不习惯吃中国菜，有时候还要带我去美国餐馆。对我来说，中国菜是很好的选择！李阿姨做的中国菜又好吃、又有营养，所以我每天都吃得很多。因为知道我没吃过北京烤鸭，他们就带我去吃。大家一边吃着饭，一边讨论北京生活的趣事。李阿姨还带我去西单购物。我在那里买了很多衣服。

　　王叔叔也非常热情，他有时候开车带我出去玩，带我去拜访他的亲戚朋友，让我了解中国人的生活。

　　子明对我也很友好。有时候，我们两个一起去北京的名胜古迹玩，还一起讨论中国和美国的不同，以及中国和美国的高中生生活。现在我们已经成为很好的朋友了！

jìsù jiātíng 寄宿家庭 *n.*		host family
yǒuqù 有趣 *adj.*		interesting
shūfu 舒服 *adj.*		comfortable
zhǔnbèi 准备 *v.*	準備	prepare
dānxīn 担心 *v.*	擔心	worry
xuǎnzé 选择 *v.; n.*	選擇	choose; choice
dàjiā 大家 *pron.*		everyone, all
shēnghuó 生活 *n.*		life
qùshì 趣事 *n.*		interesting matters
rèqíng 热情 *adj.*	熱情	enthusiastic
bàifǎng 拜访 *v.*	拜訪	to visit (people)
qīnqi 亲戚 *n.*	親戚	relatives (related by blood)
liǎojiě 了解 *v.*		to know; to understand
yǒuhǎo 友好 *adj.*		friendly
míngshèng 名胜 *n.*	名勝	scenic spot
yǔjì 古迹 *n.*	古跡	place of historic interest
yǐjí 以及 *conj.*		and
chéngwéi 成为 *v.*	成為	become

In Chinese, there are three markers to indicate whether an event or activity is completed, has occurred before, or continues. The markers are 了 (le), 过 (guo), and 着 (zhe).

了 is used after a verb to show that an action is completed, such as 你做了功课吗? (Have you done the homework?) Another example is "我爬上了长城." (I climbed the Great Wall.) A verb with 了 is often translated into English by using the simple past or the present perfect. It also often occurs with 以后 to show that a second event occurs after the completion of an earlier event, such as 吃了烤鸭以后，我们就回家。(After eating the roast duck, we [then] go home.)

The use of 过 is to denote a past experience. For instance, if you want to ask whether someone has been to China before, you can say: 你去过中国吗? If you want to say that you have never had Peking duck before, you can say 我没吃过北京烤鸭.

When a verb is followed by 着, it shows that an action or event is ongoing or continues.

For instance, ❧ 我喜欢站着，不喜欢坐着。(I like standing, not sitting.)

❧ 不要看着我。 (Don't keep looking at me.)

Look at the following sentences and determine why the markers 了, 着, and 过 are used. Decide if the reason is to describe a completed action, a past experience, or an ongoing action.

Examples: ❶ 我没吃过北京烤鸭，所以他们就带我去吃。
❷ 我们吃着饭，聊着周末要去哪儿。
❸ 吃了烤鸭，他们带我去西单商场买一些衣服。

CULTURAL HIGHLIGHTS

Eating at Home or in a Restaurant

The custom of eating at home or in a restaurant is changing in China. Previously, if the host asked, "我们在家吃还是出去吃?" the answer would have been simple. The guest would most likely have said "在家吃吧," because the guest was thinking not to make the host spend unnecessarily. It is the custom in China that the host *(the person who extended the invitation)* will pay for the meal. Nowadays, it is more complicated. Often the guest will reply, "都行，还是客从主便吧！" This change has taken place because, as China's economy grows, more people have larger disposable incomes, and they can afford to eat out in restaurants more often.

However, eating at home has turned into a different type of custom because it shows that people are willing to spend time and energy, as well as money, to prepare a special meal. So, what used to be a way to save money becomes a way to show respect to a guest. Eating at home can also be healthier than eating in a restaurant.

Try This!

1. Fill in the blanks with 了, 着, or 过.

❶ A: 你吃＿＿＿北京烤鸭吗？

B: 嗯，去年在北京的时候。

❷ A: 几点＿＿＿？

B: 五点半。

❸ A: 在北京的时候，你去＿＿＿
颐和园吗？

B: 没有，去了圆明园和故宫，
但是没去＿＿＿颐和园。

❹ A: 你现在在干什么？

B: 我正吃＿＿＿热狗呢！

❺ A: 你已经去＿＿＿西安了吗？

B: 我在去西安的火车上。

❻ A: 你在哪里啊？！电影开始啦！

B: 我马上就到了，等＿＿＿我！

❼ A: 今天天气好冷啊！

B: 是啊，今天就应该呆在家里，
看＿＿＿电视，吃＿＿＿火锅！

❽ A: 北京烤鸭、糖葫芦、炸酱面，
这些你哪个没吃＿＿＿？

B: 哈哈，我都吃＿＿＿了！

❾ A: 丁强，你在哪儿？

B: 我已经到＿＿＿杭州了！

❿ A: 吃＿＿＿饭，我们就去看电影！

B: 我已经吃＿＿＿饭了。

2. Read the following sentences and determine the reason the marker 了, 着, or 过 is used. Decide if the reason is to describe a completed action, a past experience, or an ongoing action.

❶ 妹妹一边吃着面包，一边写着功课。

❷ 今天早上八点，丁强去了圆明园。

❸ 丁强上个月已经吃过烤鸭。

❹ 昨天晚上，我们全家去了中国餐馆吃中餐。

❺ 他去年就去过西安了，不想再去了。

❻ 过年的时候，全家人在一起聊着天，吃着饺子，是最开心的事！

❼ 你去年不是去过故宫了吗？怎么又去？

❽ 我没吃过炸酱面，我想试一试。

❾ A: 你寒假去哪里了啊？
B: 我们全家去了北京。

❿ 我上个月去过长城，不想再去了。

A Meeting the extended family

李阿姨： 丁强，我们一会儿就快到了，上星期我父母听到我们说起你，都很想见见你。你还会见到我好几个亲戚。

王叔叔： 是啊，子明知道今天咱们有家庭聚会，所以一大早就去外公外婆家了。

（到了外公外婆家。）

王叔叔、

李阿姨： 爸爸、妈妈，这是丁强。

外公： 太好了，丁强来了，快进来！

丁强： 外公好、外婆好！我是丁强，非常高兴见到您。我带了水果送给你们。

外婆： 丁强，你太客气啦！我来给你介绍一下。这是健伟，他是子明的表哥。

外公： 健伟和子明是表兄弟。你们见过了吧？

丁强： 还没见过面。健伟，你好！你也姓王吗？

子明： 丁强，健伟是我舅舅的儿子，他姓李，我们不同姓。除了健伟，我还有三四个表兄弟。

健伟： 我爷爷姓李，是子明的外公，所以我是子明妈妈的侄子。子明的爸爸是我的姑父。

tīng...shuōqǐ... 听…说起…	聽…說起…	heard that (someone) mentioned (something)
zánmen 咱们 *pron.*	咱們	we, us
jiātíng jùhuì 家庭聚会 *n.*	家庭聚會	family gathering
jièshào 介绍 *v.*	介紹	introduce
jiànmiàn 见面 *v.*	見面	meet

nòng hútu 弄糊涂 *phr.*	弄糊塗	get confused
qīnshǔ chēnghu 亲属称呼 *n.*	親屬稱呼	kinship terms
fùzá 复杂 *adj.*	複雜	complicated
zhòngshì 重视 *v.*	重視	attach importance to, value something
hémù 和睦 *adj.*	和睦	to be in harmony
xiāngchǔ 相处 *v.*	相處	to get along with others
jiātíng xìngfú 家庭幸福 *phr.*		a happy family
érnǚ zǐsūn 儿女子孙 *phr.*	兒女子孫	children and grandchildren

外公：丁强，没把你<u>弄糊涂</u>吧！你知道中国人的<u>亲属称呼</u>比较<u>复杂</u>，但是<u>重视</u> <u>和睦</u> <u>相处</u>、<u>家庭幸福</u>。每当家庭聚会，<u>儿女子孙</u>就都回来，一家好几十个人在一块，热热闹闹的。今天你能来看我们，大家特别高兴。

LANGUAGE FOCUS

To indicate that you are talking about an approximate quantity, use two or more numbers in sequence followed by the measure word. For example, if you want to say that there are about three or four people in each group, you say "三四个人." You use the numbers plus the word 个 before the object. To say six or seven apples, say "六七个苹果." By placing two numbers in sequence, the other person automatically understands that it is an approximation. Be sure to use the correct measure word with the objects. If you have five or six books, say "五六本书."

The expression 好几个 also refers to an unspecified quantity and translates as "several" or "quite a few." For example, 家里有好几个人 means that there are many people in the house, but fewer than ten. If there are really a lot of people in the house, we say "家里有好几十个人！"

Look at the following sentences and determine their meaning.

❶ 我的寄宿家庭有很多亲戚。芳芳有三四个表兄弟，还有好几个堂姐。
❷ 在北京首都机场，有好几十个登机口。
❸ 我吃过三四种中国的小吃。
❹ 我的中国朋友有五六个人都姓张。
❺ 他们好几个月没有发电邮给我了。

Maternal Line

外祖父 / 外公 wàizǔfù / wàigōng
maternal grandfather

外祖母 / 外婆 wàizǔmǔ / wàipó
maternal grandmother

母亲 母親 mǔqīn
mother

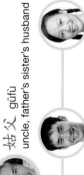

舅舅 jiùjiu
uncle, mother's brother

舅妈 舅媽 jiùmā
aunt, mother's brother's wife

表姐 / 表妹 biǎojiě / biǎomèi
female cousin
(maternal)

表哥 / 表弟 biǎogē / biǎodi
male cousin
(maternal)

姨妈 姨媽 yímā
aunt, mother's sister

姨父 yífù
aunt, mother's sister's husband

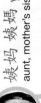

侄女 zhínǚ
niece, brother's daughter

外甥女 wàishengnǚ
niece, sister's daughter

自己 / 丈夫 zìjǐ / zhàngfu
myself / husband

妻子 qīzi
wife

女儿 女兒 nǚ'ér
daughter

儿子 兒子 érzi
son

哥哥 / 弟弟 gēge / dìdi
older brother / younger brother

嫂嫂 / 弟媳 sǎosao / dìxí
sister-in-law, older brother's wife /
younger brother's wife

侄子 zhízi
nephew, brother's son

姐姐 / 妹妹 jiějie / mèimei
older sister / younger sister

姐夫 / 妹夫 jiěfu / mèifu
brother-in-law, older sister's husband /
younger sister's husband

外甥 wàisheng
nephew, sister's son

Paternal Line

祖父 / 爷爷 zǔfù / yéye
paternal grandfather

祖母 / 奶奶 zǔmǔ / nǎinai
paternal grandmother

父亲 父親 fùqīn
father

姑妈 姑媽 gūmā
aunt, father's sister

姑父 gūfu
uncle, father's sister's husband

表姐 / 表妹 biǎojiě / biǎomèi
female cousin
(maternal)

表哥 / 表弟 biǎogē / biǎodi
male cousin
(maternal)

伯父 / 叔父 bófù / shūfù
uncle, father's older brother / father's younger brother

伯母 / 婶婶 婶婶 bómǔ / shěnshen
aunt, father's older brother's wife /
father's younger brother's wife

堂姐 / 堂妹 tángjiě / tángmèi
female cousin
(paternal)

堂哥 / 堂弟 tánggē / tángdi
male cousin
(paternal)

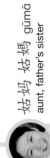

 **CULTURAL HIGHLIGHTS**

Chinese Honorific Titles

In China, when addressing (称呼, chēnghū) someone at an event, honorific titles are placed after the person's last name. The most common honorific titles are 先生 (xiānsheng, Mr.), 太太 (tàitai, Mrs.), and 小姐 (xiǎojiě, Ms.). Other common titles include 夫人 (fūrén, Madam) and 女士 (nǚshì, lady), a more polite version to address someone's wife or a female person regardless of whether she is married or not.

It is very common to use the occupation-related title after the last name. For example, a teacher is addressed as 张老师 (Zhāng lǎoshī), a school principal as 林校长 (Lín xiàozhǎng), a bank manager as 陈经理 (Chén jīnglǐ), a lawyer as 钱律师 (Qián lǜshī), and a doctor as 王医生 (Wáng yīshēng). It is also common to refer to people using their job title, particularly for those of a high rank, such as a department head 白主任 (Bái zhǔrèn) or a director 刘局长 (Liú júzhǎng).

During a social event, when addressing someone's family members, the honorific title 令 (lìng) is used. This title, 令, goes before the person's kinship term (亲属称谓, qīnshǔ chēngwèi). When talking about someone's own family members, common polite titles used are 家父家母 to refer to someone's own parents; 舍弟舍妹 is used to refer to someone's younger siblings. To help practice the proper use of the family-related honorific titles, here is a common saying in Chinese: 家大舍小令外人 (Jiā dà shè xiǎo lìng wàirén). Here is the meaning: 家 refers to your older family members, 舍 refers to younger family members of the same generation, 令 is the honorific title used to refer to other people's relatives in general.

Look at the chart below for examples of honorifics.

称别人的父亲: 令尊 lìngzūn	称自己的父亲: 家父 jiāfù
称别人的母亲: 令堂 lìngtáng	称自己的母亲: 家母 jiāmǔ
称别人的兄妹: 令兄、令妹 lìngxiōng, lìngmèi	称自己的妹弟: 舍妹、舍弟 shèmèi, shèdì
称别人的家庭: 府上 fǔshàng	称自己的家庭: 舍下、寒舍 shèxià, hánshè

1. Match the pictures with the appropriate sentences.

b

a. 有好几种北京小吃我没吃过。
famous foods
in Beijing

b. 我的邻居有五六个孩子。

c. 有好几千人参加了这次的马拉松比赛。
mǎlāsōng
marathon

d. 在北京有好几个有名的旅游景点。

e. 在马场里有五六匹马。

f. 图书馆里有三四个人在排队借书。
páiduì
queue

g. 妈妈在超市买了好几十样日常用品和食物。
daily necessities

h. 张爷爷和张奶奶有三四个孙子和孙女。

i. 在他书房的书架上放着好几十本书。

j. 这五六种水果对身体健康有好处。

k. 天快黑了，只有四五个孩子在游乐场。

2. Read the dialog and decide if the following statements are true (T) or false (F).

李阿姨： 丁强，你过来，我给你介绍认识一下，这是子明的阿姨和姨父、舅舅和舅妈。他们是我姐姐、姐夫、哥哥和嫂嫂。

丁强： 阿姨、姨父、舅舅、舅妈好！

舅妈： 丁强，在北京还习惯吗？

丁强： 嗯，挺习惯的，子明、王叔叔和李阿姨都特别照顾我！

姨父： 你喜欢吃北京小吃吗？

丁强： 李阿姨带我去吃过三四种小吃，可是我最爱吃的还是炸酱面。
zhájiàngmiàn
fried sauce noodles

舅妈： 太好了，咱们今天就吃炸酱面！

❶ 李阿姨没有兄弟姐妹。 （　　）
❷ 李阿姨的父母有一个儿子。 （　　）
❸ 子明舅舅的孩子也姓王，跟子明同姓。 （　　）
❹ 李阿姨的嫂嫂是子明的舅妈。 （　　）
❺ 李阿姨有一个妹妹。 （　　）
❻ 丁强说他在北京挺习惯的。 （　　）
❼ 丁强没有吃过北京小吃。 （　　）
❽ 丁强最喜欢吃炸酱面。 （　　）

今天，王叔叔一家带我去了子明的外公外公婆家过周末，我见到了好多子明母亲家的<u>亲人</u>。每个周末，大家<u>再</u>忙<u>也</u>要和亲人聚在一起吃饭。

家庭聚会一般来说都是在一起吃顿饭。要是不打算出去下馆子，就会先<u>商量</u>做几道什么样的家常菜，大家边做饭边聊天，聊聊工作、生活，<u>或者</u>是购物、买菜等<u>日常琐事</u>。孩子们也聚在一起聊聊学校、打打电子游戏，或者谈谈跟朋友们的趣事。如果<u>遇到</u>了什么<u>困难</u>，或者有什么好消息，都会和亲人一起分享，<u>互相</u>帮助，<u>彼此</u> <u>支持</u>。我很喜欢中国家庭这种亲人<u>相聚</u>在一起的<u>气氛</u>，<u>感觉</u>非常<u>温馨</u>和快乐！

zài...yě 再…也…		even though…still
qīnrén 亲人 *n.*	親人	one's family members
shāngliang 商量 *v.*		negotiate, discuss
huòzhě 或者 *conj.*		or
rìcháng suǒshì 日常琐事 *n.*	日常瑣事	life's trivialities
yùdào 遇到 *v.*		encounter, meet with, face
kùnnan 困难 *n.*	困難	difficulties
hùxiāng 互相 *adv.*		mutually
bǐcǐ 彼此 *pron.*		each other, both parties
zhīchí 支持 *v.*		support
xiāngjù 相聚 *v.*		gather
qìfēn 气氛 *n.*	氣氛	atmosphere
gǎnjué 感觉 *v.*	感覺	feel
wēnxīn 温馨 *adj.*	溫馨	warm, heartfelt

The expression 再…也… is used to show a contrast from one part of the sentence to the other. It is usually translated as "although," "even though," or "no matter…." 再 precedes a section that states a particular situation while 也 precedes a section that describes an action taken despite the situation mentioned earlier.

For example, the sentence 每到周末，大家再忙也要聚在一起吃饭 means that no matter how busy everybody is, they still get together to have meals on the weekend.

CULTURAL HIGHLIGHTS

Polite Expressions

As in other languages, there are expressions of politeness in Chinese, known as 客套话 (kètàohuà). Most of the phrases listed below are formulaic expressions that will help you to interact with Chinese people in a socially, culturally appropriate manner.

请问您贵姓？	What's your surname? *(When you ask someone's name)*	bàituō 拜托你！	I need your help. *(When you ask for someone's help)*
很高兴认识你！	Nice to meet you! *(When you first meet someone)*	shǎngguāng 谢谢赏光。	Thank you for coming. *(When someone accepts your invitation)*
yǎng 久仰、久仰！	I've heard so much about you. *(When you first meet someone famous)*	lín 谢谢光临！	Welcome! *(When you welcome a guest)*
哪里、哪里。	I'm flattered. *(When someone gives you compliment)*	十分感谢！	Thank you so much! *(When you thank someone)*
jiǎng 过奖了。	I'm flattered. *(When someone praises you and you accept their remarks)*	yuánliàng 请你原谅。	Please pardon me. *(When you apologize)*
		gōngxǐ 恭喜、恭喜！	Congratulations! *(When you congratulate someone)*
		请慢用。	Please enjoy. *(When you finish eating, you say to people at the table)*
		慢走、慢走。	Take care on your way home. *(When guests are leaving)*
		liú 请留步。	I'll see myself out. *(When you are leaving and the host is seeing you off)*

1. Complete the other half of the sentence by using 再…也….

   ❶ 妈妈每天工作很忙，可是，_____要去购物、买菜。

   ❷ 这些作业明天要交，我_____。

   ❸ 北京的生活很幸福，可是_____比不上在自己家里。

   ❹ 他买了一件很厚的长大衣，_____。

   ❺ 双休日上长城的人很多！可是丁强说："_____！"

   ❻ 看照片风景挺美的，可是_____不如自己去圆明园。

   ❼ 他喜欢吃北京小吃，其他小吃口味_____。

kǒuwèi
taste

   ❽ 他说他没时间，但是_____不能不吃饭！

2. Read the following sentences and choose the appropriate polite expression (客套话 kètàohuà) from the list provided that fits into the conversational exchange. An expression may be used more than once.

   客套话 (Polite expressions)

麻烦你了	十分感谢	恭喜、恭喜	谢谢赏光
请问您贵姓	请你原谅	久仰、久仰	各位请慢用
您过奖了	慢走、慢走	请留步	

   Example:　A: 让我介绍一下，这位是王教授。他是我们学校最好的老师。

   　　　　　　B: 久仰、久仰。_____

   ❶ A: 不早了，我得回去了。

   　B: 我送你。

   　A: 别客气，_____，我可以自己打车。

   　B: _____。有空常来坐坐。

❷ A: 你要买的书我帮你买到了。

  B: _____。

❸ A: 您好！我是这儿的经理。_____？
  B: 我姓高。这是我的名片。
  A: 我很高兴认识您。

❹ A: 没问题，这件事我能帮你忙。

  B: _____。

❺ A: 是谁把玻璃杯打破了？
  B: 是我不小心把玻璃杯打破了。_____。

❻ A: 你的书法写得真好。我没法跟你比。

  B: _____，我还得继续努力练习。

❼ A: 李主任，这是张校长给您的邀请信。
  B: 张校长太客气了。
  A: _____来参加我们十周年的校庆。

❽ A: 小王，我考上南京大学了。

  B: _____。

❾ A: 你家的房子真漂亮！

  B: _____。

❿ A: 请再多吃点。
  B: 谢谢，我吃饱了。_____。

BEING A PART OF THE NEIGHBORHOOD

A Exploring different activities

tīngshuō 听说 v.	聽說	hear of
shèqū huódòng 社区活动 phr.	社區活動	community program
cánjí 残疾 n.	殘疾	disabled
dǎsǎo wèishēng 打扫卫生 phr.	打掃衛生	clean up
jǔbàn 举办 v.	舉辦	organize
wényì yǎnchū 文艺演出 phr.	文藝演出	arts performance
jiēdào 街道 n.		street
jiǎn 捡 v.	撿	pick up
qīngchú túyā 清除涂鸦 phr.	清除塗鴉	clean off graffiti
yǒu yìyì 有意义 adj.	有意義	meaningful
zhīshi 知识 n.	知識	knowledge
lèisì 类似 v.	類似	similar to

外公：丁强，<u>听说</u>美国的<u>社区活动</u>特别多，是吗？

丁强：是的，我和同学都喜欢参加社区服务和志愿者活动。

表姐：那你都参加了什么活动呀？

丁强：嗯…比如说，节日的时候给<u>残疾</u>儿童学校的小朋友送礼物，去敬老院<u>打扫卫生</u>，去儿童福利院陪小朋友一起玩，<u>举办</u>社区<u>文艺演出</u>，打扫街道和<u>捡</u>垃圾，举办社区青年服务活动，<u>清除涂鸦</u>，很多很多。

外公：听起来都很<u>有意义</u>啊！

丁强：是的！我在这些活动中学到很多学校里没有的<u>知识</u>。不知道北京有没有<u>类似</u>的活动呢？

子明：有啊！也有很多！

丁强：比如呢？

子明：我们有的会去敬老院陪老人聊天，或打扫卫生，有的放假的时候去农村给"留守儿童"补课。

丁强：什么是"留守儿童"？

外公：留守儿童就是那些父母都在<u>外地</u>打工，自己留在农村生活的孩子。

丁强：哦，那他们很需要别人的帮助。

子明：是的，他们的父母不在身边，都是亲戚照顾他们，学习、生活都<u>缺少关爱</u>，我们有时候会去帮助他们一起<u>学习</u>。

丁强：那真是很有意义的活动啊！不知道我可以参加吗？

子明：当然可以啊，你可以教他们英文！

liúshǒu értóng 留守儿童 n.	留守兒童	children in foster care of grandparents or other relatives while their parents work in other cities
bǔkè 补课 n.	補課	make up lesson; remedial lesson
wàidì 外地 n.		foreign land
quēshǎo 缺少 v.		lack
guān'ài 关爱 v.	關愛	love
xuéxí 学习 v.	學習	learn

LANGUAGE FOCUS

When talking about things that some people in a group do while other people in the group do a different activity, use the expression 有的…有的….

Example: 邻居们都喜欢参加社区活动，有的打扫街道，有的参加社区文艺演出。

Try This!

1. In groups of three, take turns reading the descriptions below and (1) state whether you have done that kind of activity, (2) write what the American equivalent is, and (3) write down your opinion of whether this idea could be implemented in the United States if there is no American equivalent.

❶ 为居民提供义诊 (yìzhěn, free clinic) 服务

❷ 举办社区文艺演出

③ 参加社区青年服务活动

④ 到敬老院打扫卫生

⑤ 到敬老院为老人们理发

⑥ 清理涂鸦

⑦ 宣传 (xuānchuán, promote) 防火 (fánghuǒ, fire prevention) 知识

⑧ 打扫街道，清除垃圾

⑨ 派发 (pàifā, distribute) 宣传资料给路人 (lùrén, passers-by)

⑩ 参加应急救护培训 (yìngjí jiùhù péixùn, emergency care training)

⑪ 捐血
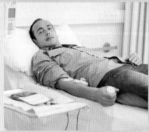

⑫ 冬衣 (dōngyī, winter clothing) 募捐 (mùjuān, collect donations) 活动

⑬ 到儿童福利院，为孤残儿童们捐赠 (juānzèng, donate) 衣物和玩具 (wánjù, toy)

⑭ 在公园捡垃圾

2. Read the following passage and answer the questions in complete sentences.

　　今年五月三日，育才中学学生参加了"走出校门，服务社会"的活动。这天，九年级一班的同学有的打扫街道，有的去敬老院服务，也有的到社区参加文艺演出。王红统计了九年级一班参加社区活动的人数，做了如下统计图。

tǒngjì
count

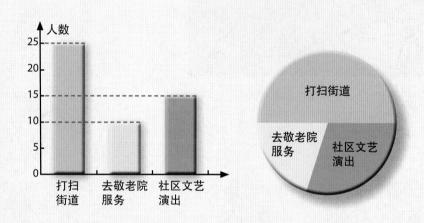

❶ 九年级一班有多少个学生？

❷ 去打扫街道的同学比去敬老院的同学多多少？

❸ 哪一种社区活动参加的学生最多？

❹ 要是九年级有800名学生，估计去敬老院的人数。

gūjì
estimate

Blog

北京人喜欢在春节的时候去逛庙会。北京的庙会有好几个，其中特别有名的包括地坛庙会，位于地坛公园。今年我也想去凑个热闹，所以今天我起得比平时早，七点就坐地铁到了地坛庙会。

那里好热闹啊！庙会有很多卖年货的地摊，比如春联、鞭炮、糖果等；有文化表演，比如抖空竹、皮影戏、口技、变戏法等，还有传统的手艺展示，比如陶艺、剪纸、织布等等。看得我眼花缭乱！

庙会上有的人是来采购年货的，有的人是来看表演的，还有的人是来看这些手艺展示的，其中还有很多像我这样的外国人！大家对这些活动都非常有兴趣！

miàohuì 庙会 n.	廟會		temple fair
qízhōng 其中 n.			among them
bāokuò 包括 v.			include
Dìtán 地坛 p.n.	地壇		Temple of Earth
còu rènao 凑热闹 phr.	湊熱鬧		join in the fun
píngshí 平时 n.	平時		normal times
mài 卖 v.	賣		sell
niánhuò 年货 n.	年貨		New Year's goods
dìtān 地摊 n.	地攤		street stall
chūnlián 春联 n.	春聯		spring couplets
biānpào 鞭炮 n.			firecrackers
tángguǒ 糖果 n.			sweets, candies
wénhuà biǎoyǎn 文化表演 phr.			cultural performance
chuántǒng 传统 n.	傳統		tradition
shǒuyì 手艺 n.	手藝		handicraft
zhǎnshì 展示 v.			exhibit
yǎnhuā liáoluàn 眼花缭乱 phr.	眼花繚亂		bedazzled
cǎigòu 采购 v.	採購		purchase

这些活动真的很<u>特别</u>，和美国的 street fairs 和 carnivals <u>实在</u>太不一样了。庙会比 street fairs 和 carnivals 的活动<u>内容</u>多得多，而且很多活动都是传统文化的展示，非常有意思。

tèbié 特别 *adj.*			special
shízài 实在 *adv.*	實在		really
nèiróng 内容 *n.*			content

EXTENDED VOCABULARY

Chinese performing arts and handicrafts

抖空竹 *phr.*		dǒu kōngzhú	Chinese yo-yo
皮影戏 *n.*	皮影戲	píyǐngxì	shadow puppet show
口技 *n.*		kǒujì	vocal mimicry
变戏法 *phr.*	變戲法	biàn xìfǎ	magic
陶艺 *n.*	陶藝	táoyì	pottery arts
剪纸 *n.*	剪紙	jiǎnzhǐ	paper cutting
织布 *n.*	織布	zhībù	weaving

LANGUAGE FOCUS

You have learned how to compare two items in Chinese using 比, in the pattern of "A + 比 + B." In this structure, an adjective is placed after B to describe the comparison.

Examples:
❶ 丁强比子明高。
❷ 他的亲戚比我的多。
❸ 变戏法比口技难学。
❹ 中文比物理容易。

To compare the extent of an action with that of another, use the particle 得 followed by 比, in the pattern of "A + Verb + 得 + 比 + B + Adjective."

Examples:
❶ 芳芳学得比玛丽快。
❷ 他吃得比我多。
❸ 子明打得比丁强好。

Another way to express the above sentences is to place an object after the verb. The same verb will occur again after the object.

Examples:
❶ 芳芳学法语学得比玛丽快。
❷ 他吃饭吃得比我多。
❸ 子明打乒乓球打得比丁强好。

1. Look at the following pictures and create a sentence that compares the differences between the two using the descriptive words provided.

Example:

  容易学

剪纸比抖空竹容易学。

①

有意思

②

难表演

③
 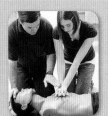
花时间

④

热闹多了

⑤
难学

⑥
费力

⑦

古老

⑧

方便

9

快得多

10

安静

2. With a partner, decide the names of two people (they can be famous people or people in your community) who can do the activities on the right. Write a sentence that expresses your opinion of who is better at that activity.

❶ 打篮球	❺ 画画
❷ 唱歌	❻ 写小说
❸ 跳舞	❼ 跑步
❹ 踢足球	❽ 游泳

Chinese Temple Fairs

The 庙会 (miàohuì) is a temple fair that has become a traditional celebration during the Chinese New Year. It started as a fair held on the grounds of a temple and originally had significance in the Taoism religion. It began to be celebrated during the Tang (618 – 907) and Song (960 – 1279) Dynasties when there was a conflict between Buddhism and Taoism, and was originally meant to attract more followers and build more temples by creating "fairs" around the temples. Sometimes there were large processions in which a highly decorated float with a figure of Buddha was paraded through the streets. This custom later transformed into a carnival where many non-religious events took place, like lion dancing, opera singing, and acrobatic performances.

The secularization of these fairs was also a boon to the local economy. Many vendors came to the fair to sell their wares. The temple fair gradually evolved into a place where people gathered for various kinds of folk performances and trading. In many parts of China, attending a temple fair is an indispensable part of the New Year's celebration. Two temple fairs that have a long history in Beijing are the White Cloud Temple (白云观) Fair and the Temple of the Earth (地坛) Temple Fair.

Step Up!

1. Read the text below and write a short reply to the students congratulating them on their community service.

北京七中寒假社区服务活动总结❶

　　在这个寒假，北京七中开展❷了丰富多彩❸的志愿活动，许多同学在鼓西社区开展了一些送温暖❹活动：给老人送福字，帮忙打扫卫生，制作电池回收箱，做一些环保宣传和演讲，还积极❺宣传提倡❻低碳生活、低碳春节等内容。这些都受到了大家的一致❼好评❽。

❶ (zǒngjié, summary)

❷ (kāizhǎn, commence)

❸ (fēngfù duōcǎi, varied and exciting)

❹ (wēnnuǎn, warmth)

❺ (jījí, actively)

❻ (tíchàng, advocate)

❼ (yízhì, unanimous)

❽ (hǎopíng, commendation)

2. Research the type of services available in your community. Based on your research, create a brochure about one of the services for Chinese immigrants who are moving to your community. You may focus on services for the elderly, educational services, recreational services, health information, or any other possible services that are available in your community.

3. In groups of three, read the brochures from the two other members of your group. Then present your brochure to the group; you will need to try to convince the other members of your group that your brochure is the most comprehensive and the best. As a group, compare the brochures and come to a consensus as to which brochure is the best and why. Finally, present your findings to the entire class. (The teacher will call on one student at random from the group to report.) All students must be able to explain which brochure is the best in the group and why.

Fun Time!

Read the recipe below and follow the steps to make the famous Beijing food, 炸酱面.

份量： Portion		2人份
准备时间： Preparation time		15分钟
烹饪时间： Cooking time		30分钟

用料 Ingredients

面条 noodles	——	200克 gram
五花肉 pork belly	——	150克 gram
黄瓜 cucumber	——	半根 half
胡萝卜 carrot	——	半根 half
姜 ginger	——	1小块 a small piece
黄豆酱 bean paste	——	3勺 tablespoon
水 water	——	适量 as appropriate
甜面酱 sweet bean paste	——	1勺 tablespoon
豆豉辣酱 chili bean paste	——	1勺 tablespoon
小葱 spring onion	——	3根 stalk
植物油 vegetable oil	——	适量 as appropriate

做法 Method

1. 五花肉切丁，放入热油锅里炒至金黄色，取出肉沫留底油备用。

   Cut the pork belly into small pieces. Heat some oil in your wok and add the pork. Cook till the pork turns golden brown at the edges. Remove the pork and keep the oil for later use.

2. 黄豆酱、甜面酱以3:1混合，再加入1勺的豆豉辣酱。

   Mix the bean paste with sweet bean paste in the ratio 3:1. Add a tablespoon of chili bean paste.

3. 炒肉留下的油加热后倒入姜葱末炒。

   Heat up the leftover oil and then add ginger.

4. 倒入调好的酱料翻炒，再加少许水继续翻炒。

   Pour in the sauce mix prepared earlier and stir fry. Add some water and continue to stir fry.

5. 将炒好的肉沫加入酱中小火翻炒。

   Add the pork into the sauce and stir fry it over a small fire.

6. 炸酱做好后，用大锅煮沸水，将面条煮好捞出，浇上炸酱，加上黄瓜丝、胡萝卜丝、小葱丝，拌好就可以吃了。

   Cook noodles in a pot of boiling water. Remove the noodles; pour sauce over; add cucumber, carrot, and spring onion; mix well before eating.

I have learned...

NEW WORDS

Verbs

进来	進來	jìnlai	come in		商量		shāngliang	negotiate, discuss
换	換	huàn	change		遇到		yùdào	encounter, meet with, face
带	帶	dài	bring		支持		zhīchí	support
出去		chūqu	go out		相聚		xiāngjù	gather
出来	出來	chūlai	come out		感觉	感覺	gǎnjué	feel
拿		ná	take out		听说	聽說	tīngshuō	hear of
进去	進去	jìnqu	go in		举办	舉辦	jǔbàn	organize
准备	準備	zhǔnbèi	prepare		捡	撿	jiǎn	pick up
担心	擔心	dānxīn	worry		类似	類似	lèisì	similar to
选择	選擇	xuǎnzé	choose		缺少		quēshǎo	lack
拜访	拜訪	bàifǎng	to visit (people)		关爱	關愛	guān'ài	love and concern
了解		liǎojiě	to know; to understand		学习	學習	xuéxí	learn
成为	成爲	chéngwéi	become		包括		bāokuò	include
介绍	介紹	jièshào	introduce		卖	賣	mài	sell
见面	見面	jiànmiàn	meet		展示		zhǎnshì	exhibit
重视	重視	zhòngshì	attach importance to, value something		采购	採購	cǎigòu	purchase
相处	相處	xiāngchǔ	to get along with others					

Nouns

礼物	禮物	lǐwù	gift		亲属称呼	親屬稱呼	qīnshǔ chēnghu	kinship terms
心意		xīnyì	regards		亲人	親人	qīnrén	one's family members
寄宿家庭		jìsù jiātíng	host family		日常琐事	日常瑣事	rìcháng suǒshì	life's trivialities
选择	選擇	xuǎnzé	choice		困难	困難	kùnnan	difficulties
生活		shēnghuó	life		气氛	氣氛	qìfēn	atmosphere
趣事		qùshì	interesting matters		残疾	殘疾	cánjí	disabled
名胜	名勝	míngshèng	scenic spot		街道		jiēdào	street
古迹	古跡	gǔjì	place of historic interest		知识	知識	zhīshi	knowledge
亲戚	親戚	qīnqi	relatives (related by blood)		留守儿童	留守兒童	liúshǒu értóng	children in foster care of grandparents or other relatives while their parents work in other cities
家庭聚会	家庭聚會	jiātíng jùhuì	family gathering		补课	補課	bǔkè	make up lesson; remedial lesson

外地		wàidì	foreign land	皮影戏	皮影戲	píyǐngxì	shadow puppet show
庙会	廟會	miàohuì	temple fair	口技		kǒujì	vocal mimicry
其中		qízhōng	among them	传统	傳統	chuántǒng	tradition
平时	平時	píngshí	normal times	手艺	手藝	shǒuyì	handicraft
年货	年貨	niánhuò	New Year's goods	陶艺	陶藝	táoyì	pottery arts
地摊	地攤	dìtān	street stall	剪纸	剪紙	jiǎnzhǐ	paper cutting
春联	春聯	chūnlián	spring couplets	织布	織布	zhībù	weaving
鞭炮		biānpào	firecrackers	内容		nèiróng	content
糖果		tángguǒ	sweets, candies				

Proper noun				**Preposition**			
地坛	地壇	Dìtán	Temple of Earth	为	為	wèi	for

Adjectives

客气	客氣	kèqì	courtesy	复杂	複雜	fùzá	complicated
有趣		yǒuqù	interesting	和睦	和睦	hémù	to be in harmony
舒服		shūfu	comfortable	温馨	溫馨	wēnxīn	warm, heartfelt
热情	熱情	rèqíng	enthusiastic	有意义	有意義	yǒu yìyì	meaningful
友好		yǒuhǎo	friendly	特别		tèbié	special

Adverbs				**Conjunctions**			
互相		hùxiāng	mutually	以及		yǐjí	and
实在	實在	shízài	really	或者		huòzhě	or

Pronouns

大家		dàjiā	everyone, all	彼此		bǐcǐ	each other, both parties
咱们	咱們	zánmen	we, us				

Phrases

敲门	敲門	qiāomén	knock on the door	文艺演出	文藝演出	wényì yǎnchū	arts performance
递给	遞給	dìgěi	to pass on	清除涂鸦	清除塗鴉	qīngchú túyā	clean off graffiti
接风	接風	jiēfēng	give a welcome dinner	凑热闹	湊熱鬧	còu rènao	join in the fun
弄糊涂	弄糊塗	nòng hútu	get confused	文化表演		wénhuà biǎoyǎn	cultural performance
家庭幸福		jiātíng xìngfú	a happy family	抖空竹		dǒu kōngzhú	Chinese yo-yo
儿女子孙	兒女子孫	érnǚ zǐsūn	children and grandchildren	变戏法	變戲法	biàn xìfǎ	magic
社区活动	社區活動	shèqū huódòng	community program	眼花缭乱	眼花繚亂	yǎnhuā liáoluàn	bedazzled
打扫卫生	打掃衛生	dǎsǎo wèishēng	clean up				

Constructions

听…说起… 聽…説起…	tīng...shuōqǐ...	heard that (someone) mentioned (something)	再…也…	zài...yě	even though...still

Members of the extended family

祖父/爷爷		zǔfù/yéye	paternal grandfather	嫂嫂/弟媳		sǎosao/dìxí	sister-in-law, older brother's wife / younger brother's wife
祖母/奶奶		zǔmǔ/nǎinai	paternal grandmother	哥哥/弟弟		gēge/dìdi	older brother / younger brother
外祖父/外公		wàizǔfù/wàigōng	maternal grandfather	自己		zìjǐ	myself
外祖母/外婆		wàizǔmǔ/wàipó	maternal grandmother	丈夫		zhàngfu	husband
姑妈	姑媽	gūmā	aunt, father's sister	妻子		qīzi	wife
姑父		gūfù	uncle, father's sister's husband	姐姐/妹妹		jiějie/mèimei	older sister/ younger sister
伯父/叔父		bófù/shūfù	uncle, father's older brother father / father's younger brother	姐夫/妹夫		jiěfu/mèifu	brother-in-law, older sister's husband/ younger sister's husband
伯母/婶婶	嬸嬸	bómǔ/shěnshen	aunt, father's older brother's wife / father's younger brother's wife	表哥/表弟		biǎogē/biǎodì	male cousins (maternal)
父亲	父親	fùqīn	father	表姐/表妹		biǎojiě/biǎomèi	female cousins (maternal)
母亲	母親	mǔqīn	mother	侄子		zhízi	nephew, brother's son
舅舅		jiùjiu	uncle, mother's brother	侄女		zhínǚ	niece, brother's daughter
舅妈	舅媽	jiùmā	aunt, mother's brother's wife	儿子	兒子	érzi	son
姨妈	姨媽	yímā	aunt, mother's sister	女儿	女兒	nǚ'ér	daughter
姨父		yífù	uncle, mother's sister's husband	外甥		wàisheng	nephew, sister's son
堂姐/堂妹		tángjiě/tángmèi	female cousins (paternal)	外甥女		wàishengnǚ	niece, sister's daughter
堂哥/堂弟		tánggē/tángdì	male cousins (maternal)				

◇◇ SENTENCE PATTERNS ◇◇

丁强，你好！你来啦！快进来！

我没吃过北京烤鸭。大家一边吃着饭，一边讨论北京生活的趣事。我在那里买了很多衣服。

你还会见到我好几个亲人。

每个周末，大家再忙也要和亲人聚在一起吃饭。

我们有的会去敬老院陪老人聊天，有的会去农村给"留守儿童"补课。

这里的活动比那里的多。

I can do!

Interpretive Communication

❑ I can understand when people talk about other members of the family.

❑ I can read and interpret blogs.

❑ I can read and understand information about community service in China.

Interpersonal Communication

❑ I can converse with family members to learn about their lives.

❑ I can interact with someone discussing past events.

❑ I can exchange information about approximate quantities.

❑ I can discuss my preferences about activities in the community.

❑ I can discuss and compare information with another person.

Presentational Communication

❑ I can explain family relationships in Chinese.

❑ I can describe a typical Chinese home.

❑ I can describe events that occurred in different time frames.

❑ I can state my opinion about community service.

❑ I can create brochures of activities that people can do to improve their communities.

❑ I can talk about approximate quantities of items.

Cultural Knowledge

❑ I can describe a Chinese temple fair.

❑ I can understand honorific expressions when they are used to address someone in Chinese.

❑ I can state some polite expressions that are used in various contexts.

❑ I can state one of Confucius' analects about friends.

My learning experience

我的学习经验

COMMUNICATIVE GOALS

- Describing after school activities
- Conversing about homework pressures and examinations
- Conversing about worries and expectations
- Comparing the homework load and college entrance examinations

Cultural Knowledge

- The imperial examination
- Private tutoring in China
- Chinese grading system

Get ready...

Below is a survey that compares parents' expectations for children's success in four different countries: Japan, Korea, China, and the United States. Study the survey and answer the following questions.

母亲对子女
寄予厚望

父亲对子女
寄予厚望

(Source: Xinhua, 2006)

子女	zǐ nǚ	children *(sons and daughters)*
寄予	jìyǔ	to place *(hope)* on
厚望	hòuwàng	great hope; high expectations

❶ 四个国家中，哪个国家的母亲对子女寄予厚望的比例最高？
proportion

❷ 四个国家中，哪个国家的父亲对子女寄予厚望的比例最低？

❸ 你觉得这是为什么？

STEPS *at a glance!*

STEP 1

PARTICIPATING IN ACADEMIC LIFE IN CHINA

A. Managing the study load in school

我看你的功课太多了，常常周末也在做作业。

B. Taking part in an academic competition

只有考到好成绩，才能进入理想的大学。

STEP 2

DEVELOPING SKILLS

A. Attending extra classes

学生每天不是在学校上课，就是去上课外补习班。

B. Finding enjoyment in learning

每天即使没有钢琴课，我也会在家练习。

STEP 3

MEETING EXPECTATIONS AND DEALING WITH PRESSURE

A. Coping with stress

这个星期的作业很多，你做得完吗？

B. Meeting expectations

由于学生不想辜负父母和老师的期望，所以每天早起晚睡，努力学习。

A Managing the study load in school

丁强和子明吃完晚饭以后聊天。

丁强：我来北京一个多月了，我看你的功课太多了，<u>常常</u>周末也在做作业。

子明：是啊！我今年高二，很忙。每天早上六点起床，吃过早餐就去学校上课。上午和下午我有九节课，晚上还有三节<u>自习</u>课，只有中午才可以休息一会儿。每天老师<u>总是</u><u>布置</u>很多功课，所以有时候晚上十二点我还在做功课。

丁强：对，我看你<u>经常</u>很晚才睡觉。那你们学校都有些什么课？

子明：除了<u>语文</u>、数学和英语三门<u>主要</u>的课以外，我们还有历史、地理、生物、化学和物理。

丁强：哦，这么多课！那你觉得可以<u>应付</u>吗？

chángcháng/jīngcháng 常常/经常 adv.	常常/經常	often
zìxí 自习 v.	自習	study by oneself in scheduled time or free time
zǒngshì 总是 adv.	總是	always
bùzhì 布置 v.	佈置	assign
yǔwén 语文 n.	語文	the Chinese language
zhǔyào 主要 adj.		main, principal
yìngfù 应付 v.	應付	to deal with, to cope with

子明：还可以吧！我常常<u>告诉</u>自己，不只我一个人<u>辛苦</u>，其他人也一样辛苦。<u>年轻</u>时多读点书、多学点<u>本事</u>是好的，将来<u>必定</u>会<u>受益</u>。

丁强：你的<u>态度</u>非常积极！这也是对<u>毅力</u>的<u>磨炼</u>！

子明：谢谢，其实我也知道不<u>能够</u><u>老是</u>读书，也需要时间<u>放松</u>一下，<u>缓解</u>功课的<u>压力</u>。这个周末我们一起到外面逛逛，好吗？

丁强：好！

gàosu 告诉 v.	告訴	tell
xīnkǔ 辛苦 adj.		strenuous, laborious
niánqīng 年轻 adj.	年輕	young
běnshì 本事 n.		skill
bìdìng 必定 adv.		surely
shòuyì 受益 v.		benefit, gain
tàidù 态度 n.	態度	attitude
jījí 积极 adj.	積極	positive
yìlì 毅力 n.		willpower, tenacity
móliàn 磨炼 n.; v.	磨煉	training; train
nénggòu 能够 aux.v.	能夠	can, be able to
lǎoshì 老是 adv.		always, all the time
fàngsōng 放松 v.	放鬆	relax
huǎnjiě 缓解 v.	緩解	relieve, alleviate
yālì 压力 n.	壓力	pressure

LANGUAGE FOCUS

常常, 经常, and 总是 are adverbs used to indicate frequency. They are normally placed before verbs to show how often an action occurs. 常常 and 经常 both mean "often" and can be used interchangeably. 总是 means "always."

- 我常常跑步。
- 她经常上网聊天。
- 他总是迟到。
- 他总是很晚才睡觉。

Other adverbs that indicate frequency include 从来不 (never), 从来没有 (never), 很少 (seldom), and 有时候 (sometimes). They are also used in the same way as those mentioned above.

1. Describe the daily routine of your family members using 总是 and 常常/经常.

   Example: 我哥哥总是很晚才起床。他早饭常常喝咖啡。

2. **Survey** The teacher will divide the board into four columns listing the Chinese adverbs expressing frequency from most frequent to least frequent. Students then take turns writing down an activity they do under each column according to the frequency with which they do it.

   Next, work in groups to summarize which activity the class does most frequently and least frequently and why. What does this information tell you about the life styles of your classmates? Each group will present the results orally to the class.

常常	有时候	很少	从来不/从来没有
打球	跑步	吃中国菜	唱歌
跑步	看电影	买东西	打球
打球	看电视	旅行	吃中国菜
上网	玩电脑游戏	跑步	打球
……	……	……	……

gāokǎo 高考 *n.*		college entrance exam
bìxū 必须 *aux. v.*	必須	must, have to
kāishǐ 开始 *v.*	開始	start
zhǐyǒu...cái 只有…才…		only by...can...
kǎo 考 *v.*		take an examination
chéngjì 成绩 *n.*	成績	grade, result
lǐxiǎng 理想 *n.*		ideal
dàxué 大学 *n.*	大學	college, university
yònggōng 用功 *adj.*		diligent, hardworking
jìngzhēng 竞争 *n.; v.*	競爭	competition; compete
jīliè 激烈 *adj.*		intense
yuánlái 原来 *adv.*	原來	so that's how it is

丁强和子明在客厅里聊天：

丁强：你还好吧？我看你天天都很忙。

子明：每个高中生都是这样，因为应付高考必须在高一高二就开始准备。只有考到好成绩，才能进入理想的大学。所以大家都非常用功，竞争非常激烈。

丁强：原来是这样。压力很大！

子明：虽然考试的压力很大，可是我爸妈和老师还是鼓励我多参加课外活动，比方说模拟联合国不但能加强我们对国际时事的认识，而且能培养我们表达意见的能力；打乒乓球不仅能锻炼身体，还能减压。

丁强：除了这些以外，我知道你还当义工，是吗？

子明：是的！我对当义工很感兴趣。我常常到老人中心服务，还在小区推动废物回收。

丁强：这些活动都很有意义。其实你的高中生活也过得非常充实。

子明：对，虽然学业很重要，但我也希望在其他方面多锻炼自己，并且为社会尽一份力。

LANGUAGE FOCUS

只有 means "only if" and is paired with 才 to emphasize that only one course of action will bring about the desired outcome. 只有 is placed at the start of the first clause to emphasize a particular course of action or condition, while 才 is placed in the second clause to indicate the desired outcome brought about by the course of action or condition mentioned earlier.

- 在中国，只有参加高考，才能报读大学。

- 只有努力学习，才会考到好成绩。

gǔlì 鼓励 v.		鼓勵	encourage
kèwài 课外 adj.		課外	extra-curricular
mónǐ liánhéguó 模拟联合国 n.		模擬聯合國	Model United Nations
jiāqiáng 加强 v.		加強	strengthen, enhance
guójì 国际 adj.		國際	international
shíshì 时事 n.		時事	current affairs
érqiě 而且 conj.			and
péiyǎng 培养 v.		培養	develop, cultivate
biǎodá 表达 v.		表達	express
yìjiàn 意见 n.			opinion, view
nénglì 能力 n.			ability
duànliàn 锻炼 v.		鍛煉	train
tuīdòng 推动 v.		推動	promote
chōngshí 充实 adj.		充實	fulfilling
xuéyè 学业 n.		學業	studies
zhòngyào 重要 adj.			important
xīwàng 希望 v.			hope
bìngqiě 并且 conj.		並且	and

Try This!

1. Match the sentences.

❶ 只有多运动，•   • a. 才会明白老师在说什么。

❷ 只有做完作业，•   • b. 才能考到好成绩。

❸ 只有用功读书，•   • c. 才可以出去玩。

❹ 只有认真听课，•   • d. 才会有健康的身体。

❺ 只有多看新闻，•   • e. 病才会好。

❻ 只有多练习，•   • f 这里才会下雪。

❼ 只有到了十二月，•   • g. 才会知道天下事。

❽ 只有去看医生，•   • h. 中文才会进步。
jìnbù
improve

2. Complete the dialogs using 只有…才….

A A mother has high expectations of her child and hopes he/she will study hard and perfect his/her skills in playing musical instruments.

孩子: 我想看一会儿电视，可以吗？

妈妈: _____。

孩子: 我可以出去玩吗？

妈妈: _____。

B Your friend is not very healthy as he/she does not like to exercise, often eats fast food, and does not eat fruit and vegetables.

朋友: 我希望身体健康。

你: _____。

C Your friend plans to save up for a trip. He/she often buys expensive clothes and dines in expensive restaurants.

朋友：我想出国旅行，可是我没有那么多钱，我怎么做才可以省钱？

你：_____。

D You are a Chinese high school student, while your friend is an American high school student. Your friend does not understand the college entrance examination system in China.

朋友：高考重要吗？

你：很重要，_____。

朋友：那高考难不难？考一个好成绩容易吗？

你：很难，_____。

朋友：你压力这么大，今天跟我出去玩一玩吧。

你：对不起，我星期一到星期六都得学习，_____

_____。

The Imperial Examination (科举制)

The Chinese have a long history of examination systems. The imperial examination was a civil service examination system in Imperial China to select candidates for state official positions. It began during the Han Dynasty (206 BC — 220 AD) and remained in effect until its abolition in 1905. The examination was based on the Four Books and Five Classics (四书五经), the authoritative books of Confucianism. The examination was held in counties, provinces, and then every three years in the capital city. The top three candidates would be interviewed by the emperor, and the selection process would take place in the Forbidden City. The top three candidates would be given the following titles: 状元 (zhuàngyuán), 榜眼 (bǎngyǎn), and 探花 (tànhuā). This kind of rigid selection process was blamed for contributing to the narrowness of intellectual life and the repression of creativity.

DEVELOPING SKILLS

A Attending extra classes

Blog

　　在中国，大部分学生每天不是在学校上课，就是去上课外补习班。

　　补习班有很多种，一种是传统的英语、语文、数学等高考科目的补习班。上这种补习班的目的是希望通过课外的辅导，学生可以取得进步。

　　另外一种常见的补习班是特长补习班，像舞蹈班、绘画班、钢琴班、小提琴班等等。上这种特长补习班是要培养孩子的特长，特别是在艺术方面。

　　很多父母想让自己的孩子在跟同龄人的竞争中有优势，或者培养孩子的毅力以及陶冶性情，所以从小就让他们上这样的补习班。

bùfèn 部分 n.		part, section
kēmù 科目 n.		subject
mùdì 目的 n.		aim, objective
tōngguò 通过 prep.	通過	through, by means of
fǔdǎo 辅导 n.; v.	輔導	coaching; coach
qǔdé 取得 v.		achieve
jìnbù 进步 n.; v.	進步	improvement, progress; improve, progress
chángjiàn 常见 adj.	常見	commonly seen
tècháng 特长 n.	特長	specialty
huìhuà 绘画 v.	繪畫	drawing
xiǎotíqín 小提琴 n.		violin
tónglíng 同龄 v.	同齡	of the same age
yōushì 优势 n.	優勢	advantage
táoyě 陶冶 v.		mold, cultivate
xìngqíng 性情 n.		temperament

To describe a situation as being one of only two possibilities, you can use the paired conjunctions 不是…就是…, in the pattern of "不是 + A, 就是 + B." Here A and B refer to the two possibilities and the structures of A and B are the same. If A is a verb object compound, B should be the same. If A is a noun, B should be a noun as well.

Examples: **1** 她什么时候去北京？不是明天就是后天。

(Both 明天 and 后天 are nouns.)

2 他整天不是上网就是看书。

(Both 上网 and 看书 are verb-object compounds.)

This pattern is useful in providing elaboration or concrete examples for the previous sentence.

Examples: **1** 马克是一个很聪明的学生，每次考试不是第一就是第二。

(The second sentence explains why Mark is an intelligent student.
He gets either the highest or the second highest grade in the class.)

2 芳芳很用功，不是复习功课，就是准备考试。

(The second sentence explains why Fangfang is a hard-working student.
She is either doing her homework or preparing for tests.)

Private Tutoring in China

Due to the emphasis on academic success in China, private tutoring has become increasingly popular. Seen as an effective way to ensure academic excellence, and with the desire to  secure the best possible education for their children in a highly competitive global market, many Chinese parents send their children to numerous private classes after school. The demand for private tutoring classes in English is especially high, given the importance of English as the international language and as a compulsory subject in *gaokao* (高考).

New Oriental School (新东方学校), an educational company, was established as a provider of private educational services in China. It is the most popular test preparation school. Many Chinese students have taken English courses there or used their TOEFL or SAT test preparation services. According to statistics, there were about 20,000,000 students who had studied in New Oriental School as of 2014.

1. Complete the sentences below.

❶ 中国的学生学习压力很大，不是＿＿＿＿＿＿＿＿＿＿＿＿＿＿就是

＿＿＿＿＿＿＿＿＿＿。

❷ 学生们的生活很没意思，每天不是＿＿＿＿＿＿＿＿＿＿＿＿就是

＿＿＿＿＿＿＿＿＿＿。

❸ 昨天我去逛商场，一件衣服都没买，那儿的衣服不是＿＿＿＿＿

＿＿＿＿＿就是＿＿＿＿＿＿＿＿＿＿。

❹ 我不喜欢坐飞机，因为坐飞机很无聊，不是＿＿＿＿＿＿＿＿＿

就是＿＿＿＿＿＿＿＿＿。

❺ 飞机餐也不好吃，没有太多的选择，不是＿＿＿＿＿＿＿＿就

是＿＿＿＿＿＿＿＿。

2. Read the text and answer the following questions.

补习班

学生：小学1-6年级
人数：每班10人

shōufèi
收费：1-4年级250元/月；5-6年级300元/月；
fee
周末班500元/学期/门

◆ 各科作业辅导＋复习＋新课预习
yùxí
preview
◆ 课课清，周周考。

学习时间：周日下午两点到晚上十点；周末上午十点到晚上十点
联系电话：158 6107 5331, 138 5725 8036　　联系人：张老师

❶ 几年级的学生可以上这个补习班？

❷ 这个补习班可以辅导学生做什么？

❸ 这补习班怎么收费？

❹ 这个补习班的学习时间是什么时候？

❺ 要是你想上这个补习班，可以给谁打电话？电话号码是什么？

子明和同学李伟在聊天。

李伟：子明，今天下午有空吗？我们一起去打球吧。

子明：不行，我下午有钢琴课。

李伟：哦，原来你在学琴啊！

子明：是的，我已经学了很多年，很喜欢弹钢琴。每天<u>即使</u>没有钢琴课，我<u>也</u>会在家<u>练习</u>。

李伟：哦，都<u>养</u>成<u>习惯</u>了！有个爱好真不错！

子明：兴趣是最好的老师。每次学了新的<u>乐曲</u>之后，我都会花时间练习，有时会练上三四个小时。

李伟：练习这么长时间，不觉得累吗？

子明：虽然有点累，但是最后能把曲子弹好，还是很有<u>成就感</u>的。

jíshǐ...yě... 即使…也…		even if...
liànxí 练习 v.	練習	practice
yǎng 养 v.	養	develop
xíguàn 习惯 n.	習慣	habit
yuèqǔ 乐曲 n.	樂曲	musical piece
chéngjiùgǎn 成就感 n.		sense of achievement

李伟： 看来学琴不仅能培养<u>才艺</u>，
　　　 还能磨炼<u>意志</u>！

子明： 你说得对！

cáiyì			
才艺 n.	才藝	talent
yìzhì			
意志 n.		will

LANGUAGE FOCUS

The pattern 即使…也… expresses concession. The first clause with 即使 is used to raise a condition which has not yet occurred or is the opposite of what has happened. The second clause with 也 describes an outcome that will happen regardless of the condition in the first clause.

Examples:　❶ 既使下午没有课，你也要自己温习功课。

　　　　　　❷ 即使我很累，我也要把功课做完。

　　　　　　❸ 即使我不说，别人也会说。

Try This!

1. Complete the following sentences.

❶ 即使_____，也不能骄傲。

❷ 即使明天下雨，_____。

❸ 即使_____，也吃不完这些菜。

❹ 即使我们今晚不睡觉，_____。

❺ 即使_____，也看不完这么多书。

❻ 即使你们不同意，_____。

2. Imagine that your Chinese host family has sent you and your host brother/sister to a math camp during the break. You have a very intense class schedule and the homework assignments are very repetitive. The camp is very strict with morning wake up times, lights out, and the use of the Internet. Write an email to your host family to complain about the situation. Use 常常, 总是, 不是…就是…, and 即使…也… to indicate the intense schedule. Also include some of your suggestions on how to spend your break next time. Write at least 250 words.

 CULTURAL HIGHLIGHTS

Chinese Grading System

The nine category rank system (九品中正制 jiǔ pǐn zhōng zhèng zhì) was a civil service nomination system during the period of the Three Kingdoms. Local government officials selected talented candidates by categorizing them into nine grades depending on their abilities. 上 meant high, 中 meant middle, and 下 meant low. Each of these categories would then be divided into three sub-categories and thus became nine grades of 上上, 上中, 上下, 中上, 中中, 中下, 下上, 下中, and 下下.

In Taiwan today students receive the following grades: 优 (yōu), 良 (liáng), 常 (cháng), 可 (kě), 差 (chà), 劣 (liè); or 甲 (jiǎ), 乙 (yǐ), 丙 (bǐng), 丁 (dīng), 差 (chà), 劣 (liè). In mainland China, teachers usually give students numerical scores. If you were a school administrator, what system would you use for your students?

MEETING EXPECTATIONS AND DEALING WITH PRESSURE

A Coping with stress

子明和他的同学张健在聊天。

子明：这个星期的作业很多，你做得完吗？

张健：我昨天一整天在家里做，还是做不完！

子明：我也是！下个礼拜还有好几个<u>测验</u>呢。

张健：是啊，<u>课业</u>这么<u>繁重</u>，我快受不了了。

子明：压力真的很大，听说以前有一些学生因为成绩不好压力大，<u>越来越</u><u>沮丧</u>，越来越<u>抑郁</u>，最后还没参加高考就<u>崩溃</u>了。

张健：我最近常常<u>失眠</u>，我就想我<u>花</u>了那么多时间学习，可是考试成绩总是不理想，现在对高考我也没有<u>信心</u>了。如果高考考不好，进不了<u>名牌</u>大学，将来找不到工作，<u>怎么办</u>呢？

子明：对自己<u>要求</u>高是好的，可是也不要给自己那么大的压力。<u>乐观</u>一点儿，不要整天想成绩考试的事情，多想积极的方面，跟朋友聊聊天，听听音乐，出去走一走，<u>调整</u>一下<u>心情</u>。我爸妈常鼓励我多参加一些有意思的课外活动，这样可以学到很多在书本上学不到的东西，对我们将来<u>做人处事</u><u>更</u>有帮助。

cèyàn 测验 n.	測驗	test
kèyè 课业 n.	課業	study load
fánzhòng 繁重 adj.		heavy
yuèláiyuè 越来越 adv.	越來越	more and more
jǔsàng 沮丧 adj.	沮喪	dejected, dispirited
yōuyù 忧郁 adj.	憂鬱	depressed
bēngkuì 崩溃 v.	崩潰	break down
shīmián 失眠 v.		unable to sleep
huā 花 v.		spend
xìnxīn 信心 n.		confidence
míngpái 名牌 n.		famous
zěnmebàn 怎么办 phr.	怎麼辦	how
yāoqiú 要求 v.		request, expect
lèguān 乐观 adj.	樂觀	optimistic
tiáozhěng 调整 v.	調整	adjust
xīnqíng 心情 n.		feelings, mood
zuòrén chǔshì 做人处事 phr.	做人處事	relating to people
gèng 更 adv.		even more

Potential complements are used to express the possibility of achieving an expected outcome. They come in two forms: positive and negative. The positive form has 得 placed between the verb and the complement, while the negative form uses 不 between the verb and the complement.

Examples:

<table>
<tr><td colspan="2">Positive form</td><td colspan="2">Negative form</td></tr>
</table>

❧ 我听得懂。
I can understand (from listening).

❧ 我听不懂。
I can't understand (from listening).

❧ 我吃得完。
I can finish (eating the food).

❧ 我吃不完。
I can't finish (eating the food).

Questions containing potential complements can be formed in the following ways:

❶ With a question word:

❧ 你听得懂吗?
Can you understand?

❧ 你吃得完吗?
Can you finish (eating the food)?

❷ With a positive-negative structure:

❧ 你听得懂听不懂?
Can you understand?

❧ 你吃得完吃不完?
Can you finish (eating the food)?

了 (liǎo) is often used as a potential complement, expressing whether or not an action can be carried out.

Examples: **❶** 下个星期五是小李的生日,你来得了吗?
Next Friday is Xiao Li's birthday party. Can you come?

❷ 下星期五我正好有事,对不起,我来不了了。
Next Friday I am not available. I am sorry, I can't come.

❸ 功课那么多,我真的受不了。
There is too much homework. I just can't bear it.

1. Fill in the blanks with the appropriate complements of possibility.

❶ 我妈妈从来没学过英文，英文的电视剧她 _____。

diànshìjù
drama serial

（听得懂、听不懂）

❷ 她的英文非常好，连英文报刊都 _____。

bàokān
newspaper

（看得懂、看不懂）

❸ 今天我们的作业不太多，我半个小时 _____。

（做得完、做不完）

❹ 我们只有两个人，点六个菜 _____。

（吃得完、吃不完）

❺ 你可以跟我一起准备测验吗？我一个人 _____。

（准备得好、准备不好）

❻ 你生病了，两个星期没上课，明天的考试你自己 _____吗？

（准备得好、准备不好）

❼ 我最近学习压力太大，每天晚上都 _____。

（睡得好、睡不好）

❽ 我想自己做中国菜，做中国菜的调料美国 _____吗？

tiáoliào
condiment

（买得到、买不到）

❾ 老师写的字太小了，我坐在后面 _____。

（看得到、看不到）

❿ 课业太繁重，学习压力太大，很多学生都 _____。

（受得了、受不了）

2. Work with a partner and describe how you felt during a busy period (exams, competitions, etc.). Use the words you just learned to express your feelings. Each of you will need to speak at least two sentences.

Blog

　　很多父母都希望孩子能考上好学校，所以孩子都承受着很大的压力。老师对学生的要求也很严格，希望他们把所有的精力都放在学习上，以最好的状态去应考。由于学生不想辜负父母和老师的期望，所以每天早起晚睡，上课专心听讲做笔记，下课认真做作业，周末还要去上父母为他们报名的各种补习班。

　　不过，现在有越来越多父母认为孩子的身心发展更重要，而且成才的路并不只有上名校这一条，所以避免给予他们太大的压力，觉得只要孩子尽力就可以了。他们更希望孩子能够快乐，所以会多跟孩子沟通，了解他们的想法，并提供适当的鼓励与支持。

chéngshòu 承受 v.		bear, withstand
yángé 严格 adj.	嚴格	strict
suǒyǒu 所有 pron.		all, entire
jīnglì 精力 n.		energy
zhuàngtài 状态 n.	狀態	state, condition
yìngkǎo 应考 v.	應考	sit for examinations
yóuyú...suǒyǐ... 由于…所以…	由於…所以…	because of, (so)...
gūfù 辜负 v.	辜負	let down
qīwàng 期望 n.; v.		expectation, hope; expect, hope
bàomíng 报名 v.	報名	sign up
búguò 不过 conj.	不過	however, but
shēnxīn 身心 n.		body and mind
fāzhǎn 发展 n.; v	發展	development; develop
chéngcái 成才 v.		become a useful person
bìmiǎn 避免 v.		avoid
jǐyǔ 给予 v.	給予	give
jìnlì 尽力 v.	盡力	do one's best
gōutōng 沟通 v.	溝通	communicate
tígōng 提供 v.		provide
shìdàng 适当 adj.	適當	appropriate
yǔ 与 conj.	與	and

There are many expressions in Chinese for cause and effect. One of them is 由于…所以…. The first clause indicates the cause and the second clause indicates the effect.

Example: 由于他很关心别人，所以常常参加社区服务的活动。

由于 is similar to 因为, however there are a few differences:

- 由于 is normally used in written Chinese, while 因为 is used in spoken Chinese though it can be used in written Chinese as well.
- 由于 usually pairs with 所以, 因此, and 因而. However, 因为 only pairs with 所以, and does not pair with 因此 or 因而.
- 由于 can only be used in the first clause, not the second clause.

Here are more examples that illustrate the similarities and differences between 由于 and 因为:

❶ 由于地铁人太多，所以我迟到了。
(因为…所以… may be used here.)

❷ 由于她热心社区服务，因此受到老师和同学的尊敬。
(因为 cannot be used here as it does not pair with 因此.)

❸ 我今天不能参加你的生日会，因为家里有点事。
(由于 cannot be used here as it cannot be placed in the second clause.)

1. Match the sentences on the left with the correct ones on the right.

❶ 由于父母和老师的要求很高 •	• a. 所以找工作很难
❷ 由于学生压力太大 •	• b. 所以飞机晚点了 delay
❸ 由于天气情况不好 qíngkuàng condition •	• c. 所以学生承受着很大的压力
❹ 由于经济情况不好 jīngjì economy •	• d. 所以变得沮丧、抑郁，甚至崩溃 shènzhì even to the extent that
❺ 由于高考的成绩不理想 •	• e. 所以他没能进入好大学
❻ 由于昨天晚上睡得不好 •	• f. 所以成绩提高了很多 tígāo improve
❼ 由于他努力学习 •	• g. 所以学校里一个人也没有
❽ 由于学校放假 •	• h. 所以他今天早上迟到了

2. Read the dialog and answer the following questions.

A：你不想上补习班，为什么还要去上？

B：因为我不想辜负我爸爸妈妈的期望。他们希望我通过上补习班，能很快地提高学习成绩。由于补习班的费用很高，所以他们为我花了很多钱。
fèiyòng
cost

A：可是你每天都在学校学习八九个小时，再说，你的成绩不错，根本不需要花钱上补习班。
gēnběn
at all

B：妈妈说我应该对自己有更高的要求，不要觉得八十几分就可以了，要努力考到九十甚至满分。

A：那你的压力太大了，你受得了吗？

B：没办法，受不了也得努力学习，我不想让我的爸爸妈妈失望。
shīwàng
disappointed

❶ B 想上补习班吗？他为什么上补习班？
❷ A 觉得 B 需不需要上补习班？为什么？
❸ 在学习上，妈妈对 B 的要求高不高？从哪里可以看出？
❹ 爸爸妈妈对孩子要求高，你觉得这对孩子来说好还是不好？为什么？

Step Up!

1. Read Ding Qiang's blog entry and determine whether the following statements are true (T) or false (F).

11月6日

　　那天和子明聊他的学习生活，发现中国的高中教育和美国有些不同。第一，中国高中生每年要读的科目比较多，有语文、数学、英语、历史、地理、生物、化学和物理。美国的高中生每年只需要学一门理科（比方说九年级学物理，十年级学化学，十一年级学生物）和一门文科（十年级学世界历史，十一年级学美国历史），加上语文、数学和外语就是五门课。如果有兴趣，可以选读经济、环保科学、艺术历史等等。

jiàyù — education
jīngjì — economics

　　第二，每个中国高中生都需要参加高考。只有通过这个统一考试，才能进大学。而在美国就没有统一的大学入学考试，但是有SAT。不过如果第一次考得不好，还可以再考，每个月都有一次考试，所以同学可以选择最适合自己的时间。

tǒngyī — standardized

　　虽然有这两点不同，但我觉得中国和美国高中生都一样辛苦。比如，在课业方面，子明的功课很多，周末还常常需要做作业，有时候做到晚上12点还没做完。我在美国时，每门课也都有作业，还有阅读和论文写作，这样也花费不少时间。在升学方面，子明基本上只有一次机会，所以一定要考好高考，压力特别大。而美国大学录取学生，除了SAT分数以外，还考虑平时在学校的成绩、课外活动、兴趣和个性等等，在各方面都有要求，所以对学生也造成不少压力。

jīběnshàng — basically
lùqǔ — admit
yídìng — surely
kǎolù — consider
gèxìng — personality

True or false?

① 中国高中生每年要读八门课。 ( )

② 美国高中生每年都要读物理、化学和生物。 ( )

③ 中国高中没有统一的大学入学考试。 ( )

④ SAT 每个月都有一次考试。 ( )

⑤ 中国高中生的课业很繁重。 ( )

⑥ 美国高中生需要写论文。 ( )

⑦ 美国大学只看 SAT 分数。 ( )

⑧ 丁强觉得中国学生比美国学生辛苦。 ( )

2. With a partner, discuss the strengths and weaknesses of the education system in China and the United States. Next, based on your discussion, choose your preferred education system and explain why.

3. Research on the high school education system in another country other than China and the United States. Respond to Ding Qiang's blog entry by telling him what the high school education system in that country is like. Make appropriate comparisons to the systems in China and the United States where necessary. Write at least 10 sentences.

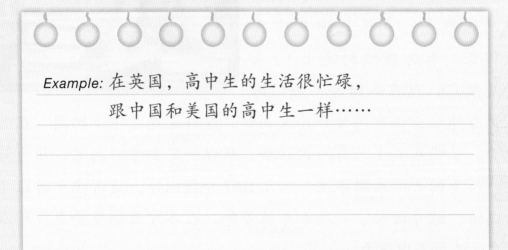

Example: 在英国，高中生的生活很忙碌，
跟中国和美国的高中生一样……

Fun Time!

Philosophical sayings are an important part of Chinese culture and reflect the values that make up the social fabric of society. The following Chinese sayings are common adages which emphasize the importance of education in China. The major themes presented in these sayings are as follows:

★ Learning is fun.

★ Knowledge and critical thinking skills are both important.

★ Learning is a lifelong process.

★ Diligence is an essential characteristic.

The above concepts are an integral part of the Chinese approach to education. Take them to heart and you will soon gain a deeper appreciation for Chinese culture! Read the English sayings on education as well and discuss if they are similar to or different from the Chinese sayings.

Chinese sayings:

1 学然后知不足
Meaning: 通过学习才知道自己知识的不足。The more one learns, the more one sees one's own ignorance.

2 温故而知新
Meaning: 复习学过的知识会学到新的知识，有新的发现。When reflecting on what one has learned, one discovers new knowledge.

3 好学不倦 (juàn)
Meaning: 喜欢学习，不觉得累。If you are eager to learn, you will never become tired of studying.

4 学而时习之 (zhī)
Meaning: 学习了知识要常常复习，常常练习。You must constantly practice what you have learned.

5 学如逆水行舟，不进则退 (nì) (zhōu) (zé tuì)
Meaning: 学习好像逆水行驶的小船，如果不努力向前进，就会向后退。学习得一直努力。Learning is like rowing upstream: not advancing is to fall behind.

6 书山有路勤为径，学海无涯苦作舟 (jìng) (yá)
Meaning: 勤奋是一条路，可以带你到达知识山峰；努力是一条船，可以帮你到达知识海洋的海岸。学习得努力。Diligence is the boat that will guide you across the sea of learning.

7 开卷有益 (juàn) (yì)
Meaning: 只要看书，就会有好处。So long as you read, there will be benefits.

8 学海无涯勤是岸 (qín) (àn)
Meaning: 知识海洋没有限。常常可以长见识。There are no limits to what one has yet to learn.

English sayings:

1 A book holds a house of gold.

2 A good mind possesses a kingdom.

3 Diligence is the mother of good fortune.

4 He who knows nothing doubts nothing.

5 Knowledge in youth is wisdom in age.

6 Knowledge is power.

7 Learning is a treasure that will follow its owner everywhere.

8 You are never too old to learn.

I have learned...

Verbs

自习	自習	zìxí	study by oneself in scheduled time or free time	同龄	同齡	tónglíng	of the same age
布置	佈置	bùzhì	assign	陶冶		táoyě	mold, cultivate
应付	應付	yìngfù	to deal with, to cope with	练习	練習	liànxí	practice
告诉	告訴	gàosu	tell	养	養	yǎng	develop
受益		shòuyì	benefit, gain	崩溃	崩潰	bēngkuì	break down
磨炼	磨煉	móliàn	train	失眠		shīmián	unable to sleep
放松	放鬆	fàngsōng	relax	花		huā	spend
缓解	緩解	huǎnjiě	relieve, alleviate	要求		yāoqiú	request, expect
开始	開始	kāishǐ	start	调整	調整	tiáozhěng	adjust
考		kǎo	take an examination	承受		chéngshòu	bear, withstand
竞争	競爭	jìngzhēng	compete	应考	應考	yìngkǎo	sit for examinations
鼓励	鼓勵	gǔlì	encourage	辜负	辜負	gūfù	let down
加强	加強	jiāqiáng	strengthen, enhance	期望		qīwàng	expect, hope
培养	培養	péiyǎng	develop, cultivate	报名	報名	bàomíng	sign up
表达	表達	biǎodá	express	发展	發展	fāzhǎn	develop
锻炼	鍛煉	duànliàn	train	成才		chéngcái	become a useful person
推动	推動	tuīdòng	promote	避免		bìmiǎn	avoid
希望		xīwàng	hope	给予	給予	jǐyǔ	give
辅导	輔導	fǔdǎo	coach	尽力	盡力	jìnlì	do one's best
取得		qǔdé	achieve	沟通	溝通	gōutōng	communicate
进步	進步	jìnbù	improve, progress	提供		tígōng	provide
绘画	繪畫	huìhuà	drawing				

Nouns

语文	語文	yǔwén	the Chinese language	磨炼	磨煉	móliàn	training
本事		běnshì	skill	压力	壓力	yālì	pressure
态度	態度	tàidù	attitude	高考		gāokǎo	college entrance exam
毅力		yìlì	willpower, tenacity	成绩	成績	chéngjì	grade, result

理想		lǐxiǎng	ideal	习惯	習慣	xíguàn	habit
大学	大學	dàxué	college, university	乐曲	樂曲	yuèqǔ	musical piece
竞争	競爭	jìngzhēng	competition	成就感		chéngjiùgǎn	sense of achievement
模拟联合国	模擬聯合國	mónǐ liánhéguó	Model United Nations	才艺	才藝	cáiyì	talent
时事	時事	shíshì	current affairs	意志		yìzhì	will
能力		nénglì	ability	测验	測驗	cèyàn	test
意见		yìjiàn	opinion, view	课业	課業	kèyè	study load
学业	學業	xuéyè	studies	信心		xìnxīn	confidence
部分		bùfèn	part, section	名牌		míngpái	famous
科目		kēmù	subject	心情		xīnqíng	feelings, mood
目的		mùdì	aim, objective	精力		jīnglì	energy
辅导	輔導	fǔdǎo	coaching	状态	狀態	zhuàngtài	state, condition
进步	進步	jìnbù	improvement, progress	期望		qīwàng	expectation, hope
特长	特長	tècháng	specialty	身心		shēnxīn	body and mind
小提琴		xiǎotíqín	violin	发展	發展	fāzhǎn	development
优势	優勢	yōushì	advantage	支持		zhīchí	support
性情		xìngqíng	temperament				

Adjectives

主要		zhǔyào	main, principal	重要		zhòngyào	important
辛苦		xīnkǔ	strenuous, laborious	常见	常見	chángjiàn	commonly seen
年轻	年輕	niánqīng	young	繁重		fánzhòng	heavy
积极	積極	jījí	positive	沮丧	沮喪	jǔsàng	dejected, dispirited
用功		yònggōng	diligent, hardworking	忧郁	憂鬱	yōuyù	depressed
激烈		jīliè	intense	乐观	樂觀	lèguān	optimistic
课外	課外	kèwài	extra-curricular	严格	嚴格	yángé	strict
国际	國際	guójì	international	适当	適當	shìdàng	appropriate
充实	充實	chōngshí	fulfilling				

Adverbs

常常/经常	常常/經常	chángcháng /jīngcháng	often	原来	原來	yuánlái	so that's how it is
总是	總是	zǒngshì	always	越来越	越來越	yuèláiyuè	more and more
必定		bìdìng	surely	更		gèng	even more
老是		lǎoshì	always, all the time				

Auxiliary verbs

能够	能夠	nénggòu	can, be able to
必须	必須	bìxū	must, have to

Phrases

怎么办	怎麼辦	zěnmebàn	how
做人处事	做人處事	zuòrén chǔshì	relating to people

Conjunctions

而且		érqiě	and
并且	並且	bìngqiě	and
不过	不過	búguò	however, but

Constructions

只有…才…		zhǐyǒu…cái	only by…can…
即使…也…		jíshǐ…yě…	even if…
由于…所以…	由於…所以…	yóuyú…suǒyǐ…	because of, (so)…

Preposition

通过	通過	tōngguò	through, by means of

Pronoun

所有		suǒyǒu	all, entire

SENTENCE PATTERNS

我看你的功课太多了，常常周末也在做作业。

只有考到好成绩，才能进入理想的大学。

学生每天不是在学校上课，就是去上课外补习班。

每天即使没有钢琴课，我也会在家练习。

这个星期的作业很多，你做得完吗？

由于学生不想辜负父母和老师的期望，所以每天早起晚睡，努力学习。

I can do!

Interpretive Communication

❑ I can read and understand the fliers on different programs of test preparation.

❑ I can get information on the daily homework load.

❑ I can read and understand blogs and dialogs on the academic life in different countries.

Interpersonal Communication

❑ I can converse about the pressures on examinations.

❑ I can talk to others about how I deal with pressure.

❑ I can ask questions and get information about the examination system in different cultures.

❑ I can give and get information on the value of homework.

Presentational Communication

❑ I can make an oral presentation to convince my teachers to use alternative assessments instead of examinations.

❑ I can write a short essay comparing the education system in China and the US.

❑ I can write about the pressures that a heavy workload creates.

Cultural Knowledge

❑ I can talk about the imperial examination in ancient China.

❑ I can understand the nine categories in the Chinese grading system.

❑ I can describe one of the most popular private educational service providers in China.

Shopping in Chinese markets

在中国市场购物

COMMUNICATIVE GOALS

- Conversing about the prices of goods and services
- Bargaining to get the best deals
- Discussing advantages and disadvantages of in-store and online shopping
- Describing a shopping experience
- Describing bargaining strategies and procedures

Cultural Knowledge

- Bargaining skills and procedures
- Chinese silk
- Chinese consumerism
- Chinese specialty products

Get ready...

Shopping for souvenirs is an important part of the travel experience. Travel souvenirs will bring back many wonderful memories of places you visited and people you met there. Some locally produced items are unique to the locale and cannot be found anywhere else. Look at the following travel souvenirs from China and match them with locations where the souvenirs would most likely be found/produced.

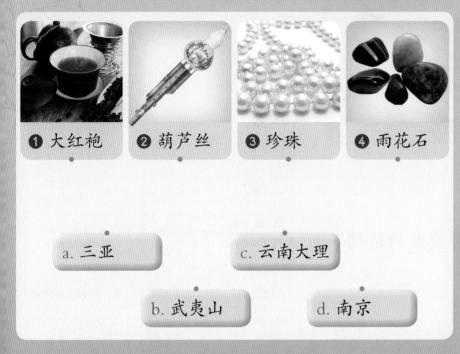

❶ 大红袍　　❷ 葫芦丝　　❸ 珍珠　　❹ 雨花石

a. 三亚　　　　　c. 云南大理

b. 武夷山　　　　d. 南京

❺ 紫砂陶　　❻ 瓷器　　❼ 仿兵马俑　　❽ 绢扇

e. 景德镇　　　　f. 宜兴

g. 苏州　　　　　h. 陕西

STEP 1

SHOPPING AND BARGAINING

A. Understanding the Chinese money system

这双蓝色的运动鞋多少钱？
原价400块。现在我们有促销。

B. Bargaining

50块太贵了！25块卖不卖？

STEP 2

PURCHASING NEW ARTICLES

A. Shopping

我想看看这件蓝色的上衣。

B. Getting the things you want

只要学会讨价还价，就能买到价廉物美的商品。

STEP 3

UNDERSTANDING CONSUMERISM

A. Buying goods and services

网购除了节省时间以外，东西也比较便宜。

B. Spending wisely

我一共花了1000元。
什么打折我就买什么。

A Understanding the Chinese money system

kuǎnshì 款式 *n.*		style, design
duōshao qián 多少钱 *pron.*	多少錢	how much *(money)*
yuánjià 原价 *n.*	原價	original price
yuán/kuài 元/块 *m.w.*	元/塊	yuan, dollar
cùxiāo 促销 *n.*	促銷	promotion
yílù 一律 *adv.*		all, without exception
dǎ bā zhé 打八折 *v.*		give 20% discount
díquè 的确 *adv.*	的確	really, indeed
jiàqián 价钱 *n.*	價錢	price
jiǎo/máo 角/毛 *m.w.*		fractional unit of Chinese currency, equal to 1/10 of a yuan
fēn 分 *m.w.*		cent, fractional unit of Chinese currency, equal to 1/100 of a yuan

A：您好！请问您想买什么？

B：我想买运动鞋。

A：这边请。我们有很多不同<u>款式</u>的运动鞋，您慢慢看。

B：这双蓝色的运动鞋<u>多少钱</u>？

A：<u>原价</u>400块。现在我们有<u>促销</u>，买两双<u>一律</u><u>打八折</u>。

B：这双鞋<u>的确</u>很不错，可是<u>价钱</u>有点儿贵，而且我只想买一双。请问，那双绿色的要多少钱？

A：那双比较便宜，只要299块9<u>毛</u>5(分)。

¥400
(400元)

¥299.95
(299元9角5分)

B：好，我就要这双。请问，你们<u>收</u><u>信用卡</u>吗？

A：<u>收</u>，我们可以<u>刷卡</u>。

B：这是我的信用卡。

A：<u>请</u><u>签个字</u>。谢谢，这是您的鞋，请拿好！

B：谢谢，再见！

A：再见！

shōu		
收 *v.*		accept
xìnyòngkǎ		
信用卡 *n.*		credit card
shuākǎ		
刷卡 *phr.*		swipe a card
qiānzì (qiān gè zì)		
签字 (签个字) *phr.*	簽字 (簽個字)	sign one's name

LANGUAGE FOCUS

1. **The Chinese money system**

   The primary unit of Chinese currency is the 元. One 元 is divided into 10 角, and one 角 is divided into 10 分. 块 and 毛, referring to 元 and 角 respectively, are more commonly used in spoken Chinese. The last unit is often omitted in spoken Chinese when the price contains two or more units. Below are some examples of how prices are expressed in Chinese:

	Written	Spoken		Written	Spoken
¥50：	五十元	五十块	¥0.60：	六角	六毛
¥0.35：	三角五分	三毛五(分)	¥10.30：	十元三角	十块三(毛)

2. **Asking prices in Chinese**

   To ask how much an item costs in Chinese, use the interrogative pronoun 多少钱. To reply, replace 多少钱 with the actual price.

   Examples: ❶ 这条裙子多少钱？这条裙子200块。

   ❷ 这件 T 恤多少钱？这件 T 恤120块。

   Alternatively, you can use 怎么卖 to ask for prices.

   Examples: ❶ 这双鞋怎么卖？400块。

   ❷ 那把雨伞怎么卖？30块。

DO YOU KNOW... 你知道吗？

Discounts in Chinese are expressed differently from the way they are in English. For example 打八折 means that you pay 80% of the original price and the discount is 20%; 打七五折 means that you pay 75% of the original price and the discount is 25%; 打五折 (打对折) means that you pay 50% of the original price or half price. So, you will get a really great deal when something is 打三折 or 打一折.

1. Express the following prices in both written and spoken Chinese.

❶ ¥1.35 _____

❷ ¥0.5 _____

❸ ¥7.00 _____

❹ ¥14.30 _____

❺ ¥180.99 _____

❻ ¥102.00 _____

❼ ¥109.05 _____

❽ ¥478.20 _____

❾ ¥2500 _____

❿ ¥4789.99 _____

2. With a partner, ask and answer questions on the prices of the following items in Chinese. Refer to the sentence patterns you learned in the earlier section.

Example:

A: 这双鞋多少钱？

B: 这双鞋400块。

¥400

❶

¥380

❷

¥20

❸

¥650

❹

¥299

❺

¥24.99

❻

¥369.90

❼

¥420.80

❽

¥30.50

❾

¥159.50

❿

¥49.90

B Bargaining

对话一

A：这条丝巾要多少钱？

B：要50块一条。

A：50块太贵了！25块卖不卖？

B：不卖。35块怎么样？

A：还是太贵了，我不买。我还是到别家去吧。

B：别走别走，你最高能给多少钱？

A：30块卖不卖？

B：好吧，30块。

sījīn 丝巾 n.	絲巾	scarf
bié 别 adv.		don't
guānglín 光临 v.	光臨	(polite form) coming to (a place)
shǒushì 首饰 n.	首飾	jewelry
suíbiàn 随便 adj.	隨便	casual, informal
xiàngliàn 项链 n.	項鏈	necklace
yǎnguāng 眼光 n.		one's taste in fashion
xīnkuǎn 新款 n.		new design
jiàgè 价格 n.	價格	price

对话二

A：欢迎光临我们首饰店。请问，您想买点儿什么？

B：不买什么，随便看看。

A：好的，请慢慢看。

B：请问，这条项链多少钱？

A：您真有眼光，这是新款，八千八一条。

B：这条项链好是好，可是价格实在是太高了。

A：八千五吧。不赚钱。

B：还是太贵了。再便宜点儿我就买一条。八千怎么样？

A：卖不了，您不能让我赔钱卖您吧？

B：那算了吧！本来我也没打算买项链。

A：别走！就八千赔本卖您一条吧。您真会讲价！

zhuànqián 赚钱 v.	賺錢	make a profit
péiqián 赔钱 phr.	賠錢	take a loss
suàn le 算了 phr.		forget it
běnlái 本来 adv.	本來	originally
péiběn 赔本 v.	賠本	take a loss
jiǎngjià 讲价 phr.	講價	bargain

EXTENDED VOCABULARY

Accessories

耳环 n.	耳環	ěrhuán	earring	钱包 n.	錢包	qiánbāo	wallet, purse
手镯 n.	手鐲	shǒuzhuó	bracelet	手提包 n.		shǒutíbāo	handbag
戒指 n.		jièzhǐ	ring	公文包/公事包 n.		gōngwénbāo/gōngshìbāo	briefcase
发夹 n.	髮夾	fàjiā	hairpin				

❖ EXPRESSIONS FOR BARGAINING ❖

There are a variety of expressions for bargaining in Chinese. Depending on your own situation and the items you would like to purchase, you can use some of the following expressions to bargain with the seller.

❶ "太贵了！"

❷ "还是太贵了。"

❸ "我是穷学生，没有多少钱。"

❹ "价格实在是太高了，便宜点我就买一件。"

❺ "你最低多少钱？"

❻ "X 块？(the price quoted by the seller) 我再到别的地方去看看。"

❼ "Y 块。(the final price you are willing to pay) 卖就卖，不卖拉倒。"

❽ "我买一件，我朋友也买一件，能不能再多打点折？"

Bargaining in China

Bargaining is very common in China. When shopping for goods (for example, clothes, gifts, art, and jade) at a local market or an independently owned business, locals and foreigners alike will usually engage in bargaining with the sellers. However, bargaining is normally not allowed in large stores, corporate chains, or department stores. The prices are fixed and employees have neither the authority nor the incentive to bargain with buyers.

The Chinese expression for bargaining is 讨价还价, which literally means "One asks for as much as one thinks one can get, and the other person wants to pay as little as possible." Another common Chinese saying about shopping is "货比三家不吃亏" which means "You will not suffer a loss if you compare prices before buying."

Here are some bargaining strategies: After the seller quotes an initial price, tell him/her that the price is too high and ask for the bottom price. Hide your enthusiasm or excitement, and pretend that you don't like the item. Offer a much lower price and continue bargaining. You may improve your leverage by pointing out defects or poor workmanship in the item. If the price offered is still not the price you want, pretend to walk away and tell the seller that you would like to go to other shops to see other products. Tell the seller you are buying in large quantities and ask for better discounts by comparing prices.

Try This!

1. Complete the dialog with the appropriate options from the word bank.

> 讲价　　最低价格　　那算了吧　　赔本　　怎么卖　　光临　　便宜

顾客A: 这家店写着"清仓大甩卖"，咱们进去看看吧！
cāng shuǎi
stock clearance sales

顾客B: 好呀！

售货员: 欢迎 ＿＿＿＿＿＿＿＿！要买点什么？

顾客A: 这件衣服＿＿＿＿＿＿＿？

售货员: 100块，已经是 ＿＿＿＿＿＿＿了。

顾客B: 可以再＿＿＿＿＿＿一点吗？

售货员: 今天已经是亏本大减价，我们不＿＿＿＿＿＿。

顾客A: 啊? 90块怎么样?

售货员: 100块已经是 ＿＿＿＿＿＿了，不能再低了。

顾客B: ＿＿＿＿＿＿，我们去别的店再看看。

顾客A: 好吧。

2. Look at the prices of the following items shown below and say if you find them reasonable or not and suggest other prices if they appear too expensive to you. Use the words and expressions you have learned.

1 $70

2 $35

3 $27

4 $1050

5 $4500

6 $105

7 $30

8 $100

9 $54

10 $7

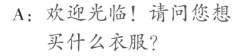

A Shopping

A：欢迎光临！请问您想买什么衣服？

B：我想看看这件蓝色的上衣。

A：先生眼光真好，这是我们刚到的新款上衣，很流行，卖得非常火。您穿很适合。

B：谢谢。这个款式的上衣显得很有时尚感。

A：您要什么号的？特大号、大号、中号都有，没有小号。

B：麻烦您给我看一下大号的。

A：这是大号的，您可以试试。

B：请问，试衣间在哪儿？

A：就在那边。

B：谢谢！我觉得大号的宽松了点儿。请给我拿一件中号的。

A：这是中号的。

B：我再试试。

A：您穿中号的很合适。

B：多少钱一件？

A：两百八十八一件。

B：能打点折吗？

xiānsheng 先生 n.		Mr., sir
liúxíng 流行 adj.; v.		popular; get popular
huǒ 火 adj.		prosperous, flourishing
shìhé 适合 adj.	適合	suitable
xiǎnde 显得 v.	顯得	look, seem
shíshànggǎn 时尚感 n.	時尚感	trendy, fashionable
tèdàhào 特大号 n.	特大號	size XL
dàhào 大号 n.	大號	size L
zhōnghào 中号 n.	中號	size M
xiǎohào 小号 n.	小號	size S
shì 试 v.	試	try on
shìyījiān 试衣间 n.	試衣間	fitting room
kuānsōng 宽松 adj.	寬鬆	loose

A：对不起，我们店的衣服都是<u>明码</u><u>标价</u>，不讲价。

B：好吧，这是三百块。

A：找您十二块。衣服请您拿好，穿得好下次再来我们店逛逛。

B：谢谢。再见！

míngmǎ 明码 *n.*	明碼	price clearly marked
biāojià 标价 *v.*	標價	mark a price

LANGUAGE FOCUS

Verb duplication is a unique Chinese structure that can indicate one of the following three meanings.

❶ Short duration of time
- 请您在这儿等等，我马上就回来。
- 让我看看这本书。

❷ Trying to do an action
- 这件衣服不错，你试试。
- 这首歌真不错，你听听！

❸ Making the tone of suggestions and requests softer and more polite
- 请你给我看看那双鞋。
- 请你来我家坐坐。

The numeral — can be inserted between the duplicated monosyllabic verb form to express the same meanings.

- 请您在这儿等一等，我马上就回来。
- 这件衣服不错，你试一试。
- 请你给我看一看那双鞋。

Another alternative form that has the same effect as verb duplication can be made by placing the expression 一下 immediately after the verb.

- 请您在这儿等一下，我马上就回来。
- 这件衣服不错，你试一下。
- 请你给我看一下那双鞋。

Try This!

1. Read the following communicative situations. Fill in the blanks with the appropriate duplicated verb forms from the word bank that most logically fit the situation.

吃吃　　喝喝　　看看　　听听　　坐坐

等等　　试试　　穿穿　　做做　　戴戴

Example: 弟弟刚上网买了一首流行歌曲，他特别喜欢。

他看我走过来，就对我说："这首新歌好听极了，

你__听听__。"

❶ 我妈妈做的炸酱面非常好吃，你_____。

❷ 这种茶真的很不错，你_____。

❸ 你_____，我马上就来。

❹ A: 你想买什么东西？

　　B: 不买什么，就随便_____。

❺ 这条丝巾好漂亮！你要不要_____？

❻ 阿姨，我妈妈马上就回家了，您先_____。

❼ 这种蛋糕很简单，你在家也可以试着_____。

❽ 你的帽子看上去很暖和，我可以_____吗？

❾ 你_____这件外套，我觉得你穿上一定很时尚。

2. Read the dialog and answer the following questions.

李阿姨：丁强，这几天天气冷了，我觉得你需要一件外套，我今天带你去买一件吧！

丁强：谢谢李阿姨！太好了，我也正想去买一件外套呢，您能带我去太好了！

（李阿姨和丁强一起坐地铁到西单购物。）

李阿姨：麻烦您给我看看那件外套。丁强，来，试一下。

丁强：好的。

李阿姨：你觉得怎么样？大小合适吗？这款衣服最近好像很流行。

丁强：嗯，我看到很多人穿，很有时尚感。

李阿姨：那你喜欢吗？有点儿大，不太合适，请问有没有中号的？

售货员：请您稍等一下，我去库里找找。
　　　　kù
　　　　storeroom

（售货员递给丁强一件中号。）

丁强：这件很合适。

李阿姨：嗯，不错，这件穿上显得很精神。

售货员：是啊，非常合适！我们这款衣服卖得很火！

丁强：可是……

李阿姨：怎么了？

丁强：我觉得有很多人穿这款衣服，我不想和他们都穿得一样。

李阿姨：哈哈，既然你这么想，那我们再到别家看看吧！

Questions:

❶ 李阿姨为什么要带丁强去买外套？

❷ 李阿姨觉得那件外套怎么样？

❸ 那件外套大小对丁强合适吗？

❹ 丁强觉得那件外套怎么样？

❺ 他们最后买了那件外套吗？为什么？

Blog

再过几个月就是圣诞节了。丁强听说空运寄包裹到美国挺贵的，所以决定早点儿把给家人、同学和老师的圣诞礼物买好，用海运寄美国，这样邮费可节省一半。丁强付不起空运的包裹费，他只付得起海运的包裹费。王叔叔告诉他，北京的秀水街市场虽然买不到全国各地的土特产，但是找得到很多有中国元素的礼物。只要他学会讨价还价，他就能买到价廉物美的商品。

丁强趁十月一号国庆节长假，去秀水街市场买了他购物单上的圣诞礼物。他给爷爷买了一条真丝领带，给奶奶买了一条丝巾，给外公买了一把画着山水画的折扇，给外婆买了青花瓷的小花瓶，给爸爸买了一套丝绸睡衣，给妈妈买了一条珍珠项链，给哥哥买了一件唐装，给姐姐

Shèngdàn Jié 圣诞节 n.	聖誕節	Christmas
kōngyùn 空运 v.	空運	air freight
bāoguǒ 包裹 n.		parcel
tǐng 挺 adv.		quite
juédìng 决定 v.		decide
hǎiyùn 海运 v.	海運	sea freight
yóufèi 邮费 n.	郵費	freight cost
jiéshěng 节省 v.	節省	save, economize
Xiùshuǐjiē Shìchǎng 秀水街市场 p.n.	秀水街市場	Silk Market
tǔtèchǎn 土特产 n.	土特產	local specialty
yuánsù 元素 n.		element
tǎo jià huán jià 讨价还价 v.	討價還價	bargain
jiàlián wùměi 价廉物美 adj.	價廉物美	(of goods) cheap and good
shāngpǐn 商品 n.		merchandise
chèn 趁 prep.		take advantage of (time, opportunity, etc.)

买了一件<u>旗袍</u>，给妹妹买了一双<u>绣花拖鞋</u>，给弟弟买了一把<u>太极剑</u>。他给中文老师买了一个画着长城的<u>漆盘</u>，还给中文班的同学们买了一些<u>中国结</u>和<u>景泰蓝钥匙链</u>。他希望大家都会喜欢这些有中国元素的圣诞礼物。从北京寄包裹海运到美国要两个多月，丁强希望他精心<u>挑选</u>的这些礼物在圣诞节前能寄到纽约。

gòuwùdān 购物单 n.	購物單	shopping list
jīngxīn 精心 adj.	精心	painstaking, meticulous
tiāoxuǎn 挑选 v.	挑選	choose

EXTENDED VOCABULARY

Chinese specialty products

zhéshàn
折扇 n.
摺扇
folding fan

qīnghuācí
青花瓷 n.
blue and white
porcelain wares

sīchóu
丝绸 n.
絲綢
silk

zhēnzhū
珍珠 n.
pearl

tángzhuāng
唐装 n.
唐裝
tangzhuang
(a Chinese jacket)

qípáo
旗袍 n.
cheongsam
(a type of Chinese dresss)

xiūhuā
绣花 *n.*
繡花
embroidery

tàijíjiàn
太极剑 *n.*
太極劍
taiji sword

qīpán
漆盘 *n.*
漆盤
lacquer plate

Zhōngguójié
中国结 *n.*
中國結
Chinese knot

jǐngtàilán yàoshiliàn
景泰蓝钥匙链 *n.*
景泰藍鑰匙鏈
cloisonné keychain

táocí
陶瓷 *n.*
ceramics

You learned about potential complements in an earlier lesson. They are used to express a possible outcome of an action. In this section on shopping for goods, potential complements can be used to express the possible outcomes of actions associated with shopping.

Positive form

- 这里买得到什么？这里买得到各种款式的运动鞋。
- 这首歌在哪里找得到？在网上找得到。
- 你拿得了这袋东西吗？这袋东西不重，我拿得了。
- 她穿得上这件衣服吗？她个子小，穿得上这件小号的衣服。

Negative form

- 我买不到我要的项链。
- 他在那里找不到你说的那家店。
- 这件T恤太贵了，我买不起。
- 东西太多了，我吃不完。

Another way to form positive potential complements is to place 能 before the verb and remove 得 after the verb:

❶ 在这里，你能买到各种各样的土特产。
❷ 这家店很有意思，你在这里能找到很多有趣的纪念品。
❸ 这么大的一碗面，你能吃完吗？

1. Fill in the blanks using the appropriate potential complements provided in the chart.

Example:

A: 看起来你特别喜欢吃中国菜，你一个人点了五个菜，你吃得完吃不完？

B: 我今天一天什么都没吃，我好久没吃到地道的中国菜了，我肯定 ____吃得完____ 。

Positive	吃得完	喝得完	进得来	出得去	买得起
	睡得着	找得到	寄得到	穿得上	拿得了
Negative	吃不完	喝不完	进不来	出不去	买不起
	睡不着	找不到	寄不到	穿不上	拿不了

❶ A: 你把我的外套放在哪儿了？

B: 就在客厅啊？你找得到吗？

A: ＿＿＿＿＿＿啊！你来帮我找。

❷ A: 这件中国陶瓷多少钱啊？

B: 一万块。

A: 一万块？谁能＿＿＿＿＿＿啊！

❸ A: 快来帮我拿东西！

B: 你又买了这么多东西！以后＿＿＿＿＿＿就不要买这么多！

❹ A: 每天晚上这里都这么吵，你能睡得着吗？

B: 根本＿＿＿＿＿＿啊！太吵了！
    gēnběn
    simply

❺ A: 这双37码的鞋怎么样？穿得上穿不上？

B: 完全＿＿＿＿＿＿，还是太小了。
    wánquán
    completely

❻ A: 你买了这么多北京小吃，吃得完吃不完啊？

B: 我们家有十口人呢，当然＿＿＿＿＿＿。

❼ A: 把你的地址给我，我给你寄杭州的土特产。
    dìzhǐ
    address

B: 啊？能寄得到吗？

A: 当然＿＿＿＿＿＿。你的地址是什么？

❽ A: 这个出口能出得去吗？
    exit

B: ＿＿＿＿＿＿，我们还是找另一个出口吧！

❾ A: 你又买了这么一大瓶可乐，喝得完喝不完？

B: 嗯，太多了，我一个人＿＿＿＿＿＿。

❿ A: 我从这个入口可以进得来吗？
    rùkǒu
    entrance

B: ＿＿＿＿＿＿，你得从北面那个入口才进得来。

2. Describe the following pictures using appropriate potential complements (positive and negative).

Example:  弟弟做不完作业。

① ② ③ ④

⑤ ⑥ ⑦ ⑧

 CULTURAL HIGHLIGHTS

Chinese Silk

Silk is considered the most beautiful of all textile fibers. It comes from the cocoon of the silk worm and requires a great deal of handling and processing, making it one of the most expensive fibers in the world. China has been the leading silk producer in the world, accounting for more than three quarters of the global raw silk production and 90 percent of the world's export market.

The vast majority of Chinese silk originates from the mulberry silkworm. During the moth stage of its life cycle, the insect feeds on the leaves of mulberry trees. The worm then starts spinning a cocoon, which is unwound by workers who unwind the fibers into silk threads. Finally, the threads are woven into cloth.

Silk's absorbency makes it comfortable to wear in warm weather. On the other hand, silk's low conductivity keeps warm air close to the skin in cold weather. Thus, silk is used for different types of clothing. Chinese embroidery art also finds expression in silk fabric and can be seen on clothing, quilt sheets, pillowcases, etc. It is no surprise that silk products are popular items in Chinese markets.

A Buying goods and services

芳芳：玛丽，你这双鞋很漂亮，在哪里买的？

玛丽：我是在西单商场的一家店里买的。那家店的鞋除了款式特别多以外，设计也非常新颖。消费超过200元，还有赠品呢！

芳芳：这么好！找一天带我去看看。

玛丽：没问题。

芳芳：其实我比较喜欢网购。网购除了节省时间以外，东西也比较便宜。

玛丽：但是网购需要付运输费。

芳芳：如果消费达到一定的数额，商家就可以免费送货。

玛丽：我还是比较喜欢去商场购物。导购员的服务也很周到，可以给你提供很好的建议。

xīnyǐng 新颖 adj.	新穎	new and original, novel
xiāofèi 消费 v.	消費	consume, spend
chāoguò 超过 v.		exceed
zèngpǐn 赠品 n.	贈品	free item
yùnshūfèi 运输费 n.	運輸費	transport fee
yídìng 一定 adj.		fixed, specified
shù'é 数额 n.	數額	amount
shāngjiā 商家 n.	商傢	merchants
miǎnfèi 免费 v.	免費	free of charge
sònghuò 送货 phr.	送貨	deliver goods
dǎogòuyuán 导购员 n.	導購員	personal shopper
fúwù 服务 n.	服務	service
zhōudào 周到 adj.		attentive and satisfactory
jiànyì 建议 n.; v.	建議	suggestion; suggest

芳芳： 去商场购物有导购员为你服务好是好，可是有时候导购员往往建议顾客买一些高价位的产品。我去商场购物，常常除了买应该要买的东西以外，还会买一些家里和我本人都不需要的东西。

玛丽： 去商场购物一定要目标明确，不要买消费计划以外的东西。

芳芳： 说起来容易，做起来难。我还是网购，需要什么就买什么吧。

jiàwèi 价位 n.	價位	price
chǎnpǐn 产品 n.	產品	product
yídìng 一定 adv.		centainly, surely
mùbiāo 目标 n.	目標	target, goal
míngquè 明确 adj.	明確	clear
jìhuà 计划 n.	計劃	plan

LANGUAGE FOCUS

除了…以外，也/还… can be used to express "not only...but also...." 以外 can be omitted without losing the meaning. However, if the sentence has two subjects, only 也 can be used to connect the two parts. If the sentence has one subject, you can use either 也 or 还.

Examples: ❶ 这双鞋子除了设计新颖(以外)，价钱也很便宜。
❷ 这家餐馆除了食物好吃(以外)，服务也很周到。
❸ 她除了买了几件衣服(以外)，还/也买了几双鞋。
❹ 丁强除了喜欢吃饺子，包子(以外)，还/也喜欢吃北京炸酱面。

Try This!

1. Match the sentences.

❶ 这个网站售卖的产品除了品种齐全
   pǐnzhǒng qíquán
   types complete
   以外，

❷ 这家服装店除了衣服价廉物美
   以外，

❸ 我除了喜欢网购，

❹ 丁强除了吃了烤鸭、小笼包以外，

❺ 除了杭州西湖、苏州园林，

a. 也喜欢去商场购物。

b. 也吃了炸酱面！他吃得太多了！

c. 还免费赠送半年的保修期。
   bǎoxiūqī
   warranty period

d. 他也去了上海外滩。

e. 服务员的服务也很周到。

❻ 这件外套除了很时尚、很合适以外， ·	· f. 还想喝什么？
❼ 你除了可乐、橙汁， ·	· g. 鱼也不吃。
❽ 这双鞋除了设计新颖，价格便宜， ·	· h. 导购员的服务也很周到。
❾ 这家商店除了打折、有赠品， ·	· i. 穿起来也很舒服！
❿ 我除了不吃虾以外， ·	· j. 价格也很低。

2. In an oral exchange with a partner, share a pleasant retail experience that you had, describing the goods or services that left an impression on you. You can talk about the quality of the product, design, price, and attentiveness of the staff. Use 除了 in your description and make at least five sentences. You may also use verb duplications and potential complements where appropriate.

Example:

去年夏天我在西单商场的一家店里买衣服。店里的衣服除了设计新颖以外，价格也不贵。服务员的服务也很周到。最后我在那里买了3件衣服，还成为他们的会员（huìyuán / member），以后买东西可以打八折！

Blog

今天我和子明到附近的商场购物，因为那里有个<u>大减价</u>。我买了很多东西，<u>收获</u>特别多！我<u>一共</u>花了1000元。什么打折我就买什么，什么便宜我就买什么，真<u>过瘾</u>！子明和我<u>差不多</u>，也买了很多东西。我们都觉得今天的确<u>不虚此行</u>。

买完东西，我觉得肚子有点<u>饿</u>，想去吃点东西，却发现我<u>只</u> <u>剩下</u>10块钱了。子明知道了，就对我说："没事儿，这<u>顿</u>饭我<u>请客</u>！"今天过得真开心！

dàjiǎnjià 大减价 n.	大減價	sale
shōuhuò 收获 n.; v.	收穫	gain; to gain
yígòng 一共 adv.		in total
guòyǐn 过瘾 adj.	過癮	satisfying
chàbuduō 差不多 adj.		about the same
bù xū cǐ xíng 不虚此行 phr.		did not make a wasted trip
è 饿 adj.; v.	餓	hungry; go hungry
zhǐ 只 adv.		only
shèngxià 剩下 v.		left (over), remain
dùn 顿 m.w.	頓	(used for meals)
qǐngkè 请客 v.	請客	give a treat

LANGUAGE FOCUS

1. Adverbs expressing scope
    一共 can be used to express "altogether," while 只 can be used to express "only."

    Example:

    上个星期，芳芳上网给家人、老师和中文班的同学们买了很多圣诞礼物，一共花了九百多块钱。她只给自己买了一件上衣，只花了六十八块钱。

2. Interrogative pronouns used as indefinite references

In Chinese, interrogative pronouns (什么, 谁, 哪个, 哪儿, 什么时候) can be used as indefinite references, similar to "wh-ever" in English. In other words, they can be used to refer in a non-specific way to people and things. To make indefinite references, interrogative pronouns are repeated in two separate but related clauses of the same sentence.

Examples: ❶ 谁先到，谁先得。
(Whoever comes first will get it.)

❷ 哪个便宜，就买哪个。
(Buy whichever is cheaper.)

❸ 哪儿大减价，我们就去哪儿买东西。
(Wherever there is a sale, we will go.)

❹ 什么时候打折，我们就什么时候去购物。
(Whenever there are discounts, we will go shopping.)

Chinese Consumerism

As the middle class rises to prominence in China, its economy is experiencing a significant shift in consumption, driven by a new generation of young, savvy consumers who value quality of life. This presents great opportunities for the luxury goods market in China.

Globally the Chinese are the biggest buyers of luxury goods, accounting for about 29% of luxury purchases in 2013. This proportion is set to continue to increase over the next few years. Almost two-thirds of Chinese spending on luxury goods takes place outside the mainland; one fifth of it takes place in Europe. Brands that are consistently favored among Chinese people include Audi, Gucci, Lancôme, Louis Vuitton, Rolex, and Tiffany.

While most luxury goods can be purchased in China, many Chinese actually prefer to buy them abroad. First, it is a little cheaper buying the products overseas, since foreign luxury goods are subject to mark-ups and hefty taxes in China. Second, counterfeit goods are very common in China, so many people believe that buying overseas is "safer." Third, the variety of products available overseas is often much wider than in China.

1. Read the dialog with a partner and answer the following questions:

A：你打算怎么买新电视机？去家用电器店买还是上网买？

B：怎么买方便，就怎么买。

A：你要买哪个品牌的？
　　　pǐnpái
　　　brand

B：我也不知道。我妈妈说哪个品牌的质量好，就买哪个品牌
　　　　　　　　　　　　　　　　zhìliàng
　　　　　　　　　　　　　　　　quality
　　的。我爸爸说哪家的免费保修期长就买哪家的。

A：听说网购便宜，那么多家用电器销售网站，你跟哪个买啊？

B：哪个网站有免费送货服务，我就跟哪个网站买。

A：我觉得应该去店里看看，然后再决定买什么牌子的。

B：你说得也对，除了价格和服务，电视机的款式也很重要。到
　　店里看了实物以后，再决定买哪个牌子的。

A：你想得没错，等你买好了，我也要向你请教。
　　　　　　　　　　　　　　　　qǐngjiào
　　　　　　　　　　　　　　　　seek advice

Questions:

❶ B一开始打算怎么买电视机？
❷ B打算买什么牌子的电视机？
❸ B的父母的建议是什么？
❹ A的建议是什么？

❺ B认为好的电视机应该注重哪些方面？
　　　　　　　　　　　zhùzhòng
　　　　　　　　　　　emphasize
❻ B最后的决定是什么？
❼ B为什么做了这个决定？

2. Fill in the blanks with the correct words that most logically match the communicative situations below, using adverbs of scope 一共 and 只, and interrogative pronouns (什么, 谁, 哪个, 哪儿, 什么时候, and 怎么) as indefinite references.

Example: 我这个月买了一件上衣288块，一条丝巾30块，两条项链1000块，
<u>一共</u> 消费1318块。他这个月 <u>只</u> 买了一双鞋，<u>只</u> 花了300块。

❶ A: 这么多家餐馆，我们应该选哪一家呢？
   B: 我不喜欢排队。＿＿＿＿＿＿＿没人，我们就去＿＿＿＿＿＿。

❷ A: 这些是你要买的衣服，＿＿＿＿＿＿1500块，谢谢。
   B: 我身上＿＿＿＿＿＿有100块现金，可以刷卡吗？
   A: 当然可以。

❸ A: 你打算去哪儿买北京小吃？可以帮我也买一点吗？我＿＿＿＿＿＿想尝尝冰糖葫芦。
   B: 好的。＿＿＿＿＿＿方便，我就去＿＿＿＿＿＿买。

❹ A: 我最喜欢大减价。＿＿＿＿＿＿有大减价，我就去＿＿＿＿＿＿看。
   B: 哦，我最不喜欢大减价，因为人太多了，而且很多时候没有你想买的东西。

❺ A: 你想点什么菜？
   B: 随便。＿＿＿＿＿＿东西好吃，就点＿＿＿＿＿＿。你决定吧！

❻ A: 你买电视机加上送货费＿＿＿＿＿＿花了多少钱？
   B: 一共2000块。

❼ A: ＿＿＿＿＿＿有这一家店打折，我们还是在这家店买吧！
   B: 可是，这家店没有保修服务，我们还是再看看吧。

❽ A: 你想吃什么？
   B: 我想吃北京炸酱面，可是＿＿＿＿＿＿有西单那里有家炸酱面店。

❾ A: 你买了这么多衣服，能穿得了吗？
   B: 我＿＿＿＿＿＿买了5件。我每天都要换一件衣服，一周正好换五件。

❿ A: 你这几天在北京旅游＿＿＿＿＿＿去了几个地方？
   B: 7个，你呢？

Step Up!

We have learned how to bargain in Chinese in this lesson. Imagine that you are studying in an international school in China. As the holiday season approaches, your school magazine editor has decided to have a special column on how to bargain in different parts of the world. You are assigned the topic "How to bargain while shopping for clothes in China." You started to do research on the Internet and found the following blog entries. Read the following suggestions on how to bargain when you are shopping for clothes and complete the following related tasks.

博客一

这要看你去哪买了。如果是去批发市场那样的地方，你就得照着一半的价格或以下去砍，不要给加价。如果不卖你就走，她们就会把你叫住，说她减点，让你加点，你就不加，还走，她还会把你叫住的，一般就能成了。我没去过那种市场买衣服，这也都是听朋友说的，她们特别能砍价。

批发 pīfā — wholesale
砍 kǎn — slash

博客二

你心中对那件衣服还满意，但必须不露声色，嘴上说这衣服还马马虎虎，就是颜色不好，或款式一般等，找点不足，看老板的态度如何。还有，你可以说，你买不买无所谓，就是随便看看，价格太高了，不想买，等等。他想你买，肯定会自动降价。

不露声色 bú lù shēngsè — not revealing any emotions
马马虎虎 mǎmǎ hūhū — average
自动降价 zìdòng jiàngjià — automatic reduce price

博客三

❶ 态度上不能表现得太热情，要淡定，让人感觉你可以要也可以不要。
　　　　　　　　　　　dàndìng
　　　　　　　　　　　composed

❷ 你喜欢的衣服裤子固然好，但是没有完美的东西，你可以挑衣服的毛病，
　　　　　　　　　gùrán　　　　　　　　　　wánměi　　　　　　　tiāo　　　　máobìng
　　　　　　　　　admittedly　　　　　　　perfect　　　　　　　pick on　　defects
比如说做工不太好、颜色太抢眼、颜色太显旧、衣服大了一点或者小了
　　　　　　　　　qiǎngyǎn　　　　xiǎnjiù
　　　　　　　　　eye-catching　　dull
一点……只要能让他觉得你不是一定要买，或者衣服裤子对你的要求来
说有不足。

❸ 狠下心来走，你走的那一刻他会产生很大的危机感，很有可能就在这一
　hěnxià xīn　　　　　　　　　　　　　　　　　　　wēijīgǎn
　harden one's heart　　　　　　　　　　　　　　　　sense of crisis
刻留住你了。

（来源：百度）

1. Answer the following questions based on the three blog entries.

   a. Write one sentence in Chinese to describe what you have found in common in all of the above three blog entries.

   b. List five things that a person should do when bargaining.

   c. What do the following underlined words mean in English?

      A: 你就得照着一半的价格或以下去砍，不要给加价。

      B: 她们特别能砍价。

      C: 你心中对那件衣服还满意，但必须不露声色。

      D: 你可以说，你买不买无所谓，就是随便看看。

      E: 他想你买，肯定会自动降价。

      F: 要淡定，让人感觉你可以要也可以不要。

      G: 你可以挑衣服的毛病，比如说做工不太好、颜色太抢眼。

   d. In your opinion, what is the most effective bargaining strategy mentioned in the three blog entries? Explain why.

2. **The #1 bargainer in class:** You are planning to submit an entry on "Bargaining while shopping for clothes" in the special holiday column of the school magazine. You have read three blog entries on the same topic. Work with a partner to role play the bargaining strategies suggested in the above three entries with each person taking a turn to be the shop owner or the customer.

3. Write an entry on the topic "How to bargain while shopping for clothes in China" for the special column of your school magazine. Your entry should suggest at least five strategies in bargaining. You should also compare these five strategies used in China with typical bargaining strategies used in your own culture. You also need to conclude your entry by analyzing the similarities and differences and the cultural perspectives and traditions that influenced the similarities and differences.

Fun Time!

1. With a partner, read the following riddles and guess the answers.

a. 拿十块钱买东西（打一字）

b. 什么东西明明是长方的，
   但好多人都称它为圆？

c. 什么东西明明是圆的，
   但好多人都说它是方的？

d. 半价出售（打一字）

e. 谢绝还价（打成语）

答案：a. 美 b. 人民币 c. 方向盘 d. 偈 e. 不折不扣

2. We have learned a lot of Chinese words and expressions containing 打, such as 打电话, 打球, 打车, 打的, 打喷嚏, 打针, and 打算. In this lesson, we have also learned 打折. Below is a list of words with 打. Work with a partner to guess the English equivalents of these words.

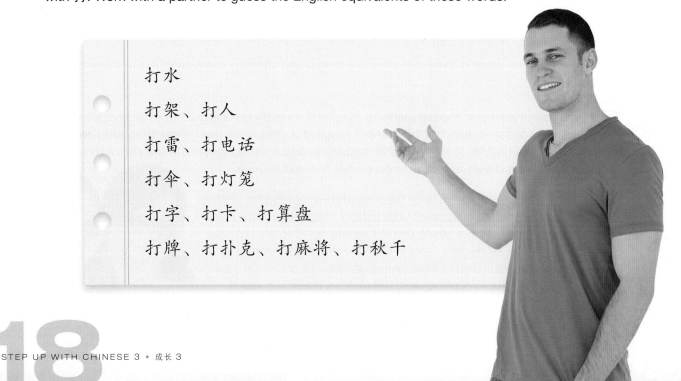

打水

打架、打人

打雷、打电话

打伞、打灯笼

打字、打卡、打算盘

打牌、打扑克、打麻将、打秋千

I have learned...

Verbs

打八折		dǎ bā zhé	give 20% discount
收		shōu	accept
光临	光臨	guānglín	(polite form) coming to (a place)
赚钱	賺錢	zhuànqián	make a profit
赔本	賠本	péiběn	take a loss
流行		liúxíng	get popular
显得	顯得	xiǎnde	look, seem
试	試	shì	try on
标价	標價	biāojià	mark a price
空运	空運	kōngyùn	air freight
决定		juédìng	decide
海运	海運	hǎiyùn	sea freight

节省	節省	jiéshěng	save, economize
讨价还价	討價還價	tǎo jià huán jià	bargain
挑选	挑選	tiāoxuǎn	choose
消费	消費	xiāofèi	consume, spend
超过	超過	chāoguò	exceed
免费	免費	miǎnfèi	free of charge
建议		jiànyì	suggest
收获		shōuhuò	gain
剩下		shèngxià	left (over), remain
饿	餓	è	go hungry
请客	請客	qǐngkè	give a treat

Nouns

款式		kuǎnshì	style, design
原价	原價	yuánjià	original price
促销	促銷	cùxiāo	promotion
价钱	價錢	jiàqián	price
信用卡		xìnyòngkǎ	credit card
丝巾	絲巾	sījīn	scarf
首饰	首飾	shǒushì	jewelry
项链	項鏈	xiàngliàn	necklace
眼光		yǎnguāng	one's taste in fashion
新款		xīnkuǎn	new design
价格	價格	jiàgè	price
耳环	耳環	ěrhuán	earring
手镯	手鐲	shǒuzhuó	bracelet
戒指		jièzhǐ	ring

发夹	髮夾	fàjiā	hairpin
钱包	錢包	qiánbāo	wallet, purse
手提包		shǒutíbāo	handbag
公文包/公事包		gōngwénbāo / gōngshìbāo	briefcase
先生		xiānsheng	Mr., sir
时尚感	時尚感	shíshànggǎn	trendy, fashionable
特大号	特大號	tèdàhào	size XL
大号	大號	dàhào	size L
中号	中號	zhōnghào	size M
小号	小號	xiǎohào	size S
试衣间	試衣間	shìyījiān	fitting room
明码	明碼	míngmǎ	price clearly marked
圣诞节	聖誕節	Shèngdàn Jié	Christmas
包裹		bāoguǒ	parcel

I have learned...

邮费	郵費	yóufèi	freight cost	景泰蓝钥匙链	景泰蓝钥匙链	jǐngtàilán yàoshiliàn	cloisonné keychain
土特产	土特產	tǔtèchǎn	local specialty	陶瓷		táocí	ceramics
元素		yuánsù	element	赠品	贈品	zèngpǐn	free item
商品		shāngpǐn	merchandise	运输费	運輸費	yùnshūfèi	transport fee
购物单	購物單	gòuwùdān	shopping list	数额	數額	shù'é	amount
折扇	摺扇	zhéshàn	folding fan	商家	商傢	shāngjiā	merchants
青花瓷		qīnghuācí	blue and white porcelain wares	导购员	導購員	dǎogòuyuán	personal shopper
丝绸	絲綢	sīchóu	silk	服务	服務	fúwù	service
珍珠		zhēnzhū	pearl	建议	建議	jiànyì	suggestion
唐装	唐裝	tángzhuāng	tangzhuang (a Chinese jacket)	价位	價位	jiàwèi	price
旗袍		qípáo	cheongsam (a type of Chinese dress)	产品	產品	chǎnpǐn	product
绣花	繡花	xiùhuā	embroidery	目标	目標	mùbiāo	target, goal
太极剑	太極劍	tàijíjiàn	taiji sword	计划	計劃	jìhuà	plan
漆盘	漆盤	qīpán	lacquer plate	大减价	大減價	dàjiǎnjià	sale
中国结	中國結	Zhōngguójié	Chinese knot	收获	收穫	shōuhuò	gain

Adjectives

随便	隨便	suíbiàn	casual, informal	新颖	新穎	xīnyǐng	new and original, novel
流行		liúxíng	popular	一定		yídìng	fixed, specified
火		huǒ	prosperous, flourishing	周到		zhōudào	attentive and satisfactory
适合	適合	shìhé	suitable	明确	明確	míngquè	clear
宽松	寬鬆	kuānsōng	loose	过瘾	過癮	guòyǐn	satisfying
价廉物美	價廉物美	jiàlián wùměi	(of goods) cheap and good	差不多		chàbuduō	about the same
精心	精心	jīngxīn	painstaking, meticulous	饿	餓	è	hungry

Adverbs

一律		yílǜ	all, without exception	挺		tǐng	quite
的确	的確	díquè	really, indeed	一定		yídìng	certainly, surely
别		bié	don't	一共		yígòng	in total
本来	本來	běnlái	originally	只		zhǐ	only

Phrases

刷卡		shuākǎ	swipe a card	讲价	講價	jiǎngjià	bargain
签字(签个字)	簽字(簽個字)	qiānzì (qiān gè zì)	sign one's name	送货	送貨	sònghuò	deliver goods
赔钱	賠錢	péiqián	take a loss	不虚此行	不虛此行	bù xū cǐ xíng	did not make a wasted trip
算了		suàn le	forget it				

Measure words

元/块	元/塊	yuán/kuài	yuan, dollar	分		fēn	cent, fractional unit of Chinese currency, equal to 1/100 of a yuan
角/毛		jiǎo/máo	fractional unit of Chinese currency, equal to 1/10 of a yuan	顿	頓	dùn	(used for meals)

Proper noun

秀水街市场	秀水街市場	Xiùshuǐjiē Shìchǎng	Silk Market

Preposition

趁	chèn	take advantage of (time, opportunity, etc.)

Pronoun

多少钱	多少錢	duōshao qián	how much (money)

◈ SENTENCE PATTERNS ◈

这双蓝色的运动鞋多少钱？原价400块。现在我们有促销。

50块太贵了！25块卖不卖？

我想看看这件蓝色的上衣。

只要学会讨价还价，就能买到价廉物美的商品。

网购除了节省时间以外，东西也比较便宜。

我一共花了1000元。什么打折我就买什么。

I can do!

Interpretive Communication

❑ I can understand different expressions on shopping and bargaining.

❑ I can read a passage about someone's shopping experiences for typical Chinese souvenirs.

❑ I can read authentic Chinese blogs on bargaining in Chinese markets.

Interpersonal Communication

❑ I can discuss places and ways to purchase things with a friend and express my preferences.

❑ I can talk about my shopping experience with a Chinese speaker.

❑ I can support my opinions and thoughts with some details.

❑ I can bargain in Chinese.

Presentational Communication

❑ I can create a role play of a bargaining scene in Chinese.

❑ I can present information on bargaining strategies in Chinese.

❑ I can write about bargaining strategies in China and compare their similarities and differences with those from my own culture.

❑ I can describe both my in-store and online shopping experience.

❑ I can compare the advantages and disadvantages of both in-store shopping and online shopping.

Cultural Knowledge

❑ I can compare how the amount of discount is presented both in China and in my own country.

❑ I can describe bargaining strategies in China.

❑ I can explain how silk is made and why it is popular in China.

❑ I can talk briefly about Chinese consumerism and the luxury goods market in China.

Maintaining health and fitness

健康与运动

COMMUNICATIVE GOALS
- Explaining how to create a healthy lifestyle
- Advising someone not to do something
- Expressing ability, permission, and necessity
- Describing frequency and duration of activities

Cultural Knowledge
- The Five Elements Theory
- Chinese martial arts – Wushu
- Square dancing by damas
- The medicine of Li Shizhen
- Relaxation with hand massage

In ancient China, one of the most important beliefs centered on the Five Elements Theory (五行, wǔxíng). It states that substances can be classified into one of five basic elements: wood (木, mù), fire (火, huǒ), water (水, shuǐ), metal (金, jīn), and earth (土, tǔ). Each element contains its own specific characteristics. Even today, the Five Elements Theory is still used as a method for analyzing changes in natural phenomena. During the 5th century BC, the Five Elements Theory was integrated into the concept of the *yin* and *yang* and became the basis for Traditional Chinese Medicine. Just as in the *yin* and *yang*, it is important for things to be in balance — the body, mind, emotions, and spirit. When they are out of balance, there is a health issue.

In the Five Elements Theory, each element is related to nature and the body. Wood, for example, corresponds to spring in the natural world and to the liver, gall bladder, and eyes in the body. Below is a chart that shows the relationship of the five elements to nature and the body. Do you see a relationship among the characteristics?

	WOOD	FIRE	EARTH	METAL	WATER
Season	Spring	Summer	Late Summer	Autumn	Winter
Yin Organ	Liver	Heart	Spleen	Lung	Kidney
Yang Organ	Gall Bladder	Small Intestine	Stomach	Large Intestine	Bladder
Orifice	Eye	Tongue	Mouth	Nose	Ear
Emotions	Anger	Joy	Pensiveness	Grief	Fear

In Europe during the Middle Ages, the underlying principle of medieval medicine was based on the theory of "humors." This was derived from ancient medical works and dominated much of Western medicine until the 19th century. The theory stated that within every individual there were four humors, or principal fluids - black bile, yellow bile, phlegm, and blood. These were produced by various organs in the body, and they had to be in balance for a person to remain healthy. Too much phlegm in the body, for example, caused lung problems; the body tried to cough up the phlegm to restore a balance. The balance of humors in humans could be achieved by diet, medicines, and by blood-letting, using leeches. The four humors were also associated with the four seasons: black bile-autumn, yellow bile-summer, phlegm-winter, and blood-spring.

STEPS *at a glance!*

HUMOR	TEMPER	ORGAN	SEASON	ELEMENT
Black bile	Melancholic	Spleen	Autumn	Earth
Yellow bile	Choleric	Gall Bladder	Summer	Fire
Phlegm	Phlegmatic	Lungs	Winter	Water
Blood	Sanguine	Head	Spring	Air

Compare the charts of the five elements in traditional Chinese medicine and the four humors of medieval European medicine and see where you find similarities and differences. Write down two similarities and two differences and compare your answers with a friend's answers.

STEP 1

DISCUSSING HEALTH ISSUES

A. Giving comments and suggestions on health

我们都叫你别熬夜了，你就是不听。

B. Discussing health

睡眠不但可以消除疲劳，而且可以提高人体的抵抗力。

KEEPING FIT THROUGH EXERCISE

A. Doing exercises

我在美国每周健身三四次。

B. Playing a sport

我已经报名参加今年的北京铁人三项比赛了。

ANALYZING ALTERNATIVE TREATMENT AND FITNESS

A. Trying out alternative medicine

既然丁强喜欢喝汤，以后我就多做一些有营养的汤给你喝。

B. Taking stock of our health

看到自己被朋友们超越了，我会再出去走一圈。

125

LESSON 5 MAINTAINING HEALTH AND FITNESS · 健康与运动

A Giving comments and suggestions on health

张健：丁强！你看起来没什么<u>精神</u>，没事吧？

丁强：哦，没事。昨晚又<u>熬夜</u>了，上网给在美国的家人<u>报</u> <u>平安</u>以后，就去<u>赶</u> <u>报告</u>，一直到今早<u>凌晨</u>两点才写完。所以现在感到有点<u>头昏脑涨</u>，不太舒服。

张健：上周我们都叫你别熬夜了，会把身体累坏的，你就是不听。你的脚怎么了？<u>绑</u>了<u>绷带</u>，是受伤了吗？

丁强：别<u>提</u>了，昨天在健身房做有氧运动时，把脚踝扭伤了，绑了绷带但是走路还是有点疼。

张健：原来是这样。你这周最好多休息，不要走太多路，<u>行动</u>要<u>小心</u>。要不要去找<u>中医师</u>做<u>推拿</u>缓解一下？

丁强：好<u>主意</u>，咱们现在就去。

jīngshen 精神 *n.*			energy, spirit
áoyè 熬夜 *phr.*			stay up late at night
bào 报 *v.*		報	report
píng'ān 平安 *n.*			safe and sound
gǎn 赶 *v.*		趕	rush through
bàogào 报告 *n.*		報告	report, assignment
língchén 凌晨 *n.*		凌晨	after midnight, before dawn
tóu hūn nǎo zhàng 头昏脑涨 *phr.*		頭昏腦漲	dizzy, not having a clear mind
bǎng 绑 *v.*		綁	bind, tie
bēngdài 绷带 *n.*		繃帶	bandage
tí 提 *v.*			mention
xíngdòng 行动 *v.*		行動	move
xiǎoxīn 小心 *adj.; v.*			careful; take care, look out
zhōngyīshī 中医师 *n.*		中醫師	Chinese physician
tuīná 推拿 *v.*			Chinese massage
zhǔyì 主意 *n.*			idea

When you want to give advice and suggestions to people, use the word 别 or 不要 to tell them not to do something. In some circumstances, in the second part of the sentence, you may use the 把–construction to indicate a possible consequence if the advice or suggestion in the first part is not followed. Look at the following sentences and determine their meaning.

Examples:

❶ 别乱吃东西！小心把肚子吃坏了。

❷ 不要运动过度，会把肌肉拉伤了。

❸ 别跳得太高，小心扭伤脚踝。

Try This!

1. Match the following pictures with the correct descriptions.

 g

a. 不要跑得太快，小心扭伤脚踝。

b. 别熬夜读书，小心把身体累坏了。

c. 别过度拉伸，小心把腰扭伤了。
　　lāshēn
　　stretching

d. 别搬太重的东西，会弄伤你的背。

e. 不要喝太多汽水，小心血糖过高。

f. 不要举太重的杠铃，会把你的肌肉拉伤。
　gànglíng　　　　　　　jīròu
　barbell　　　　　　　　muscle

g. 别吃太多油炸食物，小心胆固醇升高。

h. 不要伸直双腿做仰卧起坐，会把背弄伤的。
　　　　　　　yǎngwò qǐzuò
　　　　　　　sit-up

2. Read the following scenarios and give appropriate health advice and suggestions to the person using 别 or 不要.

　❶　A friend has sprained his ankle while running.

　❷　Your sister has worked through the night to get a report done.

　❸　Your brother drank two bottles of Coke for dinner just now.

　❹　A classmate carried a very heavy bag to school.

　❺　Your friend ate four pieces of fried chicken for lunch.

　❻　Someone has been running on the treadmill for two hours.

　❼　A friend is trying to lose weight and has been eating only salad for one week.

　❽　Your brother hurt his back while playing basketball.

CULTURAL HIGHLIGHTS

Wushu (武术)

Originating from traditional Chinese martial arts, *wushu* (武术) is a sport that has been organized and systematized into a formal branch of study in the performance arts and has become an athletic and aesthetic performance and competitive sport. Literally, "武" means military, and "术" means art. *Wushu* therefore means the art of fighting, or martial arts. It is commonly known as *kungfu* in the West. Martial arts training includes various movements, such as 踢 (tī, kicking), 打 (dǎ, punching), 摔 (shuāi, throwing), 拿 (ná, controlling), 击 (jī, hitting), and 刺 (cì, thrusting). Related to each movement are basic forms, or sequences, which may involve defensive and offensive strategies, retreating motions, mobility and immobility, speed and slowness, hard and soft postures, and emptiness and fullness, all with or without weapons.

Wushu consists of two disciplines: 套路 (tàolù, forms with or without weapons) and 散打 (sǎndǎ, free sparring). 套路 is a performance of a set of offensive and defensive *wushu* movements based on Chinese *wushu* principles. It includes the following four main categories: bare-handed forms, weapon forms, dual sparring forms, and group forms. *Taiji*, a style known for its slow, relaxed movements, belongs to the bare-handed form.

散打 is a modern fighting method and sport influenced by traditional Chinese boxing, Chinese wrestling methods (摔跤, shuāijiāo), and other Chinese grappling techniques (擒拿, qínná). Containing all of the combat aspects of *wushu*, 散打 appears much like kickboxing, or muay Thai, but includes many more grappling techniques.

Blog

今天王叔叔带我去打乒乓球。王叔叔从小就会打乒乓球，所以打得特别好。我很少打乒乓球，所以打得不好。王叔叔教了我一些打球的技巧，我觉得挺有用的。我们打了两小时的球，然后回家吃饭。

随着生活水平的提高，中国人越来越注重健康，运动和保健逐渐成为生活的一部分。王叔叔说他每个星期会跟朋友打球。他认为，运动得靠自己，把运动变成一种习惯以后，要是有一天突然停止不做了，会觉得很不自在。

王叔叔说除了锻炼以外，还要注意饮食。中国有句俗话说："吃饭七分饱"，所以不要因为好吃就吃得过多。要养成健康的生活习惯，千万不能熬夜。每天一定要睡眠充足，因为睡眠不但可以消除疲劳，而且可以提高人体的抵抗力，让我们不容易生病。

jìqiǎo 技巧 n.		technique
yǒuyòng 有用 adj.		useful
suízhe 随着 prep.	隨著	along with, in pace with
tígāo 提高 v.		increase
shuǐpíng 水平 n.		level, standard
zhùzhòng 注重 v.		place emphasis on
bǎojiàn 保健 n.		health care
zhújiàn 逐渐 adv.	逐漸	gradually
kào 靠 v.		depend
tūrán 突然 adv.		suddenly, all of a sudden
tíngzhǐ 停止 v.		stop
zìzài 自在 adj.		at ease, comfortable
zhùyì 注意 v.		pay attention to
yǐnshí 饮食 n.	飲食	diet
jù 句 n.		sentence
súhuà 俗话 n.	俗話	proverb, saying
bǎo 饱 adj.	飽	full
qiānwàn 千万 adv.	千萬	must, be sure to
shuìmián 睡眠 n.		sleep
chōngzú 充足 adj.		sufficient
xiāochú 消除 v.		remove
píláo 疲劳 n.	疲勞	fatigue
dǐkànglì 抵抗力 n.		resistance to disease

You have learned the auxiliary verbs 能, 可以, 会, and 得 (děi) in Book 2. They precede the main verb in a sentence.

1. 能   能 indicates the ability to do something.

    Examples: ❶ 他病好了，能下床走路了。

    ❷ 经过一个月的治疗，他的腿现在能动了。

2. 可以   可以 is mainly used to express permission.

    Examples: ❶ 你可以走了。   ❷ 你可以免费使用图书馆。

    可以 is also used to indicate the extent of one's ability. 能 may also be used in this instance.

    Examples: ❶ 他一分钟可以做五十个仰卧起坐。

    ❷ 他半小时能跑六公里。

3. 会   会 has very similar meanings to 能. However, it refers more to acquired skills – knowing how to do something. It also indicates possibility.

    Examples: ❶ 他会打乒乓球。   ❷ 你会说中文吗?

4. 得   得 is used to express necessity.

    Examples: ❶ 每个人都得有充足睡眠才能有精神工作。

    ❷ 你得多运动，身体才会健康。

Try This!

1. Use 能, 可以, 会, or 得 to complete the following sentences.

    ❶ 你＿＿＿＿＿＿游泳吗?

    ❷ 时间还没到，你们不＿＿＿＿＿＿走。

    ❸ 你的血糖和血压都太高了，你＿＿＿＿＿＿经常运动。
    blood sugar   blood pressure

    ❹ 每天熬夜学习对身体特别不好，你＿＿＿＿＿＿按时作息。
    ànshí
    according to time

    ❺ 他不＿＿＿＿＿＿打乒乓球，我们还是打篮球吧。

    ❻ 你生病了，＿＿＿＿＿＿好好休息。

    ❼ 我体育不太好，只＿＿＿＿＿＿做十个仰卧起坐。

    ❽ 你＿＿＿＿＿＿推拿吗? 帮我按摩脚吧。
    ànmó
    massage

    ❾ 你＿＿＿＿＿＿多运动才能保持健康的身体。

    ❿ 我＿＿＿＿＿＿问你一个问题吗?

2. Read the dialog and answer the following questions.

医生：你的脚扭伤了，明天不能上学。

子明：大概多久会好？我下个月还要参加篮球比赛。
　　　dàgài
　　　about

医生：通常要好几周才会好。你得多休息，不要走动太多。
　　　tōngcháng
　　　usually

子明：但是我这个月还有很多篮球训练。
　　　　　　　　　　　　　　　xùnliàn
　　　　　　　　　　　　　　　training

医生：你得停止训练，千万不能再做剧烈运动了，要不然你
　　　　　　　　　　　　　　　jùliè　　　　　　　　　　　yàobùrán
　　　　　　　　　　　　　　　rigorous　　　　　　　　　　otherwise
　　　的伤会更严重。

子明：但是这个比赛我已经准备了三个月了，现在突然要我
　　　fàngqì　　　　　　　　　　bù gānxīn
　　　放弃，我真的很不甘心。
　　　give up　　　　　　　　　unwilling

医生：比赛以后还会有，现在最重要的是把你的伤养好。

子明：唉，那我这三个月的努力都白费了。
　　　　　　　　　　　　　　　　　　báifèi
　　　　　　　　　　　　　　　　　　gone to waste

医生：不会白费的，等你的伤好了，你还能打篮球。

❶ 子明的脚怎么了？
❷ 医生要他做什么？
❸ 要是子明再做剧烈运动，会怎么样？
❹ 子明还想参加篮球比赛吗？为什么？
❺ 医生怎么鼓励子明？

A Doing exercises

丁强：子明，你常去<u>健身房</u>健身吗？

子明：哦，我平时喜欢打篮球，很少去健身房健身。听说美国人喜欢健身，健身是生活的一部分。你呢？你常去健身吗？

丁强：你说得很对，美国人很喜欢健身。我在美国每周健身三四次，每次健身一两个小时，锻炼身体<u>各</u> <u>部位</u>的<u>肌肉</u>。可是来了北京以后还没有健过身。在北京去健身房贵吗？

子明：北京有很多家健身<u>公司</u>，如果你<u>办</u>了其中一家的<u>会员卡</u>，去那里健身就会便宜一些。这些会员卡有年卡、半年卡和月卡。

丁强：嗯，那我先跟你一起去健身房看看吧。

子明：好的，没问题。

jiànshēnfáng 健身房 n.		gym
gè 各 pron.		each
bùwèi 部位 n.		section
jīròu 肌肉 n.		muscle
gōngsī 公司 n.		company
bàn 办 v.	辦	apply
huìyuánkǎ 会员卡 n.	會員卡	membership card

EXTENDED VOCABULARY

Gym equipment

jiànshēnchē
健身车 *n.*
健身車
exercise bike

pǎobùjī
跑步机 *n.*
跑步機
treadmill

yǎlíng
哑铃 *n.*
啞鈴
dumbbell

Stretching exercises

rèshēn yùndòng
热身运动 *phr.*
熱身運動
warm up

shōucāo yùndòng
收操运动 *n.*
收操運動
cool down exercises

lāshēn yùndòng
拉伸运动 *n.*
拉伸運動
stretching exercises

Exercises that train the arm and shoulder muscles

fǔwòchēng
俯卧撑 *n.*
俯臥撑
push-up

yǐntǐ xiàngshàng
引体向上 *n.*
chin up

jǔzhòng
举重 *n.*
舉重
weight lifting

Exercises that train the abdominal muscles

Exercise that train the leg muscles

yǎngwò qǐzuò
仰卧起坐 n.
仰臥起坐
sit ups

táituǐ / títuǐ
抬腿/提腿 phr.
擡腿/提腿
leg lift

shēndūn
深蹲 n.
squat

Others

shēnhūxī
深呼吸 v.
deep breathing

bójī
搏击 v.
搏擊
kick boxing

yújiā
瑜伽 n.
yoga

pǔlātí
普拉提 n.
pilates

yǒuyǎng yùndòng
有氧运动 n.
有氧運動
cardiovascular exercise, cardio

yǒuyǎng jiànshēncāo
有氧健身操 n.
aerobics

When you want to describe the duration of an activity in Chinese, always place the time duration after the verb.

Examples: ❶ 他每天早上游一小时泳。

❷ 我每天下午打两小时球。

❸ 我每天骑四十分钟健身车。

If you want to describe frequency, place the frequency phrase (numeral + 次) after the verb.

Examples: ❶ 他一分钟能做五十次俯卧撑。

❷ 我一周运动三次。

❸ 他一个月游四次泳。

❹ 我每两周去一次健身房。

Try This!

1. Read the following statements and decide the sequence in which you would do the routine in a gym according to what you believe a personal trainer would have you do. Number the sentences in the order in which you believe they should be. You must be able to provide a reason for why one activity comes before another.

☐ A: 做五分钟收操运动。

☐ B: 做十次俯卧撑。

☐ C: 做五十次仰卧起坐。

☐ D: 做五分钟拉伸运动。

☐ E: 骑十分钟健身车。

☐ F: 在跑步机上跑十五分钟。

☐ G: 做五十个深蹲。

2. Imagine that you have just become the assistant trainer in your school's Athletic Department. Students come into the office with problems and your job is to advise them of a workout that they can do to rebuild their muscles. Read the conditions and write up a half hour daily routine consisting of at least three different exercises with specific time allocations for each exercise. Your goal is to help them regain their strength. Choose two situations and report on what you would advise.

❶ 学生的脚踝扭伤了，他需要加强腿部肌肉。

❷ 学生的背受伤了，不能让背部再受伤。

❸ 这位学生是一个篮球运动员，刚刚做了肩膀手术。
  他需要好好保护肩膀。
  shǒushù — surgery
  bǎohù — protect

❹ 学生想加入校篮球队，她需要锻炼体能，
  参加选拔赛。
  xuǎnbásài — selection, trial
  duì — team
  tǐnéng — physical fitness

❺ 游泳队的队员要参加比赛，所以，她想要游
  得更快。

 CULTURAL HIGHLIGHTS

Square Dancing by Damas

The new pastime among older women in China is the art of dancing in the street, known as square dancing (广场舞, guǎngchǎngwǔ). These women bring their stereos and drums to a public square and dance 365 days a year. They are called "dama" (大妈) which means a middle-aged or retired woman. They can be found dancing in neighborhoods most often in the morning or the evening, often accompanied by their husbands on drums or other percussion instruments. They often dance for over an hour without taking a break, twirling fans and handkerchiefs in unison in what looks like a type of line dancing they call "yangge" (秧歌, "rice sprout song"). Sometimes people passing by will join in the dance.

Dancers organize themselves into rank and file. The most proficient dancers are usually in the front row, with the best being in the center. The rows at the back contain dancers who are less proficient. All the dancers face forward. This allows dancers to learn from those in the rows ahead.

While this activity draws concerns over noise level and disturbance from nearby residents, square dancing remains popular in China as it is good physical exercise and provides a platform for the *damas* to socialize.

Blog

我已经报名参加今年的北京铁人三项比赛了。我觉得这是一次锻炼自己体能的好机会。北京的铁人三项比赛包括740米游泳，20公里骑自行车和5公里跑步。现在我正在积极准备选拔赛。我给自己制定了一个健身计划，每天要在健身房锻炼一个小时。这一个小时里，我跑步二十分钟，骑健身车二十分钟，练举重二十分钟。

半个月过去了，我还在坚持我的健身计划。现在，我跑步和骑车的速度都提高了，体重降低了，脂肪减少了，但是我感觉自己的肌肉更有力量了，人也更有精神了。运动让我更健康、更快乐！还在等什么？挑战自己！一起加入吧！

tiěrén sānxiàng 铁人三项 n.	鐵人三項	triathlon
tǐnéng 体能 n.	體能	physical fitness
jīhuì 机会 n.	機會	opportunity
zhèngzài 正在 adv.		currently, in the process of
xuǎnbásài 选拔赛 n.	選拔賽	selection
zhìdìng 制定 v.		set up, draw up (a plan, etc.)
háizài 还在 adv.	還在	still
jiānchí 坚持 v.	堅持	persist, hang in until the end
sùdù 速度 n.		speed
tǐzhòng 体重 n.	體重	weight
jiàngdī 降低 v.		reduce
lìliàng 力量 n.		strength, power
děng 等 v.		wait
tiǎozhàn 挑战 v.	挑戰	challenge
jiārù 加入 v.		join

To express that you will do something at different times, use certain adverbs in Chinese (正在, 已经, and 还在) to indicate the aspects of different time frames. Use 正在 to indicate an action that is being done or ongoing at the present time (the English present progressive tense). Use 已经 to indicate an action that has already happened and is completed. Use 还在 to indicate an action that has been happening for some time and is still ongoing. Note that 正在, 已经, and 还在 are always placed before the verb.

Examples: ❶ 他们正在准备参加铁人三项比赛。

❷ 他们已经学会游泳和骑自行车了。

❸ 晚上十点了，他们还在健身房健身。

1. Using the list of physical activities below, interview one of your classmates to determine his/her involvement in any of these activities. Ask whether he/she is doing the activity right now, has already done it before, has done it for some time and is still doing it, or has never done it before. After the interview, write a short summary about your classmate's participation in physical activity.

Physical activity 体育项目	Doing right now 正在	Already done before 已经	Still doing 还在	Never done before 从来没有试过
打篮球				
游泳				
练武术				
打太极				
跑马拉松				
跳舞				
做瑜伽				
跳绳				
仰卧起坐				
俯卧撑				

2. Imagine that you are preparing to join a varsity team sport. You will need to talk to the coach ahead of time to discuss your training plan. In a paragraph, write up a narrative of your exercise regime over the past few years. Write in complete sentences and state the exercises that you have already done, the ones you are currently doing, and finally those that you have been doing for some time and are still doing. In your paragraph, be sure to use the words 已经, 正在, and 还在.

ANALYZING ALTERNATIVE TREATMENT AND FITNESS

A Trying out alternative medicine

王叔叔：丁强，这是莲子百合排骨汤，你要多喝点。前几天你熬夜，睡眠不足，要注意身体啊。

丁强：嗯，这汤非常好喝。我熬夜就是少睡了点觉，周末多睡几个小时就补回来啦。

王叔叔：其实熬夜对人体有很大的害处。如果熬夜不睡觉，就会抵抗力差，免疫力降低，容易生病。

丁强：听起来，熬夜的害处真大。

李阿姨：是的。咦，你的脚好多了吗？还疼不疼？

丁强：不疼了。我的同学张健带我去看了中医，做了推拿，不用打针不用吃药，现在没事了。

李阿姨：中医除了推拿以外，还有针灸和拔罐都可以用来治疗 疾病，缓解病痛。现在很多人也利用 食疗来保持身体健康和防治疾病。

qíshí 其实 adv.	其實	actually, in fact
hàichù 害处 n.	害處	harm
chà 差 adj.		bad
miǎnyìlì 免疫力 n.		immunity
zhìliáo 治疗 v.	治療	cure
jíbìng 疾病 n.		disease, illness
bìngtòng 病痛 n.		pain from illness
lìyòng 利用 v.		make use of
fángzhì 防治 v.		provide prevention and cure

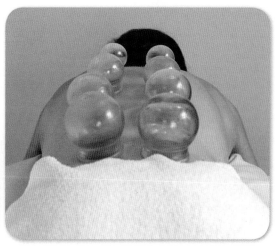

王叔叔： 你看，李阿姨今天为你煮的莲子百合排骨汤就是食疗的一种。莲子和百合都有<u>宁心安神</u>的<u>功效</u>；排骨能补<u>虚弱</u>，强<u>筋骨</u>。食疗是中国人的传统习惯，通过饮食达到<u>调理</u>身体的目的，而且食疗使用的都是我们日常生活中常见的食物。

丁强： 太好了，我们可以一边<u>享受</u>美食，一边治病。

李阿姨： <u>既然</u>丁强喜欢喝汤，以后我<u>就</u>多做一些有营养的汤给你喝。

níng xīn ān shén 宁心安神 phr.	寧心安神	calm the mind and soothe the senses
gōngxiào 功效 n.		effect, efficacy
xūruò 虚弱 adj.	虛弱	weak
jīngǔ 筋骨 n.		tendons and bone
tiáolǐ 调理 v.	調理	recuperate, nurse one's health
xiǎngshòu 享受 v.		enjoy
jìrán...jiù... 既然…就…		since...then...

EXTENDED VOCABULARY

Alternative treatment

莲子百合排骨汤 n.	蓮子百合排骨湯	liánzǐ bǎihé páigǔtāng	pork rib soup with lotus seeds and lily bulbs
针灸 n.	針灸	zhēnjiǔ	acupuncture
拔罐 phr.		báguàn	cupping
食疗 n.	食療	shíliáo	diet remedy

DO **YOU** KNOW . . .
你知道吗？

Li Shizhen (李时珍, 1518-1593), a famous Chinese doctor during the Ming Dynasty, developed a *Compendium of Materia Medica* (本草纲目, Běncǎo Gāngmù), which is a collection of information on over 300 species of plants and more than 400 species of animals that can be used to cure various illnesses. The Compendium made a significant contribution to how traditional medicine was compiled and formatted. It was also an important work in improving the credibility and scientific values of biological classification of both plants and animals.

140

LANGUAGE FOCUS

The conjunction 既然 is placed in the first part of the sentence to introduce a fact, followed by a logical conclusion or result in the second part of the sentence with 就. Look at the following sentences to see how it is used.

1. 既然食疗有帮助，你就试一试。
2. 你既然累了，就应该睡一会儿。
3. 既然你的脚疼，就应该去看医生。
4. 你既然这么累，就应该去休息。
5. 既然运动对你有好处，就应该每天运动。

Try This!

1. Match the sentences in the left column with the correct ones in the right column.

❶ 既然脚扭伤了，	a. 你就应该多去几次。
❷ 你既然这么忙，	b. 你就应该按时作息。
❸ 既然熬夜对身体不好，	c. 你就不应该去跑步。
❹ 既然推拿可以缓解酸痛，	d. 我们就应该多利用这个方法。 fāngfǎ / method
❺ 既然食疗有这么多好处，	e. 我就不要麻烦你了。
❻ 既然你身体不舒服，	f. 你就少喝一点。
❼ 你既然这么喜欢运动，	g. 就应该去看医生。
❽ 既然这么贵，	h. 我就不买了。
❾ 既然这里不卖咖啡，	i. 就应该参加铁人三项比赛。
❿ 既然可乐的糖分这么高，	j. 我们就去别的地方吧。

2. Read the following descriptions about different people's lifestyles and decide who has a healthy daily routine and who does not. If you think a daily routine is not healthy, write what you would do to change it to make it healthier. Be sure to use 既然…就…, 别/不要……, 可以…… in your suggestions. You may also use some of the words you have just learned, such as 日常作息, 睡眠充足, 疲劳, 抵抗力, 免疫力, 调理, and 防治.

康德 (Immanuel Kant)，德国哲学家，出生于1764年，1804年去世。
zhéxuéjiā 哲学家 philosopher　chūshēng 出生 born　qùshì 去世 die

康德每天早睡早起，他晚上10点睡，早上5点起床。起来后一小时喝茶提神、抽烟斗、冥想。接着写作一个小时，然后去给学生上课四个小时。11点去酒馆喝酒吃中饭，这是他每天吃的唯一的一顿正餐。吃完饭散步一个小时。下午4点到7点和他最好的朋友约瑟夫·格林见面交谈。回家后读书三个小时，然后就上床睡觉。
tíshén 提神 refresh oneself　yāndǒu 烟斗 tobacco pipe　míngxiǎng 冥想 meditate　jiēzhe 接着 next　jiǔguǎn 酒馆 wine tavern　wéiyī 唯一 only　Yuēsèfū 约瑟夫 Joseph　Gélín 格林 Green　jiāotán 交谈 talk

达尔文 (Charles Darwin)，英国生物学家，出生于1809年，1882年去世。

达尔文每天的安排很丰富，他晚上12点睡。早上8点起床后就去散步半个小时，然后一个人吃早餐半个小时。他经常先工作一个半小时，然后花一个小时时间，读读私人信件，接着再继续工作一个半小时。中午12点出去遛狗半个小时，回来吃午饭半个小时，接着阅读报纸、写信和睡午觉。下午4点睡午觉起来后再工作一个半小时，吃完晚饭后，听妻子艾玛朗读小说，然后跟她下下棋。睡前花一个小时阅读科学方面的书籍，然后躺在床上两个小时思索问题才睡觉。
ānpái 安排 arrangement　fēngfù 丰富 varied　sīrén 私人 personal　jìxù 继续 continue　Àimǎlǎng 艾玛朗 Emma　shūjí 书籍 books　tǎng 躺 lie on　sīsuǒ 思索 ponder over

冰心，中国作家，出生于1900年，1999年去世。

冰心的生活安排很有规律。她每天清晨5点左右醒后，开始收听广播，6点半起床，7点吃早饭。饭后，她习惯看报纸或者听音乐，9点写日记和接待来访者。中午12点，冰心准时吃午饭、收听午间新闻，然后午睡。下午2点，冰心起床看书、写作，晚上10点又按时上床休息。数十年如一日，冰心一直坚持这样极具规律的生活习惯，这被认为是她长寿的重要原因之一。
guīlǜ 规律 regular　guǎngbō 广播 radio broadcast　rìjì 日记 diary　jiēdài 接待 receive　láifǎngzhě 来访者 visitor　zhǔnshí 准时 on time　chángshòu 长寿 long life　yuányīn 原因 reason

Source: http://www.bundpic.com/2014/04/54567.shtml

Blog

最近，在中国流行起一种新的"游戏"——<u>晒</u> <u>步数</u>。不少中国人通过手机APP<u>微信</u> <u>记录</u>自己每天走路的步数，在<u>朋友圈</u>里展示自己每天的步行记录，还能<u>排名次</u>。<u>周围</u>的很多中国人都因为这个"游戏"而爱上了走路，好多人积极<u>参与</u>到走路的运动中来，能走路到的地方<u>坚决</u>不打车！

听说，走路这种运动对身体健康非常有好处。于是，在半个月之前，我也开始<u>关注</u>"微信运动"，<u>目前</u>已经<u>累计</u>走了194,058步，<u>平均</u>每天走的步数都在1万步以上。周围的朋友也都在用微信记录步数，每天晚上，<u>排行榜</u>上会<u>显示</u>我们的名次，非常有趣！这样还可以<u>监督</u>自己锻炼身体！如果哪一天看到自己排名<u>在最后</u>，被朋友们<u>超越</u>了，我会再出去走一圈，<u>改变</u>自己的名次。有时候，自己排名第一的时候，会非常有成就感！

shài 晒 v.	曬	to show off
bùshù 步数 n.	步數	number of steps
wēixìn 微信 n.		WeChat
jìlù 记录 v.	記錄	to record
péngyouquān 朋友圈 phr.		a group of friends *(in WeChat)*
pái míngcì 排名次 v.		rank
zhōuwéi 周围 n.	周圍	around
cānyù 参与 v.	參與	join, participate
jiānjué 坚决 adv.	堅決	firmly
guānzhù 关注 v.	關注	pay attention to
mùqián 目前 adv.		at present
lěijì 累计 v.	纍計	add up
píngjūn 平均 v.		on average
páihángbǎng 排行榜 n.		rankings
xiǎnshì 显示 v.	顯示	indicate
jiāndū 监督 v.	監督	supervise
chāoyuè 超越 v.		surpass
gǎibiàn 改变 v.	改變	change

被, unlike other passive voice markers such as 让 (to let), 给 (to give), or 叫 (to call), is traditionally used in the sense of being inflicted upon or to suffer from something undesirable or negative. It is frequently used with verbs that express adversity or an unfortunate situation such as 被打 (be beaten) or 被污染 (be polluted). However, due to the influence of Western language, the 被 sentence is no longer used exclusively to refer to negative events. Nowadays, it is also used to convey positive news such as 被选为 (be elected) or 被治好了 (be cured).

Examples: ❶ 这里的空气被工业废气污染了。

❷ 马克非常负责任，所以被选为班长。

❸ 他的病被治好了，大家都为他感到高兴。

1. Read the following sentences and change them to sentences in the passive voice.

❶ 妈妈一直监督着弟弟做功课。

❷ 丁强走路的名次超越了张健。

❸ 他拉伤了肌肉。

❹ 老师批评了玛丽的作业。
　　pīpíng
　　criticize

❺ 他们把教室弄脏了。

❻ 妹妹吃光了巧克力。

❼ 子明借了两本书。

❽ 爸爸开走了车。

❾ 芳芳喝了牛奶。

❿ 大家都关注全球变暖问题。

2. Answer the following questions based on the passage in Step 3B.

❶ "晒步数" 是什么？

❷ "晒步数" 怎么影响中国人？

❸ "我" 每天平均走多少步？

❹ 如果自己排名在最后，"我" 会怎么做？

❺ 你觉得 "晒步数" 这个游戏好吗？为什么？

CULTURAL HIGHLIGHTS

Hand Massage

Hand massage or hand acupressure is a method of therapy that has been used in China for centuries. Some people do it to help them relax and others believe that it can help to prevent and treat a range of health complaints. There are four major techniques for a hand massage: rubbing (搓, cuō), squeezing (挤, jǐ), pulling (拉, lā), and pressing (压, yā). For example, by rubbing the palms together to warm them, it is believed that you generate good energy or *qi*. The squeezing and pulling motions are often done on the fingers by pressing or pulling from the base to the finger tip. Finally, pressing can be done on pressure points on the opposite hand. None of these motions should be painful in any way.

Look at the charts below and compare the location of the pressure points. You might try doing a hand massage on yourself to see if it relaxes you.

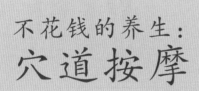

不花钱的养生：
穴道按摩

D1: nose area
D2: ear
D3: shoulder
D4: liver
D5: gall bladder
D6: waist area
D7: rectum (colon)
D8: eyes
D9: stomach

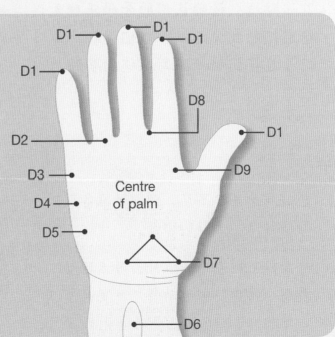

Step Up!

1. Read the following race information about the Beijing International Triathlon (北京国际铁人三项赛).
   Then answer the questions related to the material.

北京国际铁人三项赛

报到及领取运动员装备包时要带什么？
bàodào 报到 report　língqǔ 领取 collect　zhuāngbèibāo 装备包 race pack

- 身份证或护照
  shēnfènzhèng 身份证 identity card
- 报名确认邮件
  quèrèn 确认 confirmation
- 运动员必须本人报到并领取自己的运动员装备包。

运动员装备包中有什么？

- 比赛号码布：可以使用您自己的号码布，在跑步时号码朝前，可见。
  hàomǎbù 号码布 number tag
- 自行车头盔号码贴纸：请贴在头盔正前方。
  tóukuī 头盔 helmet　tiēzhǐ 贴纸 sticker
- 泳帽：运动员必须戴泳帽参加比赛。
- 身体贴纸：请确认您的号码正确无误。如果您忘记贴身体贴纸，我们将在比赛日早晨用记号笔将您的号码写在您的胳膊上。
  zhèngquè 正确 accurate　wúwù 无误 without errors
- 赛道地图
  sàidào 赛道 competition route

注意事项
shìxiàng 事项 matters

1. 您将在比赛日早晨，到游泳准备区领取计时芯片和脚踝带。
   jìshí 计时 time keeping　xīnpiàn 芯片 chip

2. 除了以上比赛用品以外，每名运动员还会得到一个运动员包，里头有一件纪念T恤和其他赞助商礼品。
   yòngpǐn 用品 items for use　jìniàn 纪念 commemorative　zànzhùshāng 赞助商 sponsors

3. 您必须参加至少一次运动员会议。在参加过运动员会议后，您将得到运动员手环。您必须一直戴着运动员手环，直到比赛结束。只有戴着运动员手环，才可以进入转换区。
   zhìshǎo 至少 at least　huìyì 会议 meeting　shǒuhuán 手环 hand band　jiéshù 结束 end　zhuǎnhuànqū 转换区 transit area

Source: http://cn.beijinginternationaltriathlon.com/packet-pick-up/

❶ 铁人三项赛中没有哪一种运动？
　Ⓐ 游泳　　　Ⓑ 跑步　　　Ⓒ 武术

❷ 参加游泳的运动员必须戴什么？
　Ⓐ 泳帽　　　Ⓑ 头盔　　　Ⓒ 太阳眼镜

❸ 人们会看见跑步队员的号码布在哪里？
　Ⓐ 前面　　　Ⓑ 背后　　　Ⓒ 左右两边

❹ 参加比赛的运动员报到的时候要带什么？
　Ⓐ 礼品　　　Ⓑ 证件　　　Ⓒ 运动员包

❺ 运动员装备包中有什么？
　Ⓐ 计时芯片　Ⓑ 脚踝带　　Ⓒ 赛道地图

❻ 运动员包里面有什么？
　Ⓐ 头盔　　　ⒷT恤衫　　　Ⓒ 记号笔

❼ 请说一说铁人三项赛是一种什么样的比赛？

❽ 在比赛日早晨，参加比赛的运动员应该去什么地方领取什么？

❾ 如果运动员忘了带身体贴纸，怎么办？

❿ 北京国际铁人三项赛有什么 guiding 规定？ 请列出至少三项。 regulations

2. You are the owner and manager of a new fitness center and you need to create a brochure to advertise your center. Make sure to include in the brochure the top 10 reasons why your new fitness center is better than others in your town/city. Be sure to include the kinds of services that your center offers. Include reasonable prices for use of the facility.

3. Imagine your friend has been suffering from a certain condition for some time. Despite treatment, there has been no marked improvement in his/her condition. You know of an alternative medicine/therapy that might help in treating the condition. In a role play of two people in which one of you is the person suffering from the condition and the other is the person offering advice and suggestions, persuade your friend to try out the alternative medicine/therapy. Use the patterns and words you have learned in this lesson: 既然…就…，别/不要…，已经, and words expressing frequency and duration.

Fun Time!

Yoga originated from India, but the practice of yoga is becoming very popular in China these days. It is a way that people learn to relax and is viewed in Traditional Chinese Medicine as beneficial. In Chinese, yoga is written as 瑜伽 and pronounced as yú jiā. Look at the yoga poses and match the poses with the Chinese names for them. Then match the Chinese names with the English names. Can you do any of these poses?

1

2

3

4

5

- a. 狗脸朝上式
- b. 树式
- c. 鹤式
- d. 莲花式
- e. 鱼式

- i. Tree pose
- ii. Upward facing dog pose
- iii. Fish pose
- iv. Lotus pose
- v. Crane pose

I have learned...

Verbs

报	報	bào	report		等		děng	wait
赶	趕	gǎn	rush through		挑战	挑戰	tiǎozhàn	challenge
绑	綁	bǎng	bind, tie		加入		jiārù	join
提		tí	mention		治疗	治療	zhìliáo	cure
行动	行動	xíngdòng	move		利用		lìyòng	make use of
小心		xiǎoxīn	take care, look out		防治		fángzhì	provide prevention and cure
推拿		tuīná	Chinese massage		调理	調理	tiáolǐ	recuperate, nurse one's health
提高		tígāo	increase		享受		xiǎngshòu	enjoy
注重		zhùzhòng	place emphasis on		晒	曬	shài	to show off
靠		kào	depend		记录	記錄	jìlù	to record
停止		tíngzhǐ	stop		排名次		pái míngcì	rank
注意		zhùyì	pay attention to		参与	參與	cānyù	join, participate
消除		xiāochú	remove		关注	關注	guānzhù	pay attention to
办	辦	bàn	apply		累计	纍計	lěijì	add up
深呼吸		shēnhūxī	deep breathing		平均		píngjūn	on average
搏击	搏擊	bójī	kick boxing		显示	顯示	xiǎnshì	indicate
制定		zhìdìng	set up, draw up (a plan, etc.)		监督	監督	jiāndū	supervise
坚持	堅持	jiānchí	persist, hang in until the end		超越		chāoyuè	surpass
降低		jiàngdī	reduce		改变	改變	gǎibiàn	change

Nouns

精神		jīngshen	energy, spirit		健身房		jiànshēnfáng	gym
平安		píng'ān	safe and sound		部位		bùwèi	section
报告	報告	bàogào	report, assignment		肌肉		jīròu	muscle
凌晨	凌晨	língchén	after midnight, before dawn		公司		gōngsī	company
绷带	繃帶	bēngdài	bandage		会员卡	會員卡	huìyuánkǎ	membership card
中医师	中醫師	zhōngyīshī	Chinese physician		健身车	健身車	jiànshēnchē	exercise bike
主意		zhǔyì	idea		跑步机	跑步機	pǎobùjī	treadmill
技巧		jìqiǎo	technique		哑铃	啞鈴	yǎlíng	dumbbell
保健		bǎojiàn	health care		收操运动	收操運動	shōucāo yùndòng	cool down exercises
饮食	飲食	yǐnshí	diet		拉伸运动	拉伸運動	lāshēn yùndòng	stretching exercises
句		jù	sentence		俯卧撑	俯臥撐	fǔwòchēng	push-up
俗话	俗話	súhuà	proverb, saying		引体向上		yǐntǐ xiàngshàng	chin up
睡眠		shuìmián	sleep		举重	舉重	jǔzhòng	weight lifting
疲劳	疲勞	píláo	fatigue		仰卧起坐	仰臥起坐	yǎngwò qǐzuò	sit ups
抵抗力		dǐkànglì	resistance to disease		深蹲		shēndūn	squat

I have learned...

深蹲		shēndūn	squat
瑜伽		yújiā	yoga
普拉提		pǔlātí	pilates
有氧运动	有氧運動	yǒuyǎng yùndòng	cardiovascular exercise, cardio
有氧健身操		yǒuyǎng jiànshēncāo	aerobics
铁人三项	鐵人三項	tiěrén sānxiàng	triathlon
体能	體能	tǐnéng	physical fitness
机会	機會	jīhuì	opportunity
选拔赛	選拔賽	xuǎnbásài	selection
速度		sùdù	speed
体重	體重	tǐzhòng	weight
力量		lìliàng	strength, power
害处	害處	hàichù	harm

Adjectives

有用		yǒuyòng	useful
自在		zìzài	at ease, comfortable
饱	飽	bǎo	full
充足		chōngzú	sufficient
差		chà	bad
虚弱	虛弱	xūruò	weak
小心		xiǎoxīn	careful

Adverbs

逐渐	逐漸	zhújiàn	gradually
突然		tūrán	suddenly, all of a sudden
千万	千萬	qiānwàn	must, be sure to
正在		zhèngzài	currently, in the process of

Preposition

随着	隨著	suízhe	along with, in pace with

Construction

既然…就…		jìrán…jiù…	since…then…

免疫力		miǎnyìlì	immunity
疾病		jíbìng	disease, illness
病痛		bìngtòng	pain from illness
功效		gōngxiào	effect, efficacy
筋骨		jīngǔ	tendons and bones
莲子百合排骨汤	蓮子百合排骨湯	liánzǐ bǎihé páigǔtāng	pork rib soup with lotus seeds and lily bulbs
针灸	針灸	zhēnjiǔ	acupuncture
食疗	食療	shíliáo	diet remedy
步数	步數	bùshù	number of steps
微信		wēixìn	WeChat
周围	周圍	zhōuwéi	around
排行榜		páihángbǎng	rankings

Phrases

熬夜		áoyè	stay up late at night
头昏脑涨	頭昏腦漲	tóu hūn nǎo zhàng	dizzy, not having a clear mind
热身运动	熱身運動	rèshēn yùndòng	warm up
抬腿/提腿	擡腿/提腿	táituǐ/títuǐ	leg lift
宁心安神	寧心安神	níng xīn ān shén	calm the mind and soothe the senses
拔罐		báguàn	cupping
朋友圈		péngyouquān	a group of friends (in WeChat)
还在	還在	háizài	still
其实	其實	qíshí	actually, in fact
坚决	堅決	jiānjué	firmly
目前		mùqián	at present

Pronoun

各		gè	each

SENTENCE PATTERNS

我们都叫你别熬夜了，你就是不听。

睡眠不但可以消除疲劳，而且可以提高
人体的抵抗力。

我每周健身三四次。

我已经报名参加今年的北京铁人三项比赛了。

既然丁强喜欢喝汤，以后我就多做一些
有营养的汤给你喝。

看到自己被朋友们超越了，我会再出去走一圈。

I can do!

Interpretive Communication

❑ I can understand when people talk or write about fitness routines.

❑ I can read and interpret dialogs and blogs about Chinese medicine.

❑ I can read and understand information about staying healthy.

Interpersonal Communication

❑ I can converse with a friend on health issues.

❑ I can interact with someone discussing events in various time frames.

❑ I can compare information about healthy lifestyles.

Presentational Communication

❑ I can explain how to keep fit.

❑ I can provide suggestions and advice to friends.

❑ I can create a plan for developing a healthy lifestyle.

❑ I can speak about the importance of following a daily exercise routine.

Cultural Knowledge

❑ I can talk about the Five Elements Theory and describe how it relates to organs in the body.

❑ I can briefly describe the characteristics of *wushu* and its disciplines.

❑ I can describe the phenomenon of "dama" or dancing in the street.

❑ I can explain how to relax using hand massage.

❑ I can explain the medicine of Li Shizhen.

Meeting the challenges of modern life

面对现代生活的挑战

COMMUNICATIVE GOALS

- Describing a positive attitude
- Explaining how to get along with others
- Analyzing and resolving conflicts
- Emphasizing a point using rhetorical questions
- Making clarifications

Cultural Knowledge

- Famous Chinese entrepreneur — Jack Ma
- The social media of WeChat
- Harmony in Chinese culture

Get ready...

Look at the following pictures of modern Beijing and write a caption in Chinese for at least five of the pictures. Tell what you see or how the picture influences your view of China. After you have written your captions, share what you have written with the class.

①

②

③

④

⑤

⑥

⑦

STEPS *at a glance!*

STEP 1

EXPERIENCING THE PRESSURES OF MODERN LIFE

A. Managing the rhythms of modern life

我们好像永远都在跟时间赛跑，做什么事都离不开一个"快"字。

B. Dealing with stress

功课这么多，这个周末恐怕哪儿都不去也应付不过来。

STEP 2

DEVELOPING A POSITIVE MINDSET

A. Learning from failure

不管失败多少次，他都不会放弃。

B. Having a positive attitude

难道你没看见我们在忙吗？

STEP 3

FINDING SOLUTIONS

A. Solving problems or conflicts

我不是身体不舒服，而是心里不舒服。

B. Getting along with others

父母越管孩子，孩子越想反抗。

A Managing the rhythms of modern life

Blog

我常常听到朋友抱怨："网速怎么那么慢！下载个音乐要等大半天。"大家越来越没有耐心了。我们的生活真的是那么忙碌吗？我们好像永远都在跟时间赛跑，做什么事都离不开一个"快"字。

一早起床洗脸刷牙之后，上班的赶快去上班，上学的赶快去上学。下午回到家，学生还要继续做作业。每次要到很晚才能做完。这就是现代人快速节奏的生活写照。因为做什么事都得讲求效率，希望用最短的时间，达成最好的效果，所以现代生活太快速，让我们喘不过气来。

bàoyuàn 抱怨 v.		grumble, complain
màn 慢 adj.		slow
mánglù 忙碌 adj.		busy
hǎoxiàng 好像 adv.		looks like, seems like
yǒngyuǎn 永远 adv.	永遠	forever
sàipǎo 赛跑 v.	賽跑	running a race
jìxù 继续 v.	繼續	continue
xiàndài 现代 n.	現代	modern times
jiézòu 节奏 n.	節奏	rhythm
xiězhào 写照 n.	寫照	portrayal
jiǎngqiú 讲求 v.	講求	be particular about, strive for
xiàolǜ 效率 n.		efficiency
xiàoguǒ 效果 n.		result, effect
chuǎn bú guò qì 喘不过气 phr.	喘不過氣	breathless

其实我们都应该把脚步放慢，享受生活里悠闲的一面。忙里偷闲跟家人一起去欣赏

一场精彩的音乐会，一起到餐馆品尝一顿丰盛美食。享受与家人相聚的美好时光。生活有忙碌紧张的一面，也有轻松愉快的一面，这是一种平衡。我们得知道什么时候应该加快脚步，什么时候应该慢下来。如果我们能掌握生活的步调，一定能够生活得更健康更幸福。

yōuxián 悠闲 *adj.*	悠閒	leisurely and carefree
máng lǐ tōu xián 忙里偷闲 *phr.*	忙裡偷閒	snatch a little leisure from a busy life
xīnshǎng 欣赏 *v.*	欣賞	appreciate
jīngcǎi 精彩 *adj.*		splendid
pǐncháng 品尝 *v.*	品嘗	taste
fēngshèng 丰盛 *adj.*	豐盛	sumptuous, rich
yǔ 与 *prep.*	與	with
qīngsōng 轻松 *adj.*	輕鬆	relaxed
yúkuài 愉快 *adj.*		happy
pínghéng 平衡 *n.;v.*		balance; to balance
zhǎngwò 掌握 *v.*		grasp, master
bùdiào 步调 *n.*	步調	pace

LANGUAGE FOCUS

You have learned potential complements in Lesson 3. Potential complements are used to express the possibility of achieving an expected result in Chinese. They can be formed by adding 得 or 不 between a verb and a resultative complement.

Examples:

Verbs containing resultative complements	Potential Complements – Positive	Potential Complements – Negative
❧ 离开	❧ 离得开	❧ 离不开
❧ 听懂	❧ 听得懂	❧ 听不懂
❧ 听见	❧ 听得见	❧ 听不见
❧ 看懂	❧ 看得懂	❧ 看不懂
❧ 做完	❧ 做得完	❧ 做不完

1. For each of the items/persons below, state whether you can live without them and explain why. Use the potential complement 离得开 / 离不开.

   ❶ 手机 ⟶ 我离得开/离不开手机，因为＿＿＿＿＿＿＿＿＿＿＿＿＿。

   ❷ 电脑 ⟶ ＿＿＿＿＿＿＿＿＿＿＿＿＿＿＿＿＿＿＿＿＿。

   ❸ 朋友 ⟶ ＿＿＿＿＿＿＿＿＿＿＿＿＿＿＿＿＿＿＿＿＿。

   ❹ 家人 ⟶ ＿＿＿＿＿＿＿＿＿＿＿＿＿＿＿＿＿＿＿＿＿。

   ❺ 咖啡 ⟶ ＿＿＿＿＿＿＿＿＿＿＿＿＿＿＿＿＿＿＿＿＿。

   ❻ 蔬菜 ⟶ ＿＿＿＿＿＿＿＿＿＿＿＿＿＿＿＿＿＿＿＿＿。

   ❼ 水 ⟶ ＿＿＿＿＿＿＿＿＿＿＿＿＿＿＿＿＿＿＿＿＿。

   ❽ 电视 ⟶ ＿＿＿＿＿＿＿＿＿＿＿＿＿＿＿＿＿＿＿＿＿。

2. **Class Survey** Find out from your classmates what is the most important thing that they cannot live without. Summarize your findings and report back to the class in Chinese.

3. In pairs, discuss the following situations with your partner and come up with a solution for each of them.

   ❶ 明天是期中考，今晚功课特别多，我担心做不完。怎么办？

   ❷ 我们新来的中文老师说话说得很快，我们都听不懂，你有什么
   办法？
   bànfǎ
   solution

   ❸ 这篇文章有很多生词，我们都看不懂。怎么办？
   wénzhāng　　　　shēngcí
   text　　　　　new words

   ❹ 我的电脑坏了，可是我一天都离不开我的电脑。怎么办？

   ❺ 我们学校请了一位大学教授来给我们谈谈中国的经济，可是
   我坐在教室后面，一点也听不见。怎么办？
   jīngjì
   economy

B Dealing with stress

张健：我真的好累！

丁强：怎么了？

张健：没想到功课那么多，下周一不但有物理考试，还要交数学课、化学课、英语课和历史课的作业。今天英文老师又通知下周二有一个小考。这个周末恐怕哪儿都不去也应付不过来。

丁强：你不要太紧张！我也遇到过同样的问题。

张健：是吗？你们功课的压力也那么大吗？

丁强：我在美国高二的时候功课也特别忙，特别是春季学期。因为我是学校网球校队的队长，每天下课以后训练两个小时，星期三和星期六都有比赛。那个时候比较累，没有精神做功课。

张健：哇，这么忙。换成是我，恐怕会吃不消。你当时是怎么样应付的？

丁强：幸亏我有一个好朋友就住在我家附近，我遇上困难的时候，首先就找他，跟他倾诉一下，这样能缓解一些压力。其次是听音乐。一边听音乐，一边做功课，心情就好起来了。

张健：我不是特别喜欢听音乐。

tōngzhī 通知 v.		inform
kǒngpà 恐怕 adv.		afraid that, probably
xiàoduì 校队 n.	校隊	school team
duìzhǎng 队长 n.	隊長	team captain
xùnliàn 训练 v.	訓練	train
chībùxiāo 吃不消 phr.		unable to bear
xìngkuī 幸亏 adv.	幸虧	luckily
shǒuxiān 首先 conj.		first of all
qīngsù 倾诉 v.	傾訴	confide in, pour out
qícì 其次 conj.		secondly

丁强：每个人缓解压力都有不同的方法。我爸爸工作紧张或者遇上困难的时候，就会去跑步。我妈妈因为<u>膝</u><u>关节</u>受伤，所以她一般不跑步，她喜欢做瑜伽。做完运动以后，出身<u>汗</u>，然后<u>泡</u>个<u>热水澡</u>，再喝点喜欢的饮料，那一定会觉得<u>精神百倍</u>。

张健：是啊！我时间不多，而且已经那么晚了，我就不运动了。泡个热水澡<u>倒</u>是个好主意。

丁强：那我为你准备一杯热<u>拿铁</u>，怎么样？

张健：那太好了！

丁强：快去泡澡吧！

xī 膝 n.			knee
guānjié 关节 n.	關節		joints
hàn 汗 n.			perspiration
pào 泡 v.			soak in
rèshuǐzǎo 热水澡 n.	熱水澡		hot shower
jīngshen bǎibèi 精神百倍 phr.			with high spirits, full of energy
dào 倒 adv.			(indicating contrast
Nátiě 拿铁 n.	拿鐵		latte

LANGUAGE FOCUS

恐怕 means "I'm afraid (that)" instead of "be afraid." It means that the speaker is making a conjecture or prediction.

Examples:

❶ 这样做，恐怕不行。

❷ 今天的功课很多，下午恐怕不能去打球了。

❸ 我最近很忙，恐怕没有时间跟你一起去看电影了。

1. Respond to the following situations with a conjecture or prediction by using 恐怕.

① 下个星期就要考试。

② 妈妈马上就要回来了。

③ 这家餐馆的菜很好吃。

④ 你经常不吃早饭。

⑤ 很多人都想去看这个电影。

⑥ 暑假到中国去。

⑦ 这个题目太难了。

⑧ 中国新年快到了。

2. Working in pairs, one person will describe a situation and the other will use 恐怕 to make a conjecture or prediction based on that situation. Switch roles and repeat the activity at least five times.

Example:

A: 他发烧了。

B: 恐怕不能参加考试。

A Learning from failure

Blog

上星期，丁强代表学校参加模拟联合国的辩论比赛，结果 输了，所以觉得很失望，也有点儿郁闷。他跟张健谈了他的感受。张健劝他，想要成功，必须要吸取 失败的教训，继续努力。

张健给丁强讲了一个马云（Mǎ Yún）的故事。马云参加了三次高考，两次都失败了。他白天打工，晚上读夜校，最后才考上了大学。1999年，他创办了阿里巴巴（Ālǐbābā），开始了电子商务的平台。经过十几年的努力，马云现在成为世界知名的企业家。

dàibiǎo 代表 v.			represent
biànlùn 辩论 v.	辯論		debate
jiéguǒ 结果 conj.	結果		in the end
shū 输 v.	輸		lose
shīwàng 失望 adj.			disappointed
yùmèn 郁闷 adj.	鬱悶		depressed
gǎnshòu 感受 n.; v.			feeling; to feel
quàn 劝 v.	勸		counsel
chénggōng 成功 v.			to succeed
xīqǔ 吸取 v.			learn
shībài 失败 n.; v.	失敗		failure; fail
jiàoxùn 教训 n.	教訓		lesson
gùshi 故事 n.			story
yèxiào 夜校 n.			night school
chuàngbàn 创办 v.	創辦		set up, found
diànzǐ shāngwù 电子商务 n.	電子商務		e-commerce
píngtái 平台 n.	平臺		platform
shìjiè 世界 n.			world

马云说他们公司曾经 犯过很多错误，以后也难免会再犯错误，可是在每一次的失败中他们要了解为什么失败，每一次的失败都是一种磨炼的机会。不管失败多少次，他都不会放弃。马云在一次演讲中鼓励大家说："我永远相信只要不放弃，我们还是有机会的。"

张健给丁强讲完了马云的经历，丁强得到了很大的启发。他知道只要坚持下去，不要放弃，总有一天可以成功的。

céngjīng 曾经 *adv.*	曾經	once, formerly
fàn 犯 *v.*		commit, make *(a mistake)*
cuòwù 错误 *n.*	錯誤	mistake
nánmiǎn 难免 *v.*	難免	hard to avoid
bùguǎn...dōu... 不管…都…		no matter what...
fàngqì 放弃 *v.*	放棄	give up
yǎnjiǎng 演讲 *v.*	演講	give a speech
xiāngxìn 相信 *v.*		believe
jīnglì 经历 *n.; v.*	經歷	experience; to experience
qǐfā 启发 *v.*	啓發	inspire

LANGUAGE FOCUS

不管 means "no matter." It is placed at the beginning of the first clause to state a possible condition. 都 is placed in the second clause to emphasize that the action or decision will not change because of the preceding condition.

Examples:

❶ 不管天气怎么样，我们每天早上都会去跑步。

❷ 不管累不累，你都要把作业做完。

❸ 不管结果怎么样，我都要试一试。

Famous Chinese Entrepreneur — Jack Ma

Jack Ma, whose Chinese name is 马云 (Mǎ Yún), is a Chinese entrepreneur and philanthropist. He is the founder and chairman of the Alibaba Group, a very successful Chinese e-commerce company. In 2014, Ma was listed as the richest man in China with a net worth of over $22.5 billion according to Bloomberg Billionaires Index.

Ma was introduced to the Internet when he was in the United States in 1995. He decided to do an Internet search for general information related to China but found none. With a friend he decided to create a website related to China. Within five hours of launching the website, he received emails from people in different parts of China wanting more information. Later that year, Ma, along with his wife and a friend, raised $20,000 to start an Internet company which created websites for other companies. They called their company "China Yellow Pages." Within three years, the company had made more than 5 million Chinese yuan, the equivalent of $800,000.

Ma worked for an information technology company from 1998 to 1999, and in 1999 decided to venture out on his own. He returned to his hometown of Hangzhou and, with a group of 17 friends, founded Alibaba. The company played an important role in improving the domestic e-commerce market and enhancing an e-commerce platform for Chinese enterprises, especially small and medium-sized enterprises. Today, Alibaba serves more than 79 million users from 240 different countries. Alibaba has a consumer-to-consumer portal called Taobao which is similar to eBay. It offers over a billion products and is one of the most visited websites globally. Taobao accounts for approximately 60% of all of the packages delivered in China and about 80% of the nation's online sales.

Try This!

1. Complete the following sentences with the construction 不管…都….

    ❶ 不管购物商场的东西贵不贵，_____。

    ❷ 不管他在哪儿，_____。

    ❸ 不管远不远，_____。

    ❹ 不管交通怎么样，_____。

    ❺ _____，我早上都跟同学一起跑步健身。

    ❻ _____，我都得吃蔬菜和水果。

    ❼ _____，我都得把功课先做好。

    ❽ _____，我都得买一双新的运动鞋。

2. With a partner, role play a scenario in which one of you encountered a setback (lost a competition, failed a test, etc.) and another tries to encourage him/her not to be affected and to continue to press on. In your role play, use 不管…都… and the words you have learned in this section.

Blog

张健这几天一直在抱怨老师不公平，因为他觉得老师不喜欢他，所以总是给他低分。丁强知道后，在微信上给张健讲了一个故事来鼓励他。

三个建筑工人在工地里砌一面墙。一个过路的人问他们说："你们在干什么？"第一个工人回答说："难道你没看见我们在忙吗？你看，刚砌上去，又倒下来了！干这种活真累！"第二个人回答说："我们在盖一栋新房子。两个月就可以建好了。"第三个人说："我们在建一座城市！这将会是我们附近最大的城市。以后有机会再回来看看！"十多年以后，第一个人还是在当工人。第二个成了工程师。第三个成了公司的总裁。他们三个人为什么有那么大的差异呢？答案就是"态度"。第一个工人总是在埋怨，第二个工人工作很认真，第三个工人不但认真，而且对工作充满热情。他盼望建筑的不单是一面墙，他更希望以后能建成一座城市。他把工作看成自己的事业，所以最后能有成就。这个故事说明了态度决定一切。只要保持良好的态度，成功一定不会遥远的。

gōngpíng 公平 adj.		fair
gōngdì 工地 n.		construction site
qì 砌 v.		build by laying bricks or stones
nándào 难道 adv.	難道	(used to give force to a rhetorical question)
dǎo 倒 v.		fall, topple
dòng 栋 m.w.	棟	(used for houses, buildings, etc.)
zǒngcái 总裁 n.	總裁	chief executive officer
chāyì 差异 n.	差異	difference
dá'àn 答案 n.		answer
mányuàn 埋怨 v.		grumble
chōngmǎn 充满 v.	充滿	be filled with
pànwàng 盼望 v.		hope
shìyè 事业 n.	事業	career
juédìng 决定 v.	決定	determine
yíqiè 一切 pron.		everything
liánghǎo 良好 adj.		good
yáoyuǎn 遥远 adj.	遙遠	faraway, distant

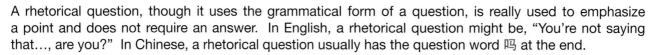
A rhetorical question, though it uses the grammatical form of a question, is really used to emphasize a point and does not require an answer. In English, a rhetorical question might be, "You're not saying that…, are you?" In Chinese, a rhetorical question usually has the question word 吗 at the end.

Examples:

❶ 难道你真的想去他的生日会吗?

You're not saying that you are going to his birthday party, are you?
(You should not go to the party.)

❷ 今天是我的生日，难道你不知道吗?

Today is my birthday; you're telling me you didn't know?
(You should know today is my birthday!)

1. Answer the following questions based on the passage in Step 2B.

❶ 张健为什么抱怨?

❷ 在丁强的故事里，三个建筑工人在做什么?

❸ 三个建筑工人在态度上有什么不同?

❹ 最后哪一个建筑工人的成就最大? 为什么?

❺ 这个故事告诉我们什么道理?
   dàolǐ
   lesson

2. Work with a partner and devise two or three different rhetorical questions for each statement. Then compare your answers with other classmates.

   Example: 小李：我有半年没有看电影了!

   ❶⟶ 难道你不喜欢看电影吗?
   ❷⟶ 难道你没有钱买戏票吗?
   ❸⟶ 难道你功课这么多吗?

❶ 我不知道学校的图书馆在哪儿。

❷ 他很少在十一点以前休息。

❸ 他早上不喝咖啡。

❹ 她妈妈不会说中文。

❺ 这个学生不想学外语。

❻ 他不喜欢数学课。

❼ 他还在运动场跑步。

❽ 小张今晚不打算回家吃饭了。

The Social Media of WeChat

Many people in China use WeChat (微信) to communicate with friends. WeChat literally means "micro message" and supports different ways of instant messaging, including text messages, voice messages, walkie-talkie, and stickers. Users can send pictures, videos, coupons, lucky money packages, or share with friends in a group chat. Besides instant messaging, WeChat also has a feature called "Moments," which allows users to post and view entries containing texts, photos, and video clips, similar to Facebook posts. WeChat has over 438 million active users, with 70 million outside of China.

FINDING SOLUTIONS

A Solving problems or conflicts ✦

子明：丁强，我有点事想跟你谈谈，你有空吗？

丁强：有什么事？看你没精打采的，不舒服吗？

子明：我不是身体不舒服，而是心里不舒服，感到很郁闷。昨晚妈妈批评我，说我成绩退步了，

她把我的吉他没收了，不许我再唱歌了。你知道我和同学组织了一个小乐队，我们经常在一起练歌。一边弹吉他一边唱歌，让我感到放松，可以忘掉不开心的事情。我的梦想就是要成为一个伟大的摇滚歌手。可是我妈妈说当歌手没有前途，要我以后当医生，你说怎么办？

丁强：我赞成你追求自己的梦想，你可以跟你妈妈保证，你会努力学习，按时完成作业，下次考试一定取得好成绩。

子明：是啊，我希望父母看到我学习态度的改变以及成绩的进步，可能会考虑把吉他还给我，让我放假的时候能和伙伴们一起唱歌。

méi jīng dǎ cǎi 没精打采 phr.	沒精打采	feel dispirited and discouraged
búshì…érshì… 不是…而是…		not…, but…
pīpíng 批评 v.	批評	criticize
tuìbù 退步 v.		deteriorate
jítā 吉他 n.		guitar
mòshōu 没收 v.	沒收	confiscate
xǔ 许 v.	許	allow, permit
zǔzhī 组织 v.	組織	form
yuèduì 乐队 n.	樂隊	music band
mèngxiǎng 梦想 n.	夢想	dream
yáogǔn 摇滚 n.	搖滾	rock (music)
qiántú 前途 n.		future, prospect
zànchéng 赞成 v.	贊成	agree
zhuīqiú 追求 v.		pursue, seek
bǎozhèng 保证 v.	保證	ensure, guarantee
ànshí 按时 adv.	按時	on time
kǎolǜ 考虑 v.	考慮	consider
huǒbàn 伙伴 n.	夥伴	partner

165

丁强：我建议你应该多和父母沟通，让他们对你的音乐爱好有深入的了解。叔叔和阿姨都是思想开明的人，他们会慢慢接受和支持你想当歌手的愿望。

子明：希望如此，谢谢你给我出主意。

sīxiǎng 思想 n.		thinking
kāimíng 开明 adj.	開明	open, liberal
jiēshòu 接受 v.		accept
yuànwàng 愿望 n.		wish
rúcǐ 如此 pron.		so, such, in this wa

LANGUAGE FOCUS

When you need to clarify that something is not one thing but another, use the expression 不是…而是… (not..., but...). The section that follows 不是 refers to something that is not true, while the section after 而是 verifies the fact. For example, 我不是不喜欢跑步，而是今天有点累不想去跑步. The sentence means "It is not that I dislike running, but today I'm a bit tired so I don't feel like running."

Look at the following sentences and try to determine their meaning.

① 不是你的父母不支持你，而是他们不了解你的兴趣和爱好。
② 你考试考得不好，不是你不聪明，而是你没有努力学习。
③ 这件事我们不是不能答应你，而是对你还不够了解。
④ 参加马拉松的运动员不是要跑得很快，而是要坚持跑到底。
⑤ 那个问题不是因为你的态度不好，而是大家都不同意，所以不能解决。

1. Match the sentences.

① 我不是要改变你的想法，	•	• a. 而是要你先把书念好，再追求梦想。
② 妈妈不是不让你追求梦想，	•	• b. 而是担心别人会不会接受。
③ 他不是不接受你的看法，	•	• c. 而是昨晚没睡好，有点累。
④ 我不是郁闷，	•	• d. 而是希望你考虑清楚再决定。

❺ 你父母不是思想不开明， •	• e. 而是现在太忙，没时间做。
❻ 我不是不喜欢吃你做的菜， •	• f. 而是觉得这样做不一定行。
❼ 芳芳不是不想解决这个问题， • 　　　　　jiějué 　　　　　solve	• g. 而是中午吃得太饱，现在吃不下。
❽ 我不是不喜欢摇滚音乐， •	• h. 而是更喜欢爵士音乐。 　　　　　　　juéshì 　　　　　　　jazz

2. Read Fangfang's blog entry and answer the following questions.

　　昨晚妈妈把我的手机没收了，她说我成绩退步了，不许我花太多时间玩手机和发微信。我感到很郁闷，平时功课已经很多了，学习压力这么大，偶尔用手机玩点游戏，或者
ǒu'ěr
occasionally
聊聊天，有什么问题？妈妈要我按时完成作业，保证下次成绩有进步，她才把手机还给我。她这么做，只会让我压力更大。为什么她一点都不了解我？

❶ 芳芳的母亲为什么没收芳芳的手机？

❷ 芳芳觉得自己用手机有错吗？为什么？

❸ 妈妈要芳芳怎样，才还她手机？

❹ 如果你是芳芳的好朋友，你会给她什么建议？

Blog

中国的父母一般对孩子的要求特别严格，所以家庭关系有时候会有点紧张。在竞争激烈的社会中，父母希望孩子好是无可非议的。儿女和父母有不同的意见和想法是常见的，而且人与人之间的相处有摩擦和争议是不可避免的。

我父母曾经反对我养宠物。后来我让他们相信，我一定会照顾好我的小狗，每天按时遛狗，他们才同意。他们现在不但鼓励，而且特别支持我有自己的理想和目标，做一个有独立思想的人。

关于子明想当摇滚歌手的梦想，我认为他应该经常和他的父母沟通，主动跟父母分享他热爱的音乐。我去看过子明的摇滚乐表演，他挺有歌手的样子，唱得也很不错。作为

父母，应该给孩子成长的空间，让孩子有自己的理想和愿望。有时候，父母越管孩子，孩子越想反抗。如果不能互相沟通，孩子就不能和父母保持亲密的关系。他们可能会感到沮丧和郁闷，对生活和学习都没有兴趣，对自己也会失去信心。这些都对孩子的心理健康有不好的影响。

guānxì 关系 n.	關係	relationship
shèhuì 社会 n.	社會	society
wúkě fēiyì 无可非议 phr.	無可非議	blameless, irreproachable
mócā 摩擦 n.; v.		conflict; rub, clash
zhēngyì 争议 n.; v.	爭議	dispute, argument; to dispute
fǎnduì 反对 v.	反對	object
lǐxiǎng 理想 n.		aspiration, dream
dúlì sīxiǎng 独立思想 phr.	獨立思想	independent mind
guānyú 关于 prep.	關於	regarding, about
zhǔdòng 主动 adj.	主動	active, initiate the action
zuòwéi 作为 prep.	作為	as, being
chéngzhǎng 成长 v.	成長	grow
kōngjiān 空间 n.	空間	space, room
yuè…yuè… 越…越…		the more…the more…
fǎnkàng 反抗 v.		resist, revolt
bǎochí 保持 v.		maintain
qīnmì 亲密 adj.	親密	close, intimate
xīnlǐ jiànkāng 心理健康 phr.		mental health

The 越…越… construction indicates a progression, similar to "the more…the more…" in English. It expresses that two situations vary together. In the 越…越… construction, the first clause introduces a situation that develops in a particular way, while the second clause describes another situation that develops in relation to the first situation.

Examples: ❶ 压力越大，越要多休息。

❷ 孩子年纪越大，越有自己的想法。

❸ 我越批评他，他就越生气。

1. Match the sentences.

❶ 功课越多，　　　　　•　　•a. 了解越深。

❷ 沟通越多，　　　　　•　　•b. 就越喜欢他。

❸ 她越了解他，　　　　•　　•c. 我的压力就越大。

❹ 你越跟他谈，　　　　•　　•d. 他就越不想听。

❺ 大家对我的要求越高，•　　•e. 就越应该多了解彼此的想法。

❻ 你们的摩擦越多，　　•　　•f. 我就越没信心。

❼ 他越批评我，　　　　•　　•g. 我们就越要想办法解决。

❽ 问题越严重，　　　　•　　•h. 我就越紧张。

2. Working in pairs, tell a partner about a conflict you had with your parents. The partner will offer advice and suggestions on how to resolve the conflict. Switch roles and repeat the activity. Use the words and patterns you have learned in this lesson to describe the conflict and to offer advice and suggestions.

 CULTURAL HIGHLIGHTS

Harmony in Chinese Culture

One of the major principles of Chinese culture is harmony. Very often, Chinese social behavior tries to avoid conflict, and if it occurs, Chinese people will seek mediation through a mutually respected third party rather than the Western preference for litigation (e.g., courts or the police). It is often said that Chinese people seek harmony, while Americans seek justice. Harmony is viewed as soft and fluid, whereas justice is firm and solid. Sometimes this can lead to problems when negotiating contracts or business dealings. In social interactions, Chinese people prefer mediated discussions and seek negotiations instead of direct confrontations.

There are several Chinese sayings that emphasize the value of harmony. 以和为贵 (yǐ hé wéi guì) means that harmony is the most precious; 和气生财 (hé qì shēng cái) means that wealth can be generated through harmony; 家和万事兴 (jiā hé wàn shì xīng) means that all things will prosper when family members are in harmony with each other. These sayings show the importance of harmony in Chinese culture.

Step Up!

1. One of your friends had an argument with his/her parents about what courses to take next year. Your friend has decided to come to you for advice, and you share about how he/she can improve the situation. With another classmate, do a spontaneous role play where you act out this conversation. Use the words you have learned in this lesson as well as the sentence structures where appropriate, such as 不是…而是…, 不管…都…, and 越…越….

2. Imagine that you are Ding Qiang and read the following email from a friend in China. She had a problem with one of her roommates and asked for your advice as to how to handle the situation. Read the email and write a response that provides both support and advice to her.

丁强：

　　你好！我最近好郁闷啊！快来帮帮我吧，我需要你的意见。是这样的，跟我一起租房子的女孩和我现在有了矛盾。这让我好烦恼啊。

máodùn
矛盾
conflict

　　首先，她经常很晚才回家，她回家的时候，我一般都睡觉了。可是，她不太注意自己的动作，常常弄出很大的声音。比如洗澡的时候唱歌，关门的声音特别大，我非常不高兴，因为我每天晚上都会被她吵醒。我曾经主动和她沟通过这个问题，我说："以后你晚上回来的时候，能不能动作轻一点，因为我经常被你吵醒了。"她每次都说"好的好的！对不起！我以后会注意的。"可是，虽然她这样说，但是每天的声音还是很大！你说我该怎么办啊？难道她不觉得声音很大吗？我真的很沮丧。

还有，她从来不打扫卫生，这也让我很不满。她的垃圾都 bùmǎn / unhappy
不按时倒，我认为这样非常不负责。大家住在一起，难免有些摩
擦，不管怎样，都应该注意保持公共空间的卫生。你说呢？我越
想这件事，就越生气。不知道该怎么办才好。

　　快给我一些建议吧！再这样下去，我恐怕很难和她住在
一起。期待你的回信！ qīdài / look forward

　　　祝
学习顺利

李琦

3. Prepare a poster or a flyer that provides suggestions as to how people can resolve conflicts. This will be displayed in the classroom so that your classmates can read it. Be sure to include at least three different ways that people can resolve their differences.

Fun Time!

1. In the following scroll entitled "莫生气," there are ways to help people not get angry about things in their lives. Many Chinese people would hang the scroll up on the wall or have a desktop version of it on a table as a daily reminder of how to maintain a happy mood throughout the day.

Read the words vertically from the right to left side of the scroll. Copy down the words you recognize and talk to another classmate about whether you agree or disagree with the meaning on the scroll. Then, working with the same classmate, write down at least five things you can do to not get angry.

莫 (mò don't) 生气

人生就像一场戏，因为有缘 (yuán fate) 才相聚，

相扶到老不容易，是否更该去珍惜 (zhēnxī cherish)，

为了小事发脾气，回头想想又何必，

别人生气我不气，气出病来无人替，

我若气死谁如意，况且 (kuàngqiě furthermore) 伤神 (shāngshén mentally exhausting) 又费力，

邻居亲朋不要比，儿孙琐事 (suǒshì trivialities) 由它去，

吃苦享乐在一起，神仙 (shénxiān fairies) 羡慕 (xiànmù envy) 好伴侣 (bànlǚ partner)。

2. There are things in our lives that make us happy and feel good about ourselves. Talk to another classmate and create a list of things or situations that can make people happy. Use the following question to ask each other: 日常生活中有什么事让你觉得很开心？

I have learned...

NEW WORDS

Verbs

抱怨		bàoyuàn	grumble, complain	相信		xiāngxìn	believe
赛跑	賽跑	sàipǎo	running a race	经历	經歷	jīnglì	to experience
继续	繼續	jìxù	continue	启发	啓發	qǐfā	inspire
讲求	講求	jiǎngqiú	be particular about, strive for	砌		qì	build by laying bricks or stones
欣赏	欣賞	xīnshǎng	appreciate	倒		dǎo	fall, topple
品尝	品嘗	pǐncháng	taste	埋怨		mányuàn	grumble
平衡		pínghéng	to balance	充满	充滿	chōngmǎn	be filled with
掌握		zhǎngwò	grasp, master	盼望		pànwàng	hope
通知		tōngzhī	inform	决定	決定	juédìng	determine
训练	訓練	xùnliàn	train	批评	批評	pīpíng	criticize
倾诉	傾訴	qīngsù	confide in, pour out	退步		tuìbù	deteriorate
泡		pào	soak in	没收	沒收	mòshōu	confiscate
代表		dàibiǎo	represent	许	許	xǔ	allow, permit
辩论	辯論	biànlùn	debate	组织	組織	zǔzhī	form
感受		gǎnshòu	to feel	赞成	贊成	zànchéng	agree
输	輸	shū	lose	追求		zhuīqiú	pursue, seek
劝	勸	quàn	counsel	保证	保證	bǎozhèng	ensure, guarantee
成功		chénggōng	to succeed	考虑	考慮	kǎolǜ	consider
吸取		xīqǔ	learn	接受		jiēshòu	accept
失败	失敗	shībài	fail	摩擦		mócā	rub, clash
创办	創辦	chuàngbàn	set up, found	争议	爭議	zhēngyì	to dispute
犯		fàn	commit, make (a mistake)	反对	反對	fǎnduì	object
难免	難免	nánmiǎn	hard to avoid	成长	成長	chéngzhǎng	grow
放弃	放棄	fàngqì	give up	反抗		fǎnkàng	resist, revolt
演讲	演講	yǎnjiǎng	give a speech	保持		bǎochí	maintain

Nouns

现代	現代	xiàndài	modern times	世界		shìjiè	world
节奏	節奏	jiézòu	rhythm	错误	錯誤	cuòwù	mistake
写照	寫照	xiězhào	portrayal	经历	經歷	jīnglì	experience
效率		xiàolǜ	efficiency	工地		gōngdì	construction site
效果		xiàoguǒ	result, effect	总裁	總裁	zǒngcái	chief executive officer
平衡		pínghéng	balance	差异	差異	chāyì	difference
步调	步調	bùdiào	pace	答案		dá'àn	answer
校队	校隊	xiàoduì	school team	事业	事業	shìyè	career
队长	隊長	duìzhǎng	team captain	吉他		jítā	guitar
膝		xī	knee	乐队	樂隊	yuèduì	music band
关节	關節	guānjié	joints	梦想	夢想	mèngxiǎng	dream
汗		hàn	perspiration	摇滚	搖滾	yáogǔn	rock (music)
热水澡	熱水澡	rèshuǐzǎo	hot shower	前途		qiántú	future, prospect
拿铁	拿鐵	nátiě	latte	伙伴	夥伴	huǒbàn	partner
感受		gǎnshòu	feeling	思想		sīxiǎng	thinking
失败	失敗	shībài	failure	愿望		yuànwàng	wish
教训	教訓	jiàoxùn	lesson	关系	關係	guānxì	relationship
故事		gùshi	story	社会	社會	shèhuì	society
夜校		yèxiào	night school	摩擦		mócā	conflict
电子商务	電子商務	diànzǐ shāngwù	e-commerce	争议	爭議	zhēngyì	dispute, argument
平台	平臺	píngtái	platform	空间	空間	kōngjiān	space, room

Adjectives

慢		màn	slow	郁闷	鬱悶	yùmèn	depressed
忙碌		mánglù	busy	公平		gōngpíng	fair
悠闲	悠閒	yōuxián	leisurely and carefree	良好		liánghǎo	good
精彩		jīngcǎi	splendid	遥远	遙遠	yáoyuǎn	faraway, distant
丰盛	豐盛	fēngshèng	sumptuous, rich	开明	開明	kāimíng	open, liberal
轻松	輕鬆	qīngsōng	relaxed	主动	主動	zhǔdòng	active, initiate the action
愉快		yúkuài	happy	亲密	親密	qīnmì	close, intimate
失望		shīwàng	disappointed				

I have learned...

Adverbs

好像		hǎoxiàng	looks like, seems like
永远	永遠	yǒngyuǎn	forever
恐怕		kǒngpà	afraid that, probably
幸亏	幸虧	xìngkuì	luckily
倒		dào	*(indicating contrast)*
曾经	曾經	céngjīng	once, formerly
难道	難道	nándào	*(used to give force to a rhetorical question)*
按时	按時	ànshí	on time

Prepositions

与	與	yǔ	with
关于	關於	guānyú	regarding, about
作为	作為	zuòwéi	as, being

Pronouns

一切		yíqiè	everything
如此		rúcǐ	so, such, in this way

Conjunctions

首先		shǒuxiān	first of all
其次		qícì	secondly
结果	結果	jiéguǒ	in the end

Constructions

不管…都…		bùguǎn...dōu...	no matter what...
不是…而是…		búshì...érshì	not..., but...
越…越…		yuè...yuè	the more...the more...

Measure word

栋	棟	dòng	*(used for houses, buildings, etc.)*

Phrases

喘不过气	喘不過氣	chuǎn bú guò qì	breathless
忙里偷闲	忙裡偷閒	máng lǐ tōu xián	snatch a little leisure from a busy life
吃不消		chībùxiāo	unable to bear
精神百倍		jīngshen bǎibèi	with high spirits, full of energy
没精打采	沒精打采	méi jīng dǎ cǎi	feel dispirited and discouraged
无可非议	無可非議	wúkě fēiyì	blameless, irreproachable
独立思想	獨立思想	dúlì sīxiǎng	independent mind
心理健康		xīnlǐ jiànkāng	mental health

SENTENCE PATTERNS

我们好像永远都在跟时间赛跑，做什么事都离不开一个"快"字。

功课这么多，这个周末恐怕哪儿都不去也应付不过来。

不管失败多少次，他都不会放弃。

难道你没看见我们在忙吗？

我不是身体不舒服，而是心里不舒服。

父母越管孩子，孩子越想反抗。

I can do!

Interpretive Communication

❑ I can read and interpret dialogs and blogs about the well being of an individual.

❑ I can read and interpret information about conflicts.

❑ I can understand when someone tells me information about maintaining a happy life.

Interpersonal Communication

❑ I can converse on solutions to handle difficult situations.

❑ I can talk with a friend on ways to reduce stress.

❑ I can discuss ways to resolve conflicts.

Presentational Communication

❑ I can provide compliments and advice to friends.

❑ I can describe how to avoid stress in my life.

❑ I can present information on resolving conflicts.

Cultural Knowledge

❑ I can talk about the success story of Jack Ma.

❑ I can describe the communication functions of WeChat.

❑ I can discuss the preferred way of resolving conflicts in China.

My favorite Chinese Entertainment

中国的娱乐

COMMUNICATIVE GOALS

- Talking about TV shows, concerts, and movies in China
- Describing famous celebrities
- Giving advice to someone and explaining consequences
- Expressing movie preferences

Cultural Knowledge

- Famous Chinese movie directors — Ang Lee and Zhang Yimou
- Famous Chinese pop singers — Faye Wong and Jay Chou
- Karaoke
- The new Chinese singing group: TFBoys

Get ready...

The following TV reality shows are very popular in China. Can you try to guess what they are about? Do you know any of them? Research online to find out what they are about and try to decide if there are similar shows in the United States. Discuss with a classmate and try to find their American equivalents.

《变形计》

《康熙来了》

《非诚勿扰》

《快乐大本营》

《十二道锋味》

《Running Man》

《爸爸去哪儿?》

《中国好声音》

《天天向上》

《我们都爱笑》

STEPS *at a glance!*

STEP 1

VIEWING CHINESE TV ENTERTAINMENT

A. Watching a performance

只要愿意认真地唱歌，普通人也能成为明星。

B. Describing popularity

这些综艺节目都很受欢迎，连孩子都成了它们的粉丝。

STEP 2

LISTENING TO CHINESE MUSIC

A. Talking about concerts

她的歌听起来旋律很优美。

B. Enjoying music and songs

第一次听这首歌，我就被它吸引住了。

STEP 3

GOING TO CHINESE MOVIES

A. Watching movies

尽管是一年多以前看的，印象还是很深刻。

B. Balancing time spent on watching movies

李阿姨不让子明常看好莱坞电影，以免分心影响功课。

A Watching a performance

 Blog

最近我迷上了《中国好声音》。它是一个大型音乐真人选秀节目，电视台播出以后非常受欢迎，收视率创了新高。

《中国好声音》这么受欢迎，原因有几个。第一，《中国好声音》的评审导师十分专业，都是现在中国最有名的歌手。当然对已经在电视上见惯了明星的观众来说，这并不是最吸引他们观看节目的原因，更吸引他们的是参加选秀的人。所以第二个

mí 迷 v.		fascinated by, engrossed in
shēngyīn 声音 n.	聲音	voice
dàxíng 大型 adj.		big scale
zhēnrén 真人 n.		reality
xuǎnxiù 选秀 v.	選秀	talent-spotting
jiémù 节目 n.	節目	show
diànshìtái 电视台 n.	電視臺	TV station
bōchū 播出 v.		broadcast
shōushìlǜ 收视率 n.	收視率	viewership
chuàng 创 v.	創	break (a record)
yuányīn 原因 n.		reason
píngshěn dǎoshī 评审导师 n.	評審導師	judge
zhuānyè 专业 adj.; n.	專業	professional; profession
yǒumíng 有名 adj.		famous
míngxīng 明星 n.		celebrity
guānzhòng 观众 n.	觀眾	audience
xīyǐn 吸引 v.		attract
guānkàn 观看 v.	觀看	view, watch

原因是，这些<u>选手</u>大多没有<u>接受</u>过专业的音乐训练，也没有明星一样的<u>外貌</u>和<u>身材</u>，可是只要爱音乐，有好的声音，<u>愿意</u>认真地唱歌，<u>普通人</u>也能成为明星。

xuǎnshǒu 选手 n.	選手	candidate
jiēshòu 接受 v.		receive
wàimào 外貌 n.		physical appearance
shēncái 身材 n.		(body) figure
pǔtōngrén 普通人 n.		common people
yuànyì 愿意 v.	願意	be willing to

EXTENDED VOCABULARY

激动 adj.	激動	jīdòng	emotional
轻 adj.		qīng	light

LANGUAGE FOCUS

In English we use adverbs to modify verbs. In Chinese we use a descriptive adverbial to provide more information about the action verb in the sentence. To form this adverbial, attach 地 (similar to "-ly" in English) to the end of a disyllabic adjective or a duplicated monosyllabic adjective (e.g., 慢 ➜ 慢慢，轻 ➜ 轻轻).

Examples: 🦋 兴奋地   🦋 激动地   🦋 慢慢地   🦋 愉快地

In a sentence, the adverbial will appear before the main verb to describe the action.

Examples: ❶ 他兴奋地叫着歌手的名。
He called out the singer's name excitedly.

❷ 她慢慢地把书放在桌子上。
She slowly put the books on the desk.

1. Describe the action in each sentence below by adding an appropriate adverbial in the sentence. Use the adjectives provided and 地 to form the adverbials.

兴奋　轻　　快　　激动　　小心　　慢　　认真　　愉快

❶ 她跳了起来。 _____

❷ 他把书放进了书包。 _____

❸ 大家叫着他的名字。 _____

❹ 他做着笔记。 _____

❺ 她把孩子放到了床上。 _____

❻ 她走进了教室。 _____

❼ 我们聊了起来。 _____

❽ 她从图书馆走回家。 _____

2. Read the dialog and answer the following questions.

丁强：最近有什么好看的电视
　　　节目？

子明：我在看台湾的一个节目，
　　　叫《康熙来了》。
　　　　Kāng Xī

丁强："康熙"来了？是说清朝那个皇帝"康熙"吗？
　　　　　　　　　　　　　　　　huángdì
　　　　　　　　　　　　　　　　emperor

子明：不是。这个节目有两位主持人，一位叫蔡康永，一位
　　　　　　　　　　　　zhǔchírén　　　　　Cài Kāngyǒng
　　　　　　　　　　　　host
　　　叫徐熙娣。从他们两位的名字里面各拿出一个字，然
　　　Xú Xīdì
　　　后合在一起就成了"康熙"。

丁强：哦，原来是这样。这是一个什么样的节目呢？

子明：这是一个访谈节目，每周三播出，每一期都会邀请
　　　　fǎngtán jiémù　　　　　　　　　　　　　　　yāoqǐng
　　　　talk show　　　　　　　　　　　　　　　　 invite
　　　几位明星嘉宾来跟主持人一起讨论一些有意思的话题。
　　　　　 jiābīn　　　　　　　　　　　　　　　　　　huàtí
　　　　　guest　　　　　　　　　　　　　　　　　　　topic
　　　通过这个节目，观众可以发现明星不为人知的一面，
　　　　　　　　　　　　　　fāxiàn
　　　　　　　　　　　　　　discover
　　　还可以了解台湾的流行文化。
　　　　　　　　　　　liúxíng wénhuà
　　　　　　　　　　　popular culture

丁强：听起来好像很有趣。

子明：对！节目播出以来，吸引了很多观众观看，创下很高
　　　的收视率。《康熙来了》的两位主持人都很专业，
　　　各有特点。徐熙娣言语犀利，十分搞笑，而蔡康永
　　　　 tèdiǎn　　　　　　　 xīlì　　　　　 gǎoxiào
　　　 characteristic　　　　 incisive　　　　funny
　　　除了是主持人以外，也是一位非常有名的作家，知识
　　　很渊博。如果有机会，你应该看一看这个节目。
　　　 yuānbó
　　　 broad and
　　　 profound

丁强：好，视频网站上有吗？今天晚上我就去找来看看。

❶ 这个节目为什么叫《康熙来了》？

❷ 《康熙来了》是一个什么样的节目？

❸ 通过这个节目，观众可以了解什么？

❹ 《康熙来了》的两位主持人各有什么特点？

Blog

　　在中国，很多综艺节目都很受欢迎，不但大人会讨论，连孩子都成了它们的粉丝，比方说，《最强大脑》、《奔跑吧兄弟》、《快乐大本营》、《爸爸去哪儿》等等。这些综艺节目怎么那么受观众喜爱呢？

　　首先，节目的阵容强大：主持人知名度高，有亲和力，常与观众互动，现在连孩子都知道他们的名字。邀请的节目嘉宾也有很高的知名度，有的人气高，有的实力强，有的特别风趣。其次，节目的内容与生活息息相关。比方说，假期怎么过；父母和孩子怎么相处；春节回乡探亲的心情。最后，节目的地点，除了在电视台以外，还利用不同的地点，有人们常去的商场、图书馆、机场，还有与节目内容有关的旅游景点、特色村镇等等，这些都给观众留下了深刻印象。

zōngyì		
综艺 n.	綜藝	variety arts
lián		
连 prep.	連	even
fěnsī		
粉丝 n.	粉絲	fan (of a pop star, etc.)
zhènróng		
阵容 n.	陣容	lineup
zhǔchírén		
主持人 n.		host
zhīmíngdù		
知名度 n.		popularity
qīnhélì		
亲和力 n.	親和力	geniality
hùdòng		
互动 v.	互動	interact
yāoqǐng		
邀请 v.	邀請	invite
jiābīn		
嘉宾 n.	嘉賓	guest
rénqì		
人气 n.	人氣	popularity
shílì		
实力 n.	實力	substance, strength
xī xī xiāngguān		
息息相关 phr.	息息相關	related, relevant
tànqīn		
探亲 phr.	探親	visit relatives
yǒuguān		
有关 v.	有關	have something to do with, relate to
tèsè		
特色 n.		characteristic
cūnzhèn		
村镇 n.	村鎮	villages and towns
shēnkè		
深刻 adj.		deep
yìnxiàng		
印象 n.		impression

连…都… is a pattern that can be used to emphasize a certain situation. It contains the meaning of "even to the extent." Normally a noun is placed after 连 and a verb placed after 都.

Examples: ❶ 这个歌手很有名，连外国人都知道他是谁。

❷ 《中国好声音》非常好看，连爷爷都喜欢看。

❸ 这首歌很受欢迎，连小孩都会唱。

1. Complete the sentences using the 连…都… pattern.

   Example: 这道题很难，<u>连班上最聪明的同学都不会做</u>。

   ❶ 这道数学题很容易，_____。

   ❷ 他非常穷_{qióng}（poor），_____。

   ❸ 最近爸爸工作很忙，_____。

   ❹ 这件衣服很漂亮，_____。

   ❺ 他太瘦了，_____。

   ❻ 这个学生太聪明了，_____。

   ❼ 我今天太累了，_____。

   ❽ 他很生气，_____。

2. Answer the following questions based on the blog entry in Step 1B.

   ❶ 中国受欢迎的综艺节目有哪些？

   ❷ 这些综艺节目的主持人有什么特点？

   ❸ 节目邀请的嘉宾怎么样？

   ❹ 节目的内容有哪些？

   ❺ 你认为在综艺节目里，主持人、嘉宾和内容，哪一个最重要？为什么？

A Talking about concerts

张健跟丁强谈王菲的演出。

张健：你猜我买到了什么票？

丁强：看你那么高兴！是什么票呀？

张健：是两张王菲 (Wáng Fēi) 演唱会的票！你知道她是谁吗？

丁强：我常常听人说，可是我不太了解，你可以给我介绍吗？

张健：王菲可以说是中国现在最有影响力的女歌手之一了。她的歌听起来旋律很优美。她独特的表演风格吸引了无数的粉丝。她的音乐得到了专业人士非常高的评价，也获得很多奖。

丁强：你以前看过她的演出吗？

张健：看过一次。去年她在上海举行演唱会的时候我去了。那真是一次完美的演出！王菲在台上魅力四射，台下的粉丝都激动得不得了，一直在鼓掌和尖叫，气氛非常热烈。

丁强：希望今天的演唱会也跟那次一样精彩！

yǎnchànghuì 演唱会 *n.*	演唱會	concert
yǐngxiǎnglì 影响力 *n.*	影響力	influence, impact
xuánlǜ 旋律 *n.*		melody
dútè 独特 *adj.*	獨特	special, unique
fēnggé 风格 *n.*	風格	style
wúshù 无数 *adj.*	無數	countless, innumerable
píngjià 评价 *n.*	評價	valuation, assessment
huòdé 获得 *v.*	獲得	receive, win
jiǎng 奖 *n.*	獎	award, prize
jǔxíng 举行 *v.*	舉行	hold
wánměi 完美 *adj.*		perfect
mèilì sì shè 魅力四射 *phr.*		charming
gǔzhǎng 鼓掌 *v.*		applaud
jiānjiào 尖叫 *v.*		scream
rèliè 热烈 *adj.*	熱烈	warm

起来 can be attached to sense verbs such as 看 and 听 to indicate an estimation based on what one sees or hears. 看起来 means "It looks/seems like that from the appearance." 听起来 means "it sounds like...." Both 看起来 and 听起来 may be used with 好像 and 似的.

Examples: ❶ 他看起来很生气。/ 他看起来好像很生气似的。

❷ 这个菜看起来很好吃。/ 这个菜看起来好像很好吃似的。

❸ 这个计划听起来很好。/ 这个计划听起来好像很好似的。

❹ 这首歌听起来很有意思。/ 这首歌听起来好像很有意思似的。

1. Divide the class into two groups. Group A will develop a scenario and Group B will use the pattern of 看起来/听起来 (好像……似的) to predict the logical result of the scenario.

For example: Group A：他昨天晚上因为准备考试很晚才睡觉。

Group B：所以他今天看起来好像很累似的。

2. State whether the following statements are true (T) or false (F) based on the dialog in Step 2A.

❶ 张健买了一张王菲演唱会的票。

❷ 丁强知道王菲是谁。

❸ 王菲的歌听起来很好听。

❹ 王菲的粉丝不多。

❺ 王菲获得了很多奖。

❻ 张健没看过王菲的演唱会。

❼ 张健很喜欢王菲。

❽ 王菲在上海的演唱会，气氛非常热烈。

丁强：你喜欢听什么样的歌曲？快的还是慢的？

张健：我比较喜欢节奏快的，听起来充满<u>活力</u>的歌曲。

丁强：那你一定喜欢周杰伦（Zhōu Jiélún）吧？

张健：美国的学生也喜欢周杰伦吗？

丁强：当然了，他可以说是最受欢迎的<u>华人</u>歌手。我们都喜欢他唱的《双截棍》（Shuāng Jié Gùn）。

张健：我也很喜欢。第一次听这首歌，我就被它吸引住了。我觉得这首歌不但旋律优美，而且<u>歌词</u>很有意义。美国的学生还喜欢什么中国歌？

丁强：老师在班上也教过我们周华健（Zhōu Huájiàn）的《朋友》。我第一次听他的歌的时候，就被他优美的歌声<u>感动</u>了。

张健：真没想到你还听过这首歌！除了周杰伦、周华健以外，你还听过哪些歌手的歌？王菲？韩红（Hán Hóng）？

huólì 活力 n.		energy
huárén 华人 n.	華人	Chinese person
gēcí 歌词 n.	歌詞	song lyrics
gǎndòng 感动 v.	感動	be moved

丁强：我只听说过她们的名字，还没听过
她们的歌曲，你以后可以给我推荐
几首。

张健：没问题。其实，我们的综艺节目
《中国好声音》里面的几位导师都
是很棒的歌手，比方说这一期的
导师：那英、汪峰、庾澄庆和周杰伦
都代表了不同的歌唱风格，有机会
再给你推荐一下他们的代表作。

tuījiàn		
推荐 v.	推薦	recommend
bàng		
棒 adj.		terrific
qī		period of time, phase, stage
期 n.		

LANGUAGE FOCUS

You have learned the 被 structure, which expresses the passive voice in Chinese. In this structure, the recipient goes first, followed by 被, the doer, and the action. This structure may also be used in talking about music and songs.

Examples: ❶ 我被这首歌感动了。　❷ 她被那优美的歌声吸引住了。

Karaoke

In China, the entertainment industry has created a very dynamic landscape of film, art, music, and theater. Although it is similar to that of the United States, perhaps one of its most unique features is also the least well-known to Western audiences: karaoke! In China, this pastime is a very popular way to spend social time with family, friends, coworkers, and business partners. These "KTVs," or karaoke establishments, come in many forms, with elaborate underground labyrinths or lavish above-ground music centers, complete with all-you-can-eat buffets. As part of the experience, karaoke-goers enjoy a private, insulated room that has speakers, a television, a large central table, and couches lining the walls. The selection of music is very diverse, including both Chinese classics and international favorites. Chinese families often know all of the lyrics to American pop songs, such as *Thriller* by Michael Jackson. Singing karaoke with a group of friends is truly a moment to remember for many foreigners who go to visit China.

1. Change the following sentences into 被 – sentences.

❶ 这首歌的歌词感动了他。

❷ 她的歌声吸引了我。

❸ 我把他的歌都下载了。

❹ 儿子把衣服弄脏了。

❺ 我把窗户擦干净了。

❻ 他把同学气哭了。

❼ 爸爸把车停在了停车场。

❽ 我没把手机带在身上。

2. Read the passage and answer the following questions.

　　在中国，TFBOYS 是一个非常受欢迎的组合^{zǔhé}，由三个充满活力的十四岁男生组成。他们唱歌的视频被放到网上，受到很多人的喜爱，他们的新歌很快地传开来，获得了成功，可以说是"一夜成名"。

　　其实，一开始也有粉丝不能理解^{lǐjiě}，十四岁应该念书、应付考试，为什么他们不上学，把时间都花在唱歌上。但是他们慢慢地被这三个小男孩的纯真^{chúnzhēn}、坚持感动了。年轻就是一种魅力，粉丝们觉得，TFBOYS 代表他们完成了他们年轻时未能实现^{shíxiàn}的梦想^{mèngxiǎng}，这也是 TFBOYS 能吸引这么多粉丝的原因。

❶ TFBOYS 是怎么样成名的？

❷ "一夜成名"是什么意思？

❸ 有些粉丝为什么一开始不能理解 TFBOYS？

❹ TFBOYS 那么受欢迎的原因是什么？

A Watching movies

张健：丁强，你喜欢看什么<u>类型</u>的电影？

丁强：类型？

张健：是啊。比方说有<u>爱情片</u>、<u>喜剧片</u>、<u>古装片</u>，还有<u>动作片</u>、<u>警匪片</u>、<u>战争片</u>、<u>恐怖片</u>、<u>科幻片</u>、<u>功夫片</u>等等。

丁强：我好像都喜欢吧。什么类型不重要，最重要的是内容。

张健：也对。那你看过什么中国电影？

丁强：我只看过两<u>部</u>中国电影，那还是在美国学中文的时候，老师给我们放的。

张健：哦？什么电影？

丁强：你知道《一个都不能少》吗？

张健：我看过！它是一个<u>励志片</u>，讲的是一个<u>贫困</u>农村的学生因为想

<u>减轻</u>家里的<u>经济</u> <u>负担</u>，所以到城里打工。他的老师<u>千辛万苦</u>地到城里把他找了回来。电视台被这对师生的故事感动，<u>进行</u>了报道，后来很多人<u>捐赠</u>了不少东西给农村的学校。

丁强：是的。这部电影让我了解到了中国城市和农村的<u>差距</u>，也看到了农村<u>教育</u>很<u>落后</u>，<u>急需</u> <u>改善</u>的一面。

lèixíng 类型 n.	類型	type, category
bù 部 m.w.		(used for movies)
pínkùn 贫困 adj.	貧困	poor
jiǎnqīng 减轻 v.	減輕	reduce
jīngjì 经济 adj.; n.	經濟	economic, financial; economy
fùdān 负担 n.	負擔	burden
qiān xīn wàn kǔ 千辛万苦 phr.	千辛萬苦	laborious
jìnxíng 进行 v.	進行	carry out
juānzèng 捐赠 v.	捐贈	donate
chājù 差距 n.		difference
jiàoyù 教育 n.		education
luòhòu 落后 adj.	落後	backward
jíxū 急需 v.		urgently need
gǎishàn 改善 v.		improve, make better

张健：那另一部电影是什么？

丁强：是《归来》。它的内容非常<u>感人</u>，<u>尽管</u>是一年多以前看的，印象<u>还</u>是很深刻。看过电影以后，我对中国这些年的改变有了更深的了解。

张健：既然你喜欢这两部电影，我想你也会喜欢其他类似的电影，比方说《红高粱》(Hóng Gāoliáng)、《大红灯笼高高挂》(Dà Hóng Dēnglong Gāo Gāo Guà)、《三峡好人》(Sānxiá Hǎorén)、《可可西里》(Kě Kě Xī Lǐ)等。

张健：听起来不错，我这个周末就上网看！

| gǎnrén 感人 adj. | | touching |
| jǐnguǎn...hái... 尽管…还… | 儘管…還… | even though... |

EXTENDED VOCABULARY

Types of movies

爱情片 n.	愛情片	àiqíngpiàn	romance film
喜剧片 n.	喜劇片	xǐjùpiàn	comedy movie
古装片 n.	古裝片	gǔzhuāngpiàn	costume film
动作片 n.	動作片	dòngzuòpiàn	action movie
警匪片 n.		jǐngfěipiàn	cops and robbers film
战争片 n.	戰爭片	zhànzhēngpiàn	war movie
恐怖片 n.		kǒngbùpiàn	horror film
科幻片 n.		kēhuànpiàn	science fiction film
功夫片 n.		gōngfūpiàn	kungfu movie
励志片 n.	勵志片	lìzhìpiàn	inspirational film

尽管···还··· is a construction that means "even though...still...." 尽管 is placed in the first clause to acknowledge a situation that has happened, while 还 is put in the second clause to state a result that contrasts with the situation in the first clause.

Examples: **❶** 尽管他已经看过这个电影，他还想再看一次。

❷ 尽管我的中文不好，我还是喜欢看中国电影。

❸ 尽管他很忙，他还是坚持每天跑步一小时。

CULTURAL HIGHLIGHTS

Ang Lee and Zhang Yimou

Contemporary Asia has much to offer the world, especially in the realm of filmmaking. Having risen through the ranks as two of the world's most celebrated contemporary filmmakers, Ang Lee and Zhang Yimou have become household names. Lee, who hails from Taiwan, has won several awards at the Academy Awards while Zhang, who hails from mainland China, bedazzled over 900 million viewers with his arrangement of the opening ceremony at the 2008 Beijing Olympics. These stunning performances are only two of their achievements among countless others.

Ang Lee pursued his higher education in the United States and got his start working on a Spike Lee student film. From that moment on, he exhibited a knack for mixing Western movie techniques with distinctly Chinese themes. Perhaps amongst his most famous movies are *Eat Drink Man Woman*; *Crouching Tiger, Hidden Dragon*; and *Life of Pi*, for which he won the Academy Award for Best Director. Throughout his career, Lee has worked on many diverse films, including *Brokeback Mountain*, *Hulk*, and *Chosen*. As a result, he has garnered many awards and recognitions at the Academy Awards and Golden Globes.

Zhang Yimou has also made a lasting impression with his debut of *Red Sorghum* in 1987, the first of his many celebrated films that depict the struggles and resilience of the Chinese people. Similar to Lee, Zhang uses skillful movie techniques to portray different aspects of Chinese culture. Indeed, he is considered part of the Fifth Generation of Chinese Filmmakers, and his work is particularly noteworthy for its rich use of color. Numerous prizes have been awarded to him, including recognition from the Cannes Film Festival, the Venice Film Festival, and the Berlin International Film Festival.

Both Ang Lee and Zhang Yimou have left their unique marks in the world of film and beyond – they have deftly translated the stories and struggles of the Chinese people into a beautiful art form, to which everyone can relate.

1. Match the sentences.

❶ 尽管他唱歌很好听，　　　　•

❷ 尽管这个电影很短，　　　　•

❸ 我除了喜欢购物，　　　　　•

❹ 尽管恐怖片很可怕，　　　　•

• a. 我对它的印象还是很深刻。

• b. 他还是坚持上学。

• c. 他还是没有红起来。

• d. 我还是喜欢看。

❺ 尽管我非常努力地学习，•

❻ 尽管天气很热，　　　　　•

❼ 尽管你很聪明，　　　　　•

❽ 尽管下雨了，　　　　　　•

• e. 我们还是坚持不开空调。

• f. 他们还在足球场踢球。

• g. 你还是要努力学习。

• h. 成绩还是不理想。

2. Do a survey to find out what types of movies your classmates like. Record your findings in a table like the one below and then present your findings to the class.

Example: 你喜欢看什么类型的电影？我喜欢……

马克	科幻片
安琪	爱情片
……	……

Blog

子明告诉我，他们的老师鼓励他们多看<u>好莱坞</u>电影，因为这样不但能提高英语水平，还能<u>增加</u>对美国文化的认识。比方说，能从中了解美国人的<u>幽默</u> <u>方式</u>、兴趣爱好、对于教育、<u>婚姻</u>、家庭的态度等等。可是李阿姨总觉得学习是最重要的，所以不让子明常看好莱坞电影，<u>以免</u> <u>分心</u>影响功课。

其实，我认为只要好好<u>安排</u>时间，<u>偶尔</u>看看电视剧和电影是不会影响学习的。我喜欢看功夫片，如李连杰 (Lǐ Liánjié)主演的《英雄》(Yīngxióng)、《霍元甲》(Huò Yuánjiǎ)和甄子丹 (Zhēn Zǐdān)

Hǎoláiwū 好莱坞 n.		好萊塢	Hollywood
zēngjiā 增加 v.			increase
yōumò 幽默 adj.			humorous
fāngshì 方式 n.			way, pattern
hūnyīn 婚姻 n.			marriage
yǐmiǎn 以免 conj.			in order to avoid, lest
fēnxīn 分心 v.			divert one's attraction
ānpái 安排 v.			arrange
ǒu'ěr 偶尔 adv.		偶爾	occasionally

主演的《叶问》。
这些片子的<u>武打</u>非
常精彩，都有中国
<u>武术</u>的特色。

Wò Hǔ Cáng Lóng

李安拍的《卧虎藏龙》也是
我很喜欢的电影。它把中国传统
的山水<u>意境</u>和武打<u>场面</u><u>结合</u>起
来，很有<u>古典</u>的美感。

Zhāng Zǐyí

章子怡在影片中的<u>表
现</u>很<u>突出</u>，也因为这
样而<u>一片成名</u>。<u>另外</u>，
我也挺喜欢武打明星成
龙。他的电影常常在武
打中加入喜剧元素，如

Jiānfēng Shíkè

《尖峰时刻》、《功夫
之王》，看了觉得很有
意思。

wǔdǎ 武打 v.		fighting
wǔshù 武术 n.	武術	Chinese martial arts
yìjìng 意境 n.		the mood of a work of art
chǎngmiàn 场面 n.	場面	scene
jiéhé 结合 v.	結合	integrate
gǔdiǎn 古典 adj.		classical
biǎoxiàn 表现 n.	表現	performance
tūchū 突出 adj.		outstanding
yí piàn chéng míng 一片成名 phr.		became famous because of a film
lìngwài 另外 conj.		in addition

LANGUAGE FOCUS

以免 is a conjunction and connects two clauses. The first clause is a piece of advice to do something; the second clause begins with 以免 and explains that the purpose of the advice is to prevent something undesirable from happening.

Examples: ❶ 你得每天好好地做功课，以免考试的时候太紧张。

❷ 我每个星期只看一两个小时的电视，以免影响学习。

❸ 你们应该早点睡觉，以免睡眠不足。

1. Complete the sentences.

   ❶ _____，以免浪费。

   ❷ _____，以免忘掉。

   ❸ _____，以免感冒。

   ❹ _____，以免影响学习。

   ❺ _____，以免上课迟到。

   ❻ 我们得努力学习，以免_____。

   ❼ 我们要保护环境，以免_____。

   ❽ 我们要多运动，以免_____。

   ❾ 在图书馆要保持安静，以免_____。

   ❿ 孩子应该帮父母做家务，以免_____。

2. Answer the following questions based on the blog entry in Step 3B.

   ❶ 为什么子明要多看好莱坞电影？

   ❷ 子明的妈妈为什么不让他常看好莱坞电影？

   ❸ 李连杰和甄子丹主演的影片有什么相同的地方？

   ❹ 丁强为什么喜欢《卧虎藏龙》？

   ❺ 成龙的电影有什么特色？

Step Up!

1. Read Fangfang's blog entry and answer the following questions.

blog

Fangfang

　　我姐姐很喜欢听歌，特别是台湾的女子组合 S.H.E，她们是由 Selina、Hebe、Ella 组成。她们有很多歌曲都很受欢迎，如《美丽新世界》、《Super Star》、《波斯猫》(Bōsī Māo)、《不想长大》和《中国话》，连我都会唱。姐姐最喜欢《中国话》，它把中国绕口令(ràokǒulìng tongue twister)和西方饶舌(ráoshé rap)结合在一起，听起来很有意思。想学好中文口语的，应该多练练这首歌。

　　Selina 长得很漂亮，看起来很温柔(wēnróu gentle)。几年前，她在上海工作时发生意外(yìwài accident)，皮肤严重烧伤(shāoshāng burn)。那时姐姐非常关注她的病情，还好她后来康复(kāngfù recover)了。Hebe 非常天真(tiānzhēn innocent)、善良，给人很实在(shízài true)的感觉。三个歌手当中，姐姐最喜欢 Ella，她既活泼(huópo lively)又外向(wàixiàng extroverted)，既调皮(tiáopí mischievous)又可爱，很平易近人(píngyì jìnrén affable)。

　　去年，她们办了一场演唱会。尽管演唱会的票不便宜，姐姐还是决定去看。她把三个月的零用钱(língyòngqián pocket money)省下来，好不容易存够钱买了演唱会的票。姐姐告诉我，在演唱会上，看着自己的偶像(ǒuxiàng idol)站在台上唱歌，她兴奋地叫着她们的名字，很多粉丝也不停地在尖叫。对姐姐来说，那是一个难忘(nánwàng memorable)的晚上。

1. S.H.E 由哪些人组成？

2. 想练习中文口语，应该练 S.H.E 哪首歌？为什么？

3. 三个歌手的性格各有什么特点？

4. 芳芳的姐姐最喜欢哪一个歌手，为什么？

5. 芳芳的姐姐怎么有钱去看 S.H.E 的演唱会？

6. 演唱会上的情况怎么样？

2. Imagine your friend is obsessed with a singer. This has affected his/her studies, health, and social life. You are concerned about this and want to give some advice. In a role play of two people in which one of you is the person who has spent too much time on the life of a singer and the other is the person offering advice, persuade your friend to manage and balance his/her time wisely. Use the patterns you have learned in this lesson:

尽管…还…，以免

3. Make a set of presentation slides introducing your favorite singer or movie star. Focus on his/her qualities and achievements, and provide possible reasons behind his/her current attainments. Share it with the class to see if the favorite singers or movie stars of your classmates share similar qualities.

Fun Time!

"小苹果," sung by 筷子兄弟, is a very popular song in China. There is even a dance to this song. Read the lyrics below and watch the online video (http://video.56.com/opera/23607.html) to dance along with the song!

红红的小脸儿温暖我的心窝，
wēnnuǎn — warm   xīnwō — heart

点亮我生命的火火火火火。
diǎnliàng — light up   shēngmìng — life

你是我的小呀小苹果儿，

就像天边最美的云朵。
yúnduǒ — cloud

春天又来到了花开满山坡，
shānpō — hill

种下希望就会收获。

我种下一颗种子，终于长出了果实。
zhǒngzi — seed   zhōngyú — finally   guǒshí — fruit

今天是个伟大日子，

摘下星星送给你拽下月亮送给你。
zhāixià — pluck   zhuàixià — pull off

让太阳每天为你升起，

变成蜡烛，燃烧自己只为照亮你。
làzhú — candle   ránshāo — burn   zhàoliàng — illuminate

把我一切都献给你，只要你欢喜，
xiàngěi — give

你让我每个明天都变得有意义。

生命虽短，爱你永远不离不弃。
qì — forsake

从不觉得你讨厌，你的一切都喜欢。

有你的每天都新鲜，

有你阳光更灿烂，有你黑夜不黑暗，
cànlàn — brilliant

你是白云我是蓝天。

你是我的小呀小苹果儿，

怎么爱你都不嫌多。
xián — complain of

夏天夜晚陪你一起看星星眨眼，
zháyǎn / blink

秋天黄昏与你徜徉在金色麦田，
huánghūn / evening　chángyáng / roam leisurely　màitián / wheat field

冬天雪花飞舞有你更加温暖。

你是我的小呀小苹果儿，

怎么爱你都不嫌多。

红红的小脸儿温暖我的心窝，

点亮我生命的火火火火火。

你是我的小呀小苹果儿，

就像天边最美的云朵。

春天又来到了花开满山坡，

种下希望就会收获。

你是我的小呀小苹果儿，

怎么爱你都不嫌多。

红红的小脸儿温暖我的心窝，

点亮我生命的火火火火火。

你是我的小呀小苹果儿，

就像天边最美的云朵。

春天又来到了花开满山坡，

种下希望就会收获。

I have learned...

NEW WORDS

Verbs

迷		mí	fascinated by, engrossed in	尖叫		jiānjiào	scream
选秀	選秀	xuǎnxiù	talent-spotting	感动	感動	gǎndòng	be moved
播出		bōchū	broadcast	推荐	推薦	tuījiàn	recommend
创	創	chuàng	break (a record)	减轻	減輕	jiǎnqīng	reduce
吸引		xīyǐn	attract	进行	進行	jìnxíng	carry out
观看	觀看	guānkàn	view, watch	捐赠	捐贈	juānzèng	donate
接受		jiēshòu	receive	急需		jíxū	urgently need
愿意	願意	yuànyì	be willing to	改善		gǎishàn	improve, make better
互动	互動	hùdòng	interact	增加		zēngjiā	increase
邀请	邀請	yāoqǐng	invite	分心		fēnxīn	divert one's attraction
有关	有關	yǒuguān	have something to do with, relate to	安排		ānpái	arrange
获得	獲得	huòdé	receive, win	武打		wǔdǎ	fighting
举行	舉行	jǔxíng	hold	结合	結合	jiéhé	integrate
鼓掌		gǔzhǎng	applaud				

Nouns

声音	聲音	shēngyīn	voice	选手	選手	xuǎnshǒu	candidate
真人		zhēnrén	reality	外貌		wàimào	physical appearance
节目	節目	jiémù	show	身材		shēncái	(body) figure
电视台	電視臺	diànshìtái	TV station	普通人		pǔtōngrén	common people
收视率	收視率	shōushìlù	viewership	综艺	綜藝	zōngyì	variety arts
原因		yuányīn	reason	粉丝	粉絲	fěnsī	fan (of a pop star, etc.)
专业	專業	zhuānyè	profession	阵容	陣容	zhènróng	lineup
评审导师	評審導師	píngshěn dǎoshī	judge	主持人		zhǔchírén	host
明星		míngxīng	celebrity	知名度		zhīmíngdù	popularity
观众	觀眾	guānzhòng	audience	亲和力	親和力	qīnhélì	geniality

嘉宾	嘉賓	jiābīn	guest	差距		chājù	difference
人气	人氣	rénqì	popularity	教育		jiàoyù	education
实力	實力	shílì	substance, strength	爱情片	愛情片	àiqíngpiàn	romance film
特色		tèsè	characteristic	喜剧片	喜劇片	xǐjùpiàn	comedy movie
村镇	村鎮	cūnzhèn	villages and towns	古装片	古裝片	gǔzhuāngpiàn	costume film
印象		yìnxiàng	impression	动作片	動作片	dòngzuòpiàn	action movie
演唱会	演唱會	yǎnchànghuì	concert	警匪片		jǐngfěipiàn	cops and robbers film
影响力	影響力	yǐngxiǎnglì	influence, impact	战争片	戰爭片	zhànzhēngpiàn	war movie
旋律		xuánlǜ	melody	恐怖片		kǒngbùpiàn	horror film
风格	風格	fēnggé	style	科幻片		kēhuànpiàn	science fiction film
粉丝	粉絲	fěnsī	fan	功夫片		gōngfūpiàn	kungfu movie
评价	評價	píngjià	valuation, assessment	励志片	勵志片	lìzhìpiàn	inspirational film
奖	獎	jiǎng	award, prize	好莱坞	好萊塢	Hǎoláiwū	Hollywood
活力		huólì	energy	方式		fāngshì	way, pattern
华人	華人	huárén	Chinese person	婚姻		hūnyīn	marriage
歌词	歌詞	gēcí	song lyrics	武术	武術	wǔshù	Chinese martial arts
期		qī	period of time, phase, stage	意境		yìjìng	the mood of a work of art
类型	類型	lèixíng	type, category	场面	場面	chǎngmiàn	scene
经济	經濟	jīngjì	economy	表现	表現	biǎoxiàn	performance
负担	負擔	fùdān	burden				

Adjectives

大型		dàxíng	big scale	棒		bàng	terrific
有名		yǒumíng	famous	贫困	貧困	pínkùn	poor
激动	激動	jīdòng	emotional	经济	經濟	jīngjì	economic, financial
轻	輕	qīng	light	落后	落後	luòhòu	backward
深刻		shēnkè	deep	感人		gǎnrén	touching
独特	獨特	dútè	special, unique	幽默		yōumò	humorous
无数	無數	wúshù	countless, innumerable	古典		gǔdiǎn	classical
完美		wánměi	perfect	突出		tūchū	outstanding
热烈	熱烈	rèliè	warm	专业	專業	zhuānyè	professional

Adverb				Preposition			
偶尔	偶爾	ǒu'ěr	occasionally	连	連	lián	even
Conjunctions				**Phrases**			
以免		yǐmiǎn	in order to avoid, lest	息息相关	息息相關	xī xī xiāngguān	related, relevant
另外		lìngwài	in addition	探亲	探親	tànqīn	visit relatives
Construction				魅力四射		mèilì sì shè	charming
尽管…还…	儘管…還…	jǐnguǎn...hái...	even though...	千辛万苦	千辛萬苦	qiānxīn wàn kǔ	laborious
				一片成名		yí piàn chéng míng	became famous because of a film

SENTENCE PATTERNS

只要愿意认真地唱歌，普通人也能成为明星。

这些综艺节目都很受欢迎，连孩子都成了它们的粉丝。

她的歌听起来旋律很优美。

第一次听这首歌，我就被它吸引住了。

尽管是一年多以前看的，印象还是很深刻。

李阿姨不让子明常看好莱坞电影，以免分心影响功课。

I can do!

Interpretive Communication

❑ I can understand when people write about their interest in songs and movies.

❑ I can read and interpret dialogs and blogs on discussions about songs and movies.

❑ I can read information about the entertainment industry.

Interpersonal Communication

❑ I can discuss TV shows and programs with a friend.

❑ I can exchange information with my friends on their movie preferences.

❑ I can compare the difference between Chinese and Americans on how they spend their leisure time.

❑ I can share information about my favorite type of Chinese entertainment.

Presentational Communication

❑ I can create a blog on a pop star.

❑ I can speak about the importance of balancing our time on school work and entertainment.

❑ I can talk about the qualities and achievements of my favorite singer.

Cultural Knowledge

❑ I can talk about famous movie directors in China.

❑ I can describe the style of a famous Chinese singer.

❑ I can explain how Chinese people spend their time on entertainment.

Celebrations in China

一起来庆祝

COMMUNICATIVE GOALS

- Conversing with others about birthday celebrations, Chinese festivals, and weddings

- Describing traditional festivals and their celebrations

- Comparing similarities and differences in birthdays, weddings, and other celebrations

- Extending invitations and responding to invitations in culturally appropriate ways

Cultural Knowledge

- Chinese traditional holidays and festivals
- Symbolic meanings of items used in Chinese festivals
- Chinese respect for the aged
- Chinese birthdays and wedding celebrations
- The Chinese practice of gift-giving

Get ready...

Read the customs and check off those customs that you practice when you celebrate birthdays and weddings. If you practice it in the United States or in your culture, write **A** before the custom; if you think people practice it in China, write **B**. If you think it is practiced in both countries, write **A & B**. If you think it is not practiced in either country, write **C** before the custom.

❶ 放鞭炮，贴大红双喜字。
　　　　　　 tiē
　　　　　paste

❷ 吃长寿面和寿桃。
　chángshòu　shòutáo
　long life　　longevity peach

❸ 吃蛋糕，唱生日歌。

❹ 去教堂举行婚礼，新娘子穿白色婚纱。
　jiàotáng　hūnlǐ　　xīnniángzi　　hūnshā
　church　wedding ceremony　bride　　wedding gown

❺ 生日会上客人送生日礼物，过生日的人收礼物。

❻ 去饭店举行婚礼，新娘子穿红色衣服。

❼ 客人参加婚宴，送红包。
　　　hūnyàn
　wedding banquet

❽ 结婚后送亲友同事喜糖。
　　　　tóngshì
　　　colleagues

❾ 婚礼那天新郎到新娘家接新娘去自己家。
　　xīnláng
　bridegroom

❿ 贴挂"寿比南山，福如东海"的寿联。
　　　　　　　　　　shòulián
　　　　　　　longevity couplet

After you have completed your checklist, compare it with a classmate and briefly discuss why you matched the country and cultural practice.

STEP 1

OBSERVING BIRTHDAYS

A. Celebrating birthdays

今天学校为三月过生日的同学办了一个集体生日会。

B. Receiving gifts

王叔叔一家人请丁强吃饭。他们送了他一把吉他。

STEP 2

ENJOYING MAJOR TRADITIONAL CHINESE FESTIVALS

A. Describing traditional Chinese festivals

中国人把农历五月初五定为端午节。

B. Celebrating traditional Chinese festivals

春节时，人们把家里打扫得干干净净。

STEP 3

EXPERIENCING MILESTONES IN LIFE

A. Celebrating weddings

我想请你参加我的婚礼。
谢谢你的邀请，我一定出席。

B. Attending a graduation ceremony

无论将来怎么样，我们都有信心去微笑面对。

A Celebrating birthdays

丁强和寄宿家庭聊今天在学校发生的事。

jítǐ shēngrìhuì 集体生日会 n.	集體生日會	group birthday party
jīngxǐ 惊喜 n.; adj.	驚喜	pleasant surprise; pleasantly surprised
wǔ yán liù sè 五颜六色 adj.	五顏六色	colorful
qìqiú 气球 n.	氣球	balloon
héchàngtuán 合唱团 n.	合唱團	choir
yuètuán 乐团 n.	樂團	music band
xiànchǎng 现场 n.	現場	site, spot
bànzòu 伴奏 v.		provide musical accompaniment
shòuxīng 寿星 n.	壽星	person whose birthday is being celebrated
píngzi 瓶子 n.		bottle
zhùfú 祝福 n.; v.		well wishes; wish someone well
zhǐtiáo 纸条 n.	紙條	slip of paper

丁强: 今天学校为我们这个月过生日的
同学办了一个集体生日会。

子明: 集体生日会？我还从来没参加过这
样的生日会呢！

丁强: 趁大家都在食堂吃午饭的时候，学
校给三月过生日的学生一个惊喜。
校长为我们准备了很多五颜六色
的气球和一个很大的蛋糕。他还为
我们请了合唱团的同学唱生日歌，
文艺表演队的小乐团还现场伴了奏
呢。

李阿姨: 你们校长还真是个有心人！

丁强: 学校还为我们每个三月出生的
"寿星"准备了一个小瓶子，
为大家准备了可以写上美好祝福
的纸条。你们看，我的瓶子里有
很多同学们给我写的祝福！

子明：你晚上可以慢慢看同学们都写了些
什么祝语给你，太有意义了！

丁强：最后，在<u>欢乐</u>的音乐声中，三月
的"寿星"们一块儿<u>吹灭</u>了<u>蜡烛</u>，
大家一起<u>切</u>蛋糕，所有的同学都吃
上了生日蛋糕，热热闹闹地<u>庆祝</u>了
我们的生日a。

王叔叔：听起来好温馨啊！

丁强：是啊，今天真是<u>难忘</u>的一天！

huānlè 欢乐 *adj.*	歡樂	joyous, happy
chuīmiè 吹灭 *phr.*	吹滅	blow off
làzhú 蜡烛 *n.*	蠟燭	candle
qiē 切 *v.*		cut
qìngzhù 庆祝 *v.*	慶祝	celebrate
nánwàng 难忘 *v.*	難忘	unable to forget, memorable

LANGUAGE FOCUS

The preposition 为 in this lesson means "(do something) for someone" and is used to identify the receiver of an action. The receiver is placed immediately after 为, followed by the action verb.

Examples: ❶ 今天李阿姨为我们做了很多菜。

❷ 为学生服务是学生中心的主要工作。

❸ 下个周六是张健的生日，我们为他办一个生日会吧！

DO YOU KNOW . . . 你知道吗？

Similar to American rites of passage into adulthood of a "sweet sixteen" birthday party, China has recently started a custom called 中学生"14岁集体生日"活动 (group birthday event for 14-year-olds) at schools. The theme of the ceremony is "与人生对话——我的中国梦" which means "a dialog with life – my Chinese dream." The sub-theme of the event is "告别金色童年，唱响青春梦想," or "bid farewell to my golden childhood, sing the dream of youth." This kind of ceremony celebrates the passage from childhood to young adulthood. Usually, students, their parents, and their teachers participate in the event in which representatives of each of the three groups give speeches or poetry recitations. The celebration often ends with someone cutting a cake and everyone singing the "Happy Birthday" song.

1. Answer the following questions based on the dialog in Step 1A.

❶ 今天丁强的学校有什么活动？

❷ 那个活动怎么样？

❸ 同学们为丁强做了什么？

❹ 那个活动是怎样结束的？

❺ 王叔叔觉得那个活动怎么样？

❻ 子明觉得那个活动怎么样？

❼ 丁强觉得那个活动怎么样？

❽ 你觉得学校举办这样的活动好不好？为什么？

2. With a partner, talk about an experience in which you organized a celebration for someone. Describe the things you did for that person. Say at least five sentences. Use 为 in your sentences.

Example:

> 我去年为我的好朋友 Mike 办了一个生日会。他喜欢吃炸鸡，所以我为他准备了很多炸鸡。我还为他订了一个很大的蛋糕。最后大家一起为他唱生日歌。生日会过后，他告诉我，他那天过得很开心，很感动。

CULTURAL HIGHLIGHTS

Respect for the Aged

Respect for the aged is a long-cherished tradition in China. The most common saying is "长幼有序" (zhǎng yòu yǒu xù) which can be translated as "Everyone knows his/her place." Chinese people believe that a long, full life brings with it much experience and wisdom. With that belief come certain traditions that honor older members of the community. For example, when you leave a room or a house, you need to formally say "Goodbye!" to the elders. When sitting down at a roundtable for a meal, the "most honored seat" or "big" seat (上座) is reserved for the oldest person. The second most important seat is for the second oldest person and so on. When eating a family meal, the oldest person at the table should start eating first and only then can the others follow. When you pour tea for elders, you should do it standing up.

The Double Ninth Festival (重阳节, Chóngyáng Jié), which falls on the ninth day of the ninth month of the lunar calendar, has been designated 中华老年节 (Seniors' Day) in mainland China since 1988. The number 九 has the exact same sound as 久, which means everlasting and symbolizes longevity. As the largest possible digit and with a sound like the word longevity, 九 is often associated with the meaning of "biggest" or "fullest" in Chinese culture.

B Receiving gifts

昨天是丁强的生日。王叔叔一家人请他吃饭。他们去了一家中餐馆，点了很多丁强喜欢吃的中国菜，还送了他一把吉他。丁强非常喜欢，一回到家就弹个不停。

现在的中国年轻人受到西方的影响，青少年、儿童过生日，除了要吃长寿面以外，也都要点蜡烛、吹蜡烛许愿、唱生日歌、切蛋糕，还会收到家人朋友送的礼物。

中国人为长辈庆祝生日叫"祝寿"，祝寿的人主要是子女、女婿、媳妇、晚辈、亲戚好友、

同事和邻居等。最常见的传统祝寿礼物有寿糕、寿烛、寿面、寿桃、寿联、百寿图、老松图等，也有送保健品的，还有送服装的。

子明的表姐在她外婆生日的时候，送了她一条自己亲手编织的围巾。她外婆说，冬天的时候用这条围巾，感到特别温暖。这说明了，生日礼物贵不贵并不重要，能表达心意的礼物才是最珍贵的。

xīfāng 西方 n.		the West
qīngshàonián 青少年 n.		youths
értóng 儿童 n.	兒童	children
xǔyuàn 许愿 phr.	許願	make a wish
zhǎngbèi 长辈 n.	長輩	elders
nǚxù 女婿 n.		son-in-law
xífù 媳妇 n.		daughter-in-law
wǎnbèi 晚辈 n.	晚輩	the younger generation
tóngshì 同事 n.		colleague
bǎojiànpǐn 保健品 n.		health product
qīnshǒu 亲手 adv.	親手	with one's own hands, personally
biānzhī 编织 v.	編織	weave
wēnnuǎn 温暖 adj.	溫暖	warm
zhēnguì 珍贵 adj.	珍貴	precious

EXTENDED VOCABULARY

Birthday celebrations for the Chinese

长寿面 n.	長壽面	chángshòumiàn	longevity noodles
祝寿 phr.	祝壽	zhùshòu	congratulate someone on his/her birthday *(for elders)*
寿糕 n.	壽糕	shòugāo	longevity cake
寿烛 n.	壽燭	shòuzhú	longevity candle
寿桃 n.	壽桃	shòutáo	longevity peach
寿联 n.	壽聯	shòulián	longevity couplet
百寿图 n.	百壽圖	bǎishòutú	longevity painting
老松图 n.	老松圖	lǎosōngtú	painting of old pine trees

LANGUAGE FOCUS

1. Sentences with double objects

   A verb taking two objects forms what is known as a "sentence with double objects." In such a sentence, the first object usually refers to a person and the second object a thing.

   Examples: ❶ 同学们要送张健一把吉他。
   (first object: 张健; second object: 一把吉他)

   ❷ 王叔叔教我中文。
   (first object: 我; second object: 中文)

   ❸ 丁强要问老师几个问题。
   (first object: 老师; second object: 几个问题)

2. Pivotal sentences

   In Chinese a sentence can contain several verbs. A pivotal sentence is one in which the object of the first verb functions as the subject of the following verb. This object therefore serves as a pivot, connecting the two verb clauses in the sentence.

   The first verb in a pivotal sentence is often a causative verb (to cause something to happen) such as 请, 让, or 叫. All three carry the meaning of asking somebody to do something. Of the three, 请 is the most polite; 让 is less so; and 叫 is the least polite. Be sure to use these verbs on the appropriate occasions.

   Examples: ❶ 叔叔阿姨请我吃饭。 ("我" functions as a pivot.)

   ❷ 老师让我们准备考试。 ("我们" functions as a pivot.)

   ❸ 爸爸叫姐姐帮妹妹穿衣服。 ("姐姐" functions as a pivot.)

The Practice of Gift-giving

Gift-giving is an important part of Chinese culture. Similar to the United States, people give gifts on birthdays, at weddings, graduation, and anniversaries. Both Chinese and Americans will bring a small gift when invited to dinner at someone's home or to thank someone for their assistance.

As in any culture, thoughtful gifts are always appreciated. What kinds of gifts make good gifts from the Chinese perspective? The answer depends on the situation of the receivers. For those people who are not financially well off, practical gifts are the most suitable ones. For loved ones and spouses, gifts that bring back happy memories are the best. For children, original and novel gifts that develop the intellect would be considered desirable. For friends, gifts with interesting qualities would always be welcomed while useful gifts are ideal for the elderly.

Popular gifts for the elderly are high quality food supplements such as multi-vitamins, Alaskan fish oil, and calcium pills. Some popular gifts for aging parents are comprehensive physical checkups at the hospital (ideally the giver accompanies the parents to the hospital).

Try This!

1. Answer the following questions based on the reading passage in Step 1B.

❶ 王叔叔一家怎么为丁强庆祝生日？

❷ 中国的年轻人怎么过生日？

❸ 中国人给年轻人过生日送什么样的礼物？

❹ 中国人怎么给长辈庆祝生日？

❺ 中国人给长辈过生日送什么样的礼物？

❻ 子明的表姐送了她外婆什么礼物？

❼ "生日礼物贵不贵并不重要，能表达心意的礼物才是最珍贵的。" 你同意这样的看法吗？为什么？

❽ 如果你有一位中国的长辈，你打算怎样给他/她庆祝生日呢？

2. Make double objects sentences by using the vocabulary below.

- ❶ 奶奶　　　丁强　　　一个寿桃
- ❷ 爸爸　　　妈妈　　　一杯茶
- ❸ 子明　　　丁强　　　中文
- ❹ 芳芳　　　妹妹　　　生日蛋糕
- ❺ 丁强　　　张健　　　一支笔
- ❻ 丁强　　　朋友　　　一把吉他
- ❼ 李阿姨　　售货员　　五十块
- ❽ 弟弟　　　姐姐　　　一双鞋

3. Combine the two sentences into one pivotal sentence.

Example: 子明教丁强。 ↔ 丁强说中文。

Answer: <u>子明教丁强说中文。</u>

- ❶ 李阿姨叫子明。　　　　↔　子明回家。
- ❷ 老师叫大家。　　　　　↔　大家安静。
- ❸ 子明请丁强。　　　　　↔　丁强来北京旅游。
- ❹ 王叔叔送丁强。　　　　↔　丁强去参观圆明园。
- ❺ 爸爸让子明回家。　　　↔　子明回家帮妈妈做饭。
- ❻ 大家帮助外公外婆。　　↔　外公外婆庆祝70岁大寿。
- ❼ 王叔叔请丁强。　　　　↔　丁强去子明的爷爷奶奶家做客。
- ❽ 丁强感谢李阿姨。　　　↔　李阿姨一直照顾他在北京的生活。

A Describing traditional Chinese festivals

丁强：子明，中国有哪些传统<u>节日</u>？

子明：中国有七大传统节日。<u>春节</u>、<u>元宵节</u>、<u>清明节</u>、<u>端午节</u>、<u>七夕节</u>、<u>中秋节</u>和<u>重阳节</u>。

丁强：哇，这么多传统节日。这些节日都在什么时候？

子明：春节是中国的<u>农历</u>新年，在农历<u>正月</u> 初一，也就是新的一年的第一天。元宵节在农历正月十五，是农历新年的第一个<u>月圆</u>之夜。<u>阳历</u>四月四、五日左右是清明节，人们<u>扫墓</u>，<u>踏青</u>。中国人把农历五月初五定为端午节，<u>纪念</u> <u>爱国</u> <u>诗人</u>屈原，^{Qū Yuán}有吃<u>粽子</u>、<u>赛龙舟</u>的<u>习俗</u>。

丁强：哦，我以前在美国上中文课时读过端午节，挺有意思的。

jiérì 节日 n.	節日	festival
nónglì 农历 n.	農曆	lunar calendar
zhēngyuè 正月 n.		first month of the lunar calendar
chū 初 n.		first (in order)
yuèyuán 月圆 n.	月圓	full moon
yánglì 阳历 n.	陽曆	the Gregorian calendar
sǎomù 扫墓 phr.	掃墓	tomb sweeping
tàqīng 踏青 v.		go on an outing in early spring
jìniàn 纪念 v.	紀念	commemorate
àiguó 爱国 v.	愛國	to be patriotic
shīrén 诗人 n.	詩人	poet
zòngzi 粽子 n.		rice dumpling
sài lóngzhōu 赛龙舟 phr.	賽龍舟	dragon boat race
xísú 习俗 n.	習俗	custom

子明：是啊，我们的传统节日都很有意思。另外，七夕节是农历七月初七，是中国传统节日中最有<u>浪漫</u>色彩的一个节日，<u>起源</u>于牛郎（Niú Láng）与织女（Zhī Nǚ）的<u>传说</u>。我们可以说七夕节是中国的情人节。

丁强：我想很多中国<u>情侣</u>应该会选在这天<u>结婚</u>吧。

子明：说得没错。七夕以后，就是中秋节了。中国人把农历八月十五日定为中秋节。中秋节家人<u>团聚</u>，一起<u>赏月</u>，吃<u>月饼</u>。过了中秋，很快就到了农历九月初九重阳节。1988年，中国把重阳定为"老人节"，这样老人们有了自己的节日。

丁强：这些传统节日听起来都很有意义，很高兴我能在中国过这些节！

lànmàn 浪漫 adj.		romantic
sècǎi 色彩 n.		characteristic, quality
qǐyuán 起源 v.		originate
chuánshuō 传说 n.	傳說	legend
qínglǚ 情侣 n.	情侶	couple
jiéhūn 结婚 v.	結婚	marry
tuánjù 团聚 v.	團聚	reunite
shǎngyuè 赏月 phr.	賞月	admire the moon
yuèbǐng 月饼 n.	月餅	mooncake

EXTENDED VOCABULARY

Traditional Chinese festivals

春节 n.	春節	Chūn Jié	Spring Festival
元宵节 n.	元宵節	Yuánxiāo Jié	Lantern Festival
清明节 n.	清明節	Qīngmíng Jié	Qingming Festival
端午节 n.	端午節	Duānwǔ Jié	Dragon Boat Festival
七夕节 n.	七夕節	Qīxī Jié	Qixi Festival
中秋节 n.	中秋節	Zhōngqiū Jié	Mid-Autumn Festival
重阳节 n.	重陽節	Chóngyáng Jié	Chongyang Festival

In Book 2, we introduced the 把 sentence. As you might remember, in this construction, 把 has the function of shifting the object of the verb to a pre-verbal position in the pattern of "subject + 把 + object + verb (phrase)." 把 is often used to indicate that something is done to an item in a certain way. There are many types of 把 sentences. We have introduced the following two types of 把 sentences: change of location and completion.

Examples: ❶ 我把台灯放在书桌上。
(change of location)

❷ 当你离开房间的时候，应该把灯关掉。
(completion)

In this lesson, we will introduce another type of 把 sentence: identification. Here the object is given a certain form of identification.

Examples: ❶ 中国人把农历五月初五定为端午节。
❷ 老师把学生看成自己的孩子。

1. Answer the following questions according to the dialog in Step 2A.

❶ 中国的传统节日有哪些？

❷ 什么时候是中国的春节？

❸ 清明节的时候人们通常做什么？

❹ 端午节有什么意义？

❺ 为什么七夕节是最有浪漫色彩的节日？

❻ 农历八月十五日是什么日子？人们在这一天通常做什么？

❼ 你最喜欢中国的哪个传统节日？为什么？

❽ 你认为中国的传统节日和美国的传统节日有什么相同的地方和不同的地方？

2. Complete the following 把 sentences using the options provided.

| 功课 | 吃光 | 当成 | 搬到 | 农历新年 |
| 看成 | 书架 | 花瓶 | 水龙头 | 关掉 |

❶ 姐姐把书放在_____上。

❷ 你得把_____做完，才能玩电脑游戏。

❸ 我把十元_____五元，给了收银员！

❹ 哥哥一口气把三明治_____了。

❺ 爸爸把桌子_____书房里。

❻ 丁强把老师_____朋友，有什么事都会跟老师说。

❼ 刷牙的时候，应该把_____关掉。

❽ 妈妈把花插在_____里。

❾ 中国人把正月初一定为_____。

❿ 看完电视以后，应该把电视机_____。

3. What are some traditional festivals in your country? With a partner, tell him/her at least three of your favorite festivals and use the 把 construction to state the dates of these festivals.

Blog

　　人们常说："有钱没钱，回家过年。"春节时，人们把家里打扫得干干净净，也把家里布置得漂漂亮亮。大家也会逛庙会，办年货，把年货市场挤得水泄不通。最重要的春节习俗有回家过年、家庭团聚、吃年夜饭、贴春联、贴门神、守岁、放鞭炮、拜年、送红包等。元宵节晚上，按民间传统，人们要点彩灯，出门赏月观灯，放烟火、猜灯谜、吃元宵。

　　在重阳节这天，有登高、赏菊花、吃重阳糕的习俗。"高"和"糕"发音一样，有步步高的吉祥之意。"高"还有高寿的意思，所人们认为"登高"可以长寿。九九重阳，因为与"久久"同音，九在数字中又是最大数，有长久和长寿的含义。

guònián 过年 *phr.*	過年	celebrate the New Year
bùzhì 布置 *v.*	佈置	decorate
shuǐ xiè bù tōng 水泄不通 *phr.*	水洩不通	packed with people
niányèfàn 年夜饭 *n.*	年夜飯	a family reunion dinner on Chinese New Year's Eve, also called 年饭
tiē 贴 *n.*	貼	paste
ménshén 门神 *n.*	門神	door god
shǒusuì 守岁 *v.*	守歲	stay up late on New Year's Eve
bàinián 拜年 *phr.*		pay a New Year's call
hóngbāo 红包 *n.*	紅包	red envelope containing money
mínjiān 民间 *n.*	民間	folk
cǎidēng 彩灯 *n.*	彩燈	colored lantern
yānhuǒ 烟火 *n.*	煙火	fireworks
cāi dēngmí 猜灯谜 *phr.*	猜燈謎	guess lantern riddles
yuánxiāo 元宵 *n.*		sweet dumpling
dēnggāo 登高 *v.*		climb a hill or mountain
júhuā 菊花 *n.*		chrysanthemum
fāyīn 发音 *n.*	發音	pronunciation
bù bù gāo 步步高 *phr.*		progressing step by step
jíxiáng 吉祥 *adj.*		auspicious
hányì 含义 *n.*	含義	meaning

In this section you will learn another type of 把 sentence which is a change in state. The doer does an action that causes the recipient to have a changed state. Note that the adjective that describes the changed state needs to be duplicated if it has two syllables.

Examples: ❶ 姐姐把房间打扫得干干净净。
(干净 → 干干净净)

❷ 妈妈把客厅布置得漂漂亮亮。
(漂亮 → 漂漂亮亮)

❸ 人们在春节时喜欢逛庙会，把那里挤得水泄不通。

1. Complete the following sentences using the 把 construction.

❶ 过年了，王叔叔和李阿姨＿＿＿＿＿＿＿＿＿＿干干净净的。

❷ 我好饿啊，我先＿＿＿＿＿＿＿＿＿吧！

❸ 春节期间，买年货的中国人＿＿＿＿＿＿＿＿＿水泄不通。

❹ 还有一块重阳糕，你＿＿＿＿＿＿＿＿＿吧！

❺ 丁强，我今天不去学校了，你帮我＿＿＿＿＿＿＿＿＿交给老师吧！

❻ 子明，你能＿＿＿＿＿＿＿＿＿递给我吗？

❼ 今天是丁强的生日，李阿姨＿＿＿＿＿＿＿＿＿得漂漂亮亮的。

❽ 丁强，垃圾太多了，你＿＿＿＿＿＿＿＿＿扔了吧！

2. How do you celebrate your favorite traditional festival? With a partner, describe to him/her the things you and your family usually do during the festival. Say at least five sentences. Use the 把 construction in your sentences.

Example:

我喜欢和家人一起过中秋节。每年中秋节，妈妈都会把花园布置得漂漂亮亮。我们会在花园里边吃月饼边赏月。中秋节的月亮很圆，很美，也很亮。我很喜欢吃月饼，所以每年都会把家里买的月饼都吃完。

CULTURAL HIGHLIGHTS

Symbolic Meaning of Items Used in Chinese Festivals

During the Spring Festival (or Chinese New Year), people in many places in China often eat "饺子" (jiǎozi, dumplings) since they look like gold ingots. People in some other places, such as Guangdong Province, like to make a special soup for the New Year's Eve banquet called "发菜汤" (fācàitāng, long thread moss soup) since 发菜 sounds like 发财 (fācái), which means "receive a fortune" or "become prosperous."

During the Lantern Festival (元宵节), people eat "元宵" (glutinous rice balls) or "汤圆," and during Mid-Autumn Festival (中秋节) people eat moon cakes. Both foods are sweet and round and express the wish that people have a sweet and perfect life ("甜蜜圆满"). During Qingming Festival (清明节), some people fly their kites high in the sky and then cut the thread and let the kites fly away. It is believed that this can help them get rid of sickness, avoid disaster, and bring them good luck.

A Celebrating weddings

Blog

　　婚礼在中国人的生活中是一个很重要的仪式。新郎 新娘会邀请亲朋好友和同事参加他们的婚礼。过去，婚礼的邀请是通过纸质的请柬，而现在，人们还会通过短信、微信以及电子邮件来邀请亲朋好友。

　　婚礼当天，新郎要去新娘家接新娘。到新郎家后，新娘给新郎的父母敬茶。然后，新郎新娘去酒店，站在酒店门口欢迎出席婚礼的来宾。主持人宣布婚礼仪式开始，新郎新娘交换戒指，三鞠躬，新人给父母敬茶，双方父母代表讲话，新人开香槟、切蛋糕、

hūnlǐ 婚礼 n.	婚禮	wedding ceremony
yíshì 仪式 n.	儀式	ceremony
xīnláng 新郎 n.		bridegroom
xīnniáng 新娘 n.		bride
zhǐzhì 纸质 n.	紙質	paper
qǐngjiǎn 请柬 n.	請柬	invitation card
jìngchá 敬茶 v.		serve someone tea
jiǔdiàn 酒店 n.		hotel
chūxí 出席 v.		attend
láibīn 来宾 n.	來賓	guest
xuānbù 宣布 v.	宣佈	announce
jiāohuàn 交换 v.	交換	exchange
jūgōng 鞠躬 v.		bow
xīnrén 新人 n.		newly wedded couple
xiāngbīn 香槟 n.	香檳	champagne

喝交杯酒。婚宴开始后，新人到各桌给客人敬酒。中国人常常把参加婚礼婚宴称为"喝喜酒"。婚礼以后，新郎新娘会送朋友和同事喜糖。

参加中国人的婚礼，亲戚朋友一般都会"随礼"，也就是送红包，红包里的钱也做"礼金"，包含了对新郎新娘结婚后美满生活的祝福。

jiāobēijiǔ 交杯酒 *n.*		nuptial wine (*"crossed-cupped wine"*)
hūnyàn 婚宴 *n.*		wedding banquet
kèrén 客人 *n.*		guest
bāohán 包含 *v.*		contain
měimǎn 美满 *adj.*	美满	fulfilling

COMMON EXPRESSIONS FOR INVITATIONS

Here are some common expressions for inviting someone to an event and responding to the invitation. They are normally used in spoken contexts. Take some time to learn them as they will be useful if you are invited to a special occasion.

Inviting

- 我想邀请你参加我的生日会。
- 可以赏光*出席我的婚礼吗？

Responding

- 谢谢你的邀请，我一定会来。
- 真是太对不起了，那天我刚好有事，无法出席。

polite expression, used when requesting someone to accept an invitation

1. Answer the following questions according to the passage in Step 3A.

   ❶ 中国人如何发出婚礼邀请？现在和过去有什么不一样？
   ❷ 中国人把参加婚礼宴会又叫做什么？
   ❸ 中国的婚礼是在教堂举行的吗？
   ❹ 中国的婚礼有什么特点？
   ❺ 婚礼当天，新郎要做什么？
   ❻ 婚礼上，新郎和新娘要做什么？
   ❼ 除了举办婚礼，新郎新娘还会做什么？
   ❽ 参加中国人的婚礼要准备什么？
   ❾ 你觉得中国的婚礼和美国的婚礼有什么不一样吗？
   ❿ 你更喜欢哪一种婚礼方式？为什么？

2. Imagine that you are having a birthday celebration at your house next Saturday. Go around the class and invite your classmates to the celebration. Your classmates will respond by indicating whether or not they will attend. Use appropriate expressions such as 邀请, 赏光, 谢谢, etc.

 **CULTURAL HIGHLIGHTS**

Comparing American and Chinese Customs: Who Pays for the Wedding?

In the United States, the tradition is for the bride's family to pay for the wedding and reception, whereas the groom's family generally pays for the rehearsal dinner the night before. Sometimes, the groom's parents will also offer to pay for some of the drinks at the wedding. In China, however, the tradition may be different and varies from one place to another. In some places, the Chinese groom and his family pay for the entire wedding and even provide a house or apartment, complete with furnishings, for the newly weds. The bride and her family are only responsible for taking care of the bedding. Depending on the financial conditions of the bride, the bride and her family may share the cost of the wedding and the house. The bride is also often expected to bring some form of dowry to the marriage.

B Attending a graduation ceremony

子明的表哥健伟高中<u>毕业</u>了。这是他的<u>毕业演讲稿</u>。

<u>尊敬</u>的校长、各位老师、各位同学：

下午好！

今天参加毕业<u>典礼</u>，我感到非常高兴。

首先，我想代表<u>全体</u>毕业班的同学感谢老师们三年来对我们的<u>辛勤</u>教育和培养。

我们<u>怀念</u>为高考而努力的每一天，我们学会了很多的知识，锻炼了毅力，也交到了很多朋友。我们感谢老师，我们感谢同学，我们感谢学校！

<u>过去</u>的生活是<u>灿烂</u>的，是美丽的，是<u>丰富</u>的。所以，现在是我们收获的时节。因为有了三年的学习，我们才有了知识和<u>技能</u>，才有了<u>面对</u>挑战<u>坚忍不拔</u>的毅力。<u>无论</u>将来怎么样，我们<u>都</u>有信心去微笑面对！

三年时间很快过去了，我们将离开<u>母校</u>，虽然我们人离开了，但我们的<u>记忆</u>不会离开。我们将在新的学校继续努力学习，将来成为社会的有用<u>人才</u>，让学校和各位老师为我们感到<u>自豪</u>。

最后，祝各位老师身体健康，工作<u>顺利</u>，每天都有好心情。<u>预祝</u>各位同学都能进入自己<u>向往</u>的学校，今后的人生成功、快乐！

谢谢大家！

Pinyin	Simplified	Traditional	English
bìyè	毕业 v.	畢業	graduate
yǎnjiǎnggǎo	演讲稿 n.	演講稿	text of a speech
zūnjìng	尊敬 adj.		distinguished
diǎnlǐ	典礼 n.	典禮	ceremony
quántǐ	全体 n.	全體	all, entire, whole
xīnqín	辛勤 adj.		industrious, hardworking
huáiniàn	怀念 v.	懷念	cherish the memory of
guòqù	过去 n.	過去	the past
cànlàn	灿烂 adj.	燦爛	brilliant, splendid
fēngfù	丰富 adj.	豐富	rich
jìnéng	技能 n.		skill
miànduì	面对 v.	面對	face, confront
jiān rěn bù bá	坚忍不拔 phr.	堅忍不拔	firm and indomitable
wúlùn...dōu	无论…都…	無論…都…	no matter...
mǔxiào	母校 n.		alma mater
jìyì	记忆 n.	記憶	memory
réncái	人才 n.		talent
zìháo	自豪 adj.		proud
shùnlì	顺利 adj.	順利	smooth sailing
yùzhù	预祝 v.	預祝	wish, congratulate beforehand
xiàngwǎng	向往 v.	嚮往	yearn for

无论…都… means "no matter..." Compared to 不管…都…, it is used in more formal contexts. The conjunction 无论 is placed at the beginning of the first clause to introduce possible conditions, while 都 is placed in the second clause to emphasize the result or action that is not affected or influenced at all by the preceding condition or possibility.

Examples: ❶ 毕业典礼是你的大日子，无论多忙，我都会来。

❷ 无论我们走到哪里，都会永远记得我们亲爱的母校。

❸ 无论子女多大了，他们在父母的眼里都永远是孩子。

1. Answer the following questions based on the passage in Step 3B.

❶ 这是一篇关于什么的演讲？

❷ 这篇演讲发生在什么地方

❸ 演讲人感谢了谁？

❹ 演讲人认为自己高中三年收获了什么？

❺ 演讲人在最后说了什么？

❻ 如果让你做毕业演讲，你会说些什么？
（200字）

2. Match the sentences.

❶ 无论天气有多冷，	a. 中国人都会去办年货。
❷ 无论面对多大的困难，	b. 父母都会为他们操心。 cāoxīn / worry
❸ 无论春节期间商场多么拥挤，	c. 只要努力都能克服。
❹ 无论孩子多大，	d. 他每天早上都要到河里去游泳。
❺ 无论刮风下雨，	e. 丁强都下定决心要学好它。 juéxīn / determined
❻ 无论大家平时多么忙，	f. 他每天都准时到学校上课。
❼ 无论中文多么难，	g. 过年的时候都会聚在一起吃饭。
❽ 无论丁强有什么困难，	h. 王叔叔一家都会尽力帮助他。

Step Up!

Imagine that your Chinese exchange school e-pal is the editor of his/her school magazine and will have a special issue for Mother's Day. The focus of this issue will be on what children from different parts of the world would say to and do for their mothers in order to show their gratitude.

1. Below are excerpts of a poem entitled "妈妈." Read them and answer the following questions.

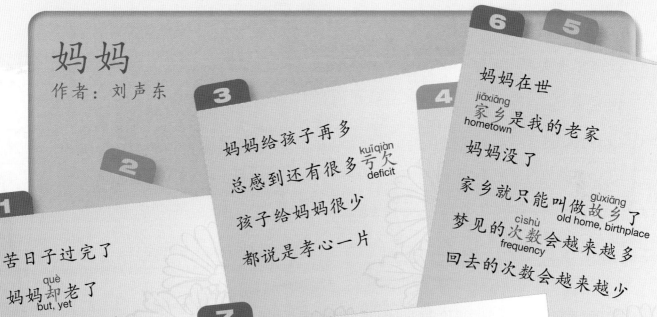

妈妈

作者：刘声东

1

苦日子过完了

妈妈却老了
què — but, yet

好日子开始了

妈妈却走了

这就是我苦命的妈妈
kǔmìng — ill-fated

妈妈健在时
jiànzài — still living

我远游了

我回来时

妈妈却远走了

这就是你不孝的儿子
xiàu — filial

3

妈妈给孩子再多

总感到还有很多亏欠
kuīqiàn — deficit

孩子给妈妈很少

都说是孝心一片

5 6

妈妈在世

家乡是我的老家
jiāxiāng — hometown

妈妈没了

家乡就只能叫做故乡了
gùxiāng — old home, birthplace

梦见的次数会越来越多
cìshù — frequency

回去的次数会越来越少

7

小时候，妈妈的膝盖是扶手
fúshǒu — handrail

我扶着它学会站立和行走

长大后，妈妈的肩膀是扶手

我扶着它学会闯荡和守候
chuǎngdàng — make a living away from home
shǒuhòu — wait

离家时，妈妈的期盼是扶手
qīpàn — longing

我扶着它历经风雨不言愁
lìjīng — experience
yán chóu — speak sorrow

回家时，妈妈的笑脸是扶手

我扶着它洗尽风尘慰乡愁
fēngchén — dust
wèi — comfort

妈妈没了

我到哪儿去寻找
xúnzhǎo — search

我依赖了一生的这个扶手
yīlài — depend on

妈妈走了

我的世界变了

世界变了

我的内心也变了

我变成了没妈的孩子

变得不如能够扎根大地的一棵小草 (zhāgēn take root)

母爱如天

我的天塌下来了 (tā collapse)

母爱如海

我的海快要枯竭了 (kūjié dry up)

慈母万滴血 (címǔ loving mother，dī droplet)

生我一条命

还送千行泪

陪我一路行 (péi accompany)

爱恨百般浓 (hèn hatred，nóng strong)

都是一样情

即便十分孝

难报一世恩 (ēn kindness, favor)

——万千百十一

一声长叹 (tàn sigh)

叹不尽人间母子情……

a. Use one sentence in Chinese to describe the main idea of this poem.

b. 刘声东为什么写这首诗？

c. 刘声东的妈妈怎么了？还在世吗？

d. 刘声东在这首诗里把母亲比作什么？

e. 为什么刘声东说他以前的家乡已经从"老家"变成"故乡"了？

f. 为什么刘声东说他现在"变得不如能够扎根大地的一棵小草"了？

g. 刘声东在这首诗里把母爱比作什么？

h. 你觉得刘声东是一个好儿子吗？为什么？

2. Discuss with your classmate about maternal or paternal love. During the discussion, share your views about what you understand from the earlier poem, your own views, and learn as much as you can about your partner's thoughts. The discussion may include your understanding of the Chinese concept of 孝 (xiào, filial piety), criteria of a good child in both China and the United States, your own personal gratitude toward your own mother or father, and other personal ideas.

3. Write an article on the topic of "Maternal/Paternal Love" in reference to the poem you have just read, focusing on how Liu Shendong expressed his love for and his remorse and regrets toward his mother. What lessons have you learned from reading his poem in reference to your relationship with your own mother or father? Compare and contrast how Liu Shengdong writes about his mother with that of a famous person in the United States (such as one of the founding fathers of the United States) or in contemporary life. Conclude your article by analyzing the similarities and differences and the cultural perspectives and traditions that influenced those similarities and differences. In your article, use the sentence structures introduced in this lesson.

Fun Time!

"生日礼物" is a very popular song in China. Take a look at the lyrics below and try to figure out the meaning. Go online to listen to the song and try to sing along with it.

生日礼物

填词、谱曲：骆驼
编曲：刘炜

星星是生日蜡烛，

歌声是我的祝福。

在你生日的那天，

你用沉默 (chénmò / silence) 告诉我你不在乎 (zàihu / care about)，

不知今生可否走出，

过去是那么的忙碌 (mánglù / busy)，

你说快乐就是礼物。

星星是生日蜡烛，

歌声是我的祝福。

月光是我的礼物，

陪伴你一生的路。

我问你要什么礼物，

你说未来有太多的苦。

这一生我们在拥有 (yōngyǒu / own, possess) 也在付出 (fùchū / pay, give)。

儿时的梦变得模糊 (móhu / blurred)，

一个拥抱 (yōngbào / hug) 就可以满足 (mǎnzú / satisfy)。

月光是我的礼物，

陪伴 (péibàn / accompany) 你一生的路。

I have learned...

Verbs

伴奏		bànzòu	provide musical accompaniment	守岁	守歲	shǒusuì	stay up late on New Year's Eve
祝福	祝福	zhùfú	wish someone well	登高		dēnggāo	climb a hill or mountain
切		qiē	cut	敬茶		jìngchá	serve someone tea
庆祝	慶祝	qìngzhù	celebrate	出席		chūxí	attend
难忘	難忘	nánwàng	unable to forget, memorable	宣布	宣佈	xuānbù	announce
编织	編織	biānzhī	weave	交换	交換	jiāohuàn	exchange
踏青		tàqīng	go on an outing in early spring	鞠躬		jūgōng	bow
纪念	紀念	jìniàn	commemorate	包含		bāohán	contain
爱国	愛國	àiguó	to be patriotic	毕业	畢業	bìyè	graduate
起源		qǐyuán	originate	怀念	懷念	huáiniàn	cherish the memory of
结婚	結婚	jiéhūn	marry	面对	面對	miànduì	face, confront
团聚	團聚	tuánjù	reunite	预祝	預祝	yùzhù	wish, congratulate beforehand
布置	佈置	bùzhì	decorate	向往	嚮往	xiàngwǎng	yearn for
贴	貼	tiē	paste	预祝	預祝	yùzhù	wish, congratulate beforehand

Nouns

集体生日会	集體生日會	jítǐ shēngrìhuì	group birthday party	儿童	兒童	értóng	children
惊喜	驚喜	jīngxǐ	pleasant surprise	长辈	長輩	zhǎngbèi	elders
气球	氣球	qìqiú	balloon	女婿		nǚxù	son-in-law
合唱团	合唱團	héchàngtuán	choir	媳妇		xífù	daughter-in-law
乐团	樂團	yuètuán	music band	晚辈	晚輩	wǎnbèi	the younger generation
现场	現場	xiànchǎng	site, spot	同事		tóngshì	colleague
寿星	壽星	shòuxīng	person whose birthday is being celebrated	保健品		bǎojiànpǐn	health product
瓶子		píngzi	bottle	长寿面	長壽面	chángshòumiàn	longevity noodles
祝福		zhùfú	well wishes	寿糕	壽糕	shòugāo	longevity cake
纸条	紙條	zhǐtiáo	slip of paper	寿烛	壽燭	shòuzhú	longevity candle
蜡烛	蠟燭	làzhú	candle	寿烛	壽桃	shòutáo	longevity peach
西方		xīfāng	the West	寿联	壽聯	shòulián	longevity couplet
青少年		qīngshàonián	youths	百寿图	百壽圖	bǎishòutú	longevity painting

老松图	老松圖	lǎosōngtú	painting of old pine trees	烟火	煙火	yānhuǒ	fireworks
节日	節日	jiérì	festival	元宵		yuánxiāo	sweet dumpling
农历	農曆	nónglì	lunar calendar	菊花		júhuā	chrysanthemum
正月		zhēngyuè	first month of the lunar calendar	发音	發音	fāyīn	pronunciation
初		chū	first (in order)	含义	含義	hányì	meaning
月圆	月圓	yuèyuán	full moon	婚礼	婚禮	hūnlǐ	wedding ceremony
阳历	陽曆	yánglì	the Gregorian calendar	仪式	儀式	yíshì	ceremony
诗人	詩人	shīrén	poet	新郎		xīnláng	bridegroom
粽子		zòngzi	rice dumpling	新娘		xīnniáng	bride
习俗	習俗	xísú	custom	纸质	紙質	zhǐzhì	paper
色彩		sècǎi	characteristic, quality	请柬	請柬	qǐngjiǎn	invitation card
传说	傳說	chuánshuō	legend	酒店		jiǔdiàn	hotel
情侣	情侶	qínglǚ	couple	来宾	來賓	láibīn	guest
月饼	月餅	yuèbǐng	mooncake	新人		xīnrén	newly wedded couple
春节	春節	Chūn Jié	Spring Festival	香槟	香檳	xiāngbīn	champagne
元宵节	元宵節	Yuánxiāo Jié	Lantern Festival	交杯酒		jiāobēijiǔ	nuptial wine ("crossed-cupped wine")
清明节	清明節	Qīngmíng Jié	Qingming Festival	婚宴		hūnyàn	wedding banquet
端午节	端午節	Duānwǔ Jié	Dragon Boat Festival	客人		kèrén	guest
七夕节	七夕節	Qīxī Jié	Qixi Festival	演讲稿	演講稿	yǎnjiǎnggǎo	text of a speech
中秋节	中秋節	Zhōngqiū Jié	Mid-Autumn Festival	典礼	典禮	diǎnlǐ	ceremony
重阳节	重陽節	Chóngyáng Jié	Chongyang Festival	全体	全體	quántǐ	all, entire, whole
年夜饭	年夜飯	niányèfàn	a family reunion dinner on Chinese New Year's Eve, also called 年饭	过去	過去	guòqù	the past
门神	門神	ménshén	door god	技能		jìnéng	skill
红包	紅包	hóngbāo	red envelope containing money	母校		mǔxiào	alma mater
民间	民間	mínjiān	folk	记忆	記憶	jìyì	memory
彩灯	彩燈	cǎidēng	colored lantern	人才		réncái	talent

Adjectives

惊喜	驚喜	jīngxǐ	pleasantly surprised	温暖	溫暖	wēnnuǎn	warm
五颜六色	五顏六色	wǔ yán liù sè	colorful	珍贵	珍貴	zhēnguì	precious
欢乐	歡樂	huānlè	joyous, happy	浪漫		làngmàn	romantic

吉祥		jíxiáng	auspicious	灿烂	燦爛	cànlàn	brilliant, splendid
美满	美滿	měimǎn	fulfilling	丰富	豐富	fēngfù	rich
尊敬		zūnjìng	distinguished	自豪		zìháo	proud
辛勤		xīnqín	industrious, hardworking	顺利	順利	shùnlì	smooth sailing

Phrases

吹灭	吹滅	chuīmiè	blow off	过年	過年	guònián	celebrate the New Year
许愿	許願	xǔyuàn	make a wish	水泄不通	水洩不通	shuǐ xiè bù tōng	packed with people
祝寿	祝壽	zhùshòu	congratulate someone on his/her birthday (for elders)	拜年		bàinián	pay a New Year's call
扫墓	掃墓	sǎomù	tomb sweeping	猜灯谜	猜燈謎	cāi dēngmí	guess lantern riddles
赛龙舟	賽龍舟	sài lóngzhōu	dragon boat race	步步高		bù bù gāo	progressing step by step
赏月	賞月	shǎngyuè	admire the moon	坚忍不拔	堅忍不拔	jiān rěn bù bá	firm and indomitable

Adverb

亲手	親手	qīnshǒu	with one's own hands, personally

Construction

无论…都…	無論…都…	wúlùn...dōu	no matter...

◆ SENTENCE PATTERNS ◆

今天学校<u>为</u>三月过生日的同学办了一个集体生日会。

王叔叔一家人<u>请</u>丁强吃饭。

他们<u>送了他一把吉他</u>。

中国人<u>把</u>农历五月初五定为端午节。

春节时，人们<u>把</u>家里<u>打扫得干干净净</u>。

我想<u>请</u>你参加我的婚礼。

谢谢你的邀请，我一定出席。

<u>无论</u>将来怎么样，我们<u>都</u>有信心去微笑面对。

I can do!

Interpretive Communication

❏ I can understand when people talk about birthday celebrations and weddings.

❏ I can read and interpret authentic materials about celebrations.

❏ I can read and comprehend information about major traditional festivals, birthday celebrations and weddings in China.

Interpersonal Communication

❏ I can converse with people about milestones in their lives.

❏ I can interact with someone about a celebration in school.

❏ I can extend and respond to invitations *(either accept or decline an invitation)*.

❏ I can compare and contrast information about birthdays, holiday celebrations, and weddings.

Presentational Communication

❏ I can describe Chinese birthdays, traditional festivals, and wedding celebrations.

❏ I can describe events that occurred in the past.

❏ I can compare and contrast similarities and differences in celebrations in different countries.

Cultural Knowledge

❏ I can talk about the symbolic meanings of items used in Chinese festivals.

❏ I can describe the Chinese respect for the aged.

❏ I can explain Chinese birthday and wedding celebrations.

❏ I can talk about the Chinese practice of gift-giving.

LESSON 9

Chinese cultural treasures

中国文化珍宝

COMMUNICATIVE GOALS

- Describing Chinese painters and calligraphers
- Comparing and contrasting different art works
- Sequencing events in a timeline
- Demonstrating consequential ideas

Cultural Knowledge

- Beijing 798 Art Zone
- Seals and seal engraving
- Famous Chinese novelist and dramatist — Lao She
- Chinese paintings
- Chinese calligraphy
- Chinese performing arts
- Famous Chinese painting — Along the River During the Qingming Festival

Get ready...

Imagine that your class is planning on creating a time capsule of art and music in the 21st century to be opened by students in the 22nd century. Think about what items you would like to put in the time capsule that represent your art and music preferences and what you want to tell future students about your life and personality through these preferences. In Chinese, list at least 10 items that you would like to put in the capsule that tell something about your likes and dislikes. You must include an item from the following list and you may add at least four more:

- a picture of a modern work of art
- a picture of a classical work of art
- a poem that you like
- a song or piece of modern music
- a piece of classical music
- a sculpture or pottery

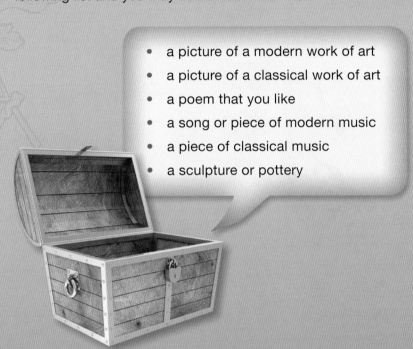

Then, compare your list with the lists of at least two other classmates and see where you agree and where you disagree. You may also create a class list and vote on ten items that should be included.

STEPS *at a glance!*

STEP 1

CHINESE PAINTINGS

A. Talking about Chinese artists

国画既是中国的国粹，也是世界的珍宝。

B. Comparing and contrasting famous painters

徐悲鸿的马虽然细节上不如素描那么具体，但是马的生命力却体现得非常到位。

STEP 2

CHINESE CALLIGRAPHY

A. Explaining the sequence of writing Chinese calligraphy

凡是学书法的人，都要有"文房四宝"。

B. Describing famous Chinese calligraphers

为了把字练好，王羲之每天都练习书法。

STEP 3

CHINESE PERFORMING ARTS

A. Experiencing the Chinese teahouse

就算是中国人，也不一定听得懂京剧。

B. Viewing the art of Chinese opera

梅兰芳能把花旦的角色演得很好，因此非常有名。

A Talking about Chinese artists

丁强：李阿姨，昨天王叔叔带我去北京798艺术区，那里有一家白石<u>茶馆</u>，里面的<u>茶具</u>和<u>陈设</u> <u>据说</u>都与中国著名画家<u>齐白石</u>（Qí Báishí）有关，真是太有特色了。

李阿姨：齐白石是中国<u>国画</u>艺术<u>大师</u>。他画的虾<u>尤其</u>出名，<u>栩栩如生</u>。可是他在开始学习画虾的时候，只会<u>临摹</u>，所以画得不好。后来自己养虾、<u>观察</u>、<u>写生</u>，经过数十年的努力，终于把虾画得<u>活灵活现</u>。

丁强：我记得上美术课的时候，老师给我们欣赏过齐白石画的虾、<u>郑板桥</u>（Zhèng Bǎnqiáo）画的<u>竹子</u>，还有<u>徐悲鸿</u>（Xú Bēihóng）画的马。

cháguǎn 茶馆 n.	茶館	teahouse
chájù 茶具 n.		tea set
chénshè 陈设 n.	陳設	set up as a display, furnish
jùshuō 据说 v.	據說	it is said
guóhuà 国画 n.	國畫	Chinese painting
dàshī 大师 n.	大師	master
yóuqí 尤其 adv.		especially
xǔ xǔ rú shēng 栩栩如生 phr.		have a life-like resemblance
línmó 临摹 v.	臨摹	copy from, facsimile
guānchá 观察 v.	觀察	observe, watch
xiěshēng 写生 v.	寫生	sketching from real life
huó líng huó xiàn 活灵活现 phr.	活靈活現	vivid, lively
zhúzi 竹子 n.		bamboo

李阿姨：国画<u>既</u>是中国的<u>国粹</u>，<u>也</u>是世界的<u>珍宝</u>。既然你对国画那么有兴趣，过几天我就带你去见一位画家。他是王叔叔和我在中学时候的美术老师。他对国画和书法都很有研究。

jì…yě… 既…也…		both…and, as well as
guócuì 国粹 n.	國粹	national treasure
zhēnbǎo 珍宝 n.	珍寶	treasure

LANGUAGE FOCUS

When describing something that has two similar qualities or attributes, use the conjunction 既…也… to create a more cohesive sentence that combines the two elements.

Examples:

- 他父亲既是律师，也是家长会会长。
- 番茄既是有营养的蔬菜，也是好吃的水果。
- 丁强既是游泳队的队长，也是足球队的队员。

Read some other examples that show the use of 既…也… and determine their meanings.

❶ 北京既是王叔叔出生的地方，也是他工作和生活的地方。

❷ 徐悲鸿既是杰出的现代画家，也是对现代中国美术教育影响最大的人。

❸ 齐白石用水墨画的虾既是他个人的发明，也是现代中国写意画的象征和标志。

❹ 徐悲鸿既是最早去欧洲学习艺术的留学生之一，也是最早把西方绘画技巧和中国水墨画结合在一起的画家。

❺ 北京既是中国的首都，也是中国的政治、文化、交通、科技创新和国际交往的中心。

Beijing 798 Art Zone

The 798 Art District is located in the northeastern part of Beijing and is named after a factory which was built and designed by German experts in the 1950s. In 2002, many artists and cultural organizations saw the vacant space and decided to develop it into an art center. Gradually, the empty spaces were transformed into galleries, artists' studios, design companies, restaurants, and even fashion shops. Today 798 is famous for its unique art exhibitions and special workshops and has become one of the landmarks of Beijing urban culture. There are over 400 cultural organizations from all over the world that have settled in the 798 Art District. In order to expand the reputation and influence of the art zone and to promote the development of modern art, the district has held the 798 Art Festival every year since 2006. Another well known festival is the 798 Creative Arts Festival. Both festivals focus on the integration of art and culture.

In addition to providing an international flavor to visitors, the 798 Art District also contrasts the present with the past. Walking down the street, visitors see mottled redbrick walls with slogans from different ages on one side and on the other side are the orderly industrial plants and crisscrossed pipelines. Here, history, reality, industry, and the arts merge together perfectly.

Try This!

1. Combine the attributes or qualities of the following people into complete sentences using 既…也….

   ❶ 郑板桥：画家，书法家

   ❷ 徐悲鸿：画家，美术教育家

   ❸ 达芬奇：雕塑家，建筑师
      <small>diāosùjiā</small>
      <small>sculptor</small>

   ❹ 芳芳：王菲的粉丝，周杰伦的粉丝

   ❺ 子明：老人院的义工，儿童福利院的义工

   ❻ 张健：丁强的好朋友，丁强的同学

   ❼ 丁强：健身室会员，篮球队队长

   ❽ 王叔叔：负责任的员工，慈爱的父亲
      <small>cí'ài</small>
      <small>loving</small>

2. Read the biographies of the two artists below. For each biography, create five cohesive sentences that combine elements from the description. You will need to use the sentence pattern and vocabulary words indicated for each sentence. Finally, re-sequence these sentences to make them into a paragraph-like report about each artist.

弗雷德里克 (Fúléidélǐkè) · 雷明顿 (Léimíngdùn) (Frederic Remington, 1861-1909) 是美国画家，插画家 (chāhuàjiā illustrator)，雕塑家，作家，出生在纽约。虽然在美国东部长大，但是他从小就喜欢画骑兵 (qíbīng horseman) 和西部牛仔 (niúzǎi cowboy)。他画奔跑的野马，逼真 (bīzhēn vivid) 和生动 (shēngdòng lively)。他的牛仔和马的雕塑非常出名。

徐悲鸿 (1895-1953) 是中国现代画家和美术教育家。小时候跟随父亲学习水墨画 (shuǐmòhuà ink painting)。24岁去法国留学，在巴黎国立美术学校学习油画、素描 (sùmiáo drawing)，以及观摩 (guānmó inspect and learn) 和研究西方美术。徐悲鸿是第一个将西方素描及油画与国画成功地结合起来的中国画家。他画的奔马不但逼真而且给人跃动 (yuèdòng vibrant) 的感觉。

❶ 既…也… _____ 。

❷ 据说 _____ 。

❸ 有特色 _____ 。

❹ 栩栩如生/活灵活现 _____ 。

❺ 尤其有名 _____ 。

Blog

中国历史上有很多的大画家，他们用毛笔画出中国的山水、人物、花草、虫鱼、鸟兽，把中国的风景和人物都栩栩如生地展现在世人眼前。

齐白石的创作非常多。光是1953这一年，他的大小作品就有600多幅。他天天努力创作，最后成为中国历史上大名鼎鼎的国画大师。不仅是国画，齐白石的书法、篆刻和诗歌也都很有名。

徐悲鸿和齐白石虽然都是画家，但是他们的绘画风格大不相同。徐悲鸿画的马，虽借用西方素描法而十分写实，但在笔墨上却注重中国传统绘画中的写意。

máobǐ 毛笔 n.	毛筆	calligraphic brush
shānshuǐ 山水 n.		mountains and rivers, landscape
rénwù 人物 n.		person, subject
chóng 虫 n.	蟲	insect
shòu 兽 n.	獸	animal
zhǎnxiàn 展现 v.		unfold before one's eyes, present
shìrén 世人 n.		common people
chuàngzuò 创作 n.; v.	創作	creative work, creation; create, produce
guāng 光 adv.		just
zuòpǐn 作品 n.		work
dà míng dǐng dǐng 大名鼎鼎 phr.		renowned, well-known
zhuànkè 篆刻 v.		carving the seal
shīgē 诗歌 n.	詩歌	poem, poetry
sùmiáo 素描 v.		sketch
xiěshí 写实 adj.	寫實	(of art style) realistic
bǐmò 笔墨 n.	筆墨	strokes and brushes
xiěyì 写意 n.	寫意	spontaneous expression

徐悲鸿的马虽然细节上<u>不如</u>素描那么<u>具体</u>，但是马的<u>生命力</u>却<u>体现</u>得非常<u>到位</u>。《<u>八骏图</u>》画了八匹马，八匹马都大不相同，非常<u>逼真</u>。

bùrú 不如 v.		not as good as
jùtǐ 具体 adj.	具體	specific
shēngmìnglì 生命力 n.		vitality
tǐxiàn 体现 v.	體現	express, demonstrate
dàowèi 到位 adj.		satisfactory
Bā Jùn Tú 八骏图 n.	八駿圖	*The Eight Horses*
bīzhēn 逼真 adj.		life-like

LANGUAGE FOCUS

You learned how to make comparisons using 比 and 跟…一样… in Book 2. Another way to compare two items and show that one is not as good as the other is to use the word 不如, in the pattern of: A + 不如 + B + (那么) + adjective. 那么 may be omitted in the sentence.

Examples:
❶ 这幅画不如那幅画逼真。
❷ 他不如这个画家有名。
❸ 他画的马不如徐悲鸿画的(那么)写意。
❹ 这幅山水画不如那幅油画(那么)写实。

Alternatively, you can use 没有 instead of 不如 in the same pattern: A + 没有 + B + (那么) + adjective.

Examples:
❶ 这里没有那里拥挤。
❷ 这家餐馆的食物没有那家的(那么)好吃。

Try This!

1. Use the expression 不如…(那么)… to compare the following pictures using the vocabulary words provided.

❶

色彩鲜艳

❷

活灵活现

❸ 栩栩如生

❹ 大

❺ 容易

❻ 吵

❼ 有营养

❽ 甜

2. Describe the two horse paintings below by completing the chart. Then, compare and contrast the two horse paintings and write two paragraphs about what you see in the paintings and how they are similar and different. Use comparative structures such as 不如···(那么)···, 没有···(那么)···, 跟···一样···, and 比.

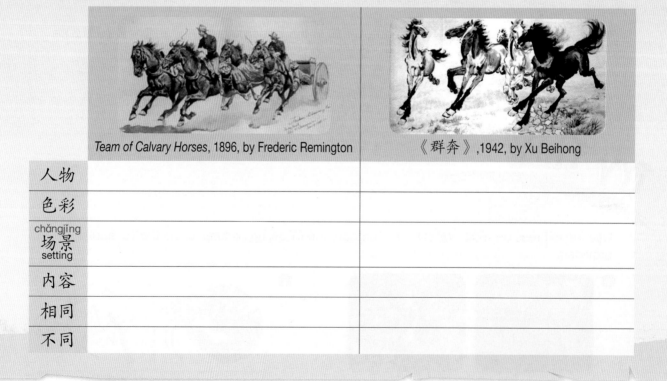

Team of Calvary Horses, 1896, by Frederic Remington　　　　《群奔》,1942, by Xu Beihong

人物		
色彩		
chǎngjǐng 场景 setting		
内容		
相同		
不同		

Blog

最近我除了喜欢上中国国画，也被中国书法吸引住了。我决定开始学习中国书法，王叔叔非常热心地教我。他说，凡是学书法的人，都要有"文房四宝"，那就是笔、墨、纸、砚。接着要根据自己喜欢的书法字体购买字帖。楷书是最规范、最通行的一种字体，也是最基础的，所以王叔叔建议我从楷书开始练习。

开始练习书法的时候，可以先练习基本的笔画，横、竖、撇、捺、点、提等，然后再练习部首，最后把部首和笔画放在字里一起练习。写毛笔字的时候千万不要心急，要静下心来一笔一画慢慢写。王叔叔说如果想要把毛笔字写好，就要坚持练习。最好每天抽出一点时间，练习至少一个小时。

fánshì 凡是 _adv._		every, any, all
jiēzhe 接着 _conj._	接著	next, thereafter
gēnjù 根据 _prep._	根據	according to, based on
zìtǐ 字体 _n._	字體	style of fonts
zìtiè 字帖 _n._		copybook for calligraphy
guīfàn 规范 _adj._	規範	standardized
tōngxíng 通行 _v._		current, general
jīchǔ 基础 _n._	基礎	foundation, basis
jīběn 基本 _adj._		basic
bùshǒu 部首 _n._		radical, compound of a character
xīnjí 心急 _adj._		anxious, impatient
chōuchū 抽出 _v._		set aside (time)
zhìshǎo 至少 _adv._		at least

书写的<u>姿势</u>很重要，王叔叔说，应该<u>挺直</u>坐着，全身各部位都要<u>自然</u>、轻松。我<u>按照</u>他的要求，坚持了不到十分钟就觉得好累！

<u>总的来说</u>，学习书法要有耐心与毅力。只要坚持每天练习，几个月后一定会有进步的。要是不信，你就试试看！

zīshì 姿势 *n.*	姿势	posture
tǐngzhí 挺直 *v.*		make upright
zìrán 自然 *adj.*		natural
ànzhào 按照 *v.*		follow
zǒng de lái shuō 总的来说 *conj.*	總的來說	in summary

EXTENDED VOCABULARY

Chinese calligraphy

文房四宝 *phr.*	文房四寶	wén fáng sì bǎo	four treasures of the study
笔 *n.*	筆	bǐ	calligraphic brush
墨 *n.*		mò	ink
纸 *n.*	紙	zhǐ	paper
砚 *n.*	硯	yàn	ink stone

Major Chinese scripts

龍	龍	龍		
kǎishū 楷书 *n.* 楷書 standard script	zhuànshū 篆书 *n.* 篆書 seal script	lìshū 隶书 *n.* 隸書 clerical script	xíngshú 行书 *n.* 行書 semi-cursive script	cǎoshū 草书 *n.* 草書 cursive script

244

Basic Chinese strokes

héng 横 *n.* 横 horizontal stroke	shù 竖 *n.* 竪 vertical stroke	piě 撇 *n.* left-falling stroke	nà 捺 *n.* right-falling stroke	diǎn 点 *n.* 點 dot	tí 提 *n.* upward stroke

LANGUAGE FOCUS

1. 凡是…都…

   The construction illustrates a relationship between a condition and a result. 凡是 is placed in the first clause to introduce the scope of a condition, while 都 is placed in the second clause to highlight a result that arises from the condition.

   Examples:
   ❶ 凡是学中国国画的人，都知道徐悲鸿是谁。

   ❷ 凡是去过北京 798 艺术区的人，应该都知道那里有个白石茶馆。

   ❸ 凡是到过这家店的人，都觉得里头的陈设很有特色。

2. Sequencing

   Sequencing refers to the order in which events and actions happen. 首先, 接着, 然后, 后来, and 最后 are some of the most common words to use for sequencing. Below is a list of sequencing words or phrases that will help you put ideas, storylines, events, or objects in a logical sequence.

Beginning	Middle/ Continuing	Interruption *(something unexpected)*	Ending
🦋 首先	🦋 然后	🦋 突然	🦋 最后
🦋 第一	🦋 接着	🦋 没想到	🦋 总的来说
🦋 有一天	🦋 其次		🦋 终于
🦋 从……开始	🦋 第二		
	🦋 另外		
	🦋 还有		
	🦋 之前		
	🦋 之后		

Holding the brush and strokes

This is the proper way to hold a brush for Chinese calligraphy. It is different from how you hold a pen or pencil. Pay attention to where you place your thumb and that you hold the brush upright.

握笔姿态

Here are the eight types of strokes that can be found in the character 永 (yǒng). Can you follow the stroke order in writing this character?

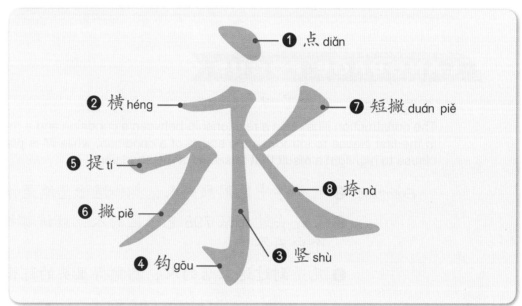

❶ 点 diǎn
❷ 横 héng
❼ 短撇 duǎn piě
❺ 提 tí
❽ 捺 nà
❻ 撇 piě
❹ 钩 gōu
❸ 竖 shù

Try This!

1. Research a Chinese artist that you are interested in. In a brief introduction to the class, tell your classmates his/her works and major accomplishments. Make sure your introduction contains at least five sentences. Use 凡是…都… in your sentences.

Example:

徐悲鸿是中国非常有名的画家。凡是中国人，都知道他是谁。他画的马很有特色，凡是看过他的画的人，都觉得那些马栩栩如生。他对中国的美术教育也有很大的影响。我觉得他是一个非常伟大的人物。

2. Complete the following sentences with actions that would follow a logical sequence.

❶ 考试以前，我先＿＿＿＿＿＿＿＿，接着＿＿＿＿＿＿＿＿，然后
＿＿＿＿＿＿＿＿，最后＿＿＿＿＿＿＿＿。

❷ 上学以前，我先＿＿＿＿＿＿＿＿，然后＿＿＿＿＿＿＿＿，接着
＿＿＿＿＿＿＿＿，最后＿＿＿＿＿＿＿＿。

❸ 睡觉前，我先＿＿＿＿＿＿＿＿，接着＿＿＿＿＿＿＿＿，然后
＿＿＿＿＿＿＿＿，最后＿＿＿＿＿＿＿＿。

❹ 参加铁人三项比赛以前，我首先＿＿＿＿＿＿＿＿，其次
＿＿＿＿＿＿＿＿，接着＿＿＿＿＿＿＿＿，最后＿＿＿＿＿＿＿＿。

❺ 去毕业舞会以前，我先＿＿＿＿＿＿＿＿，然后＿＿＿＿＿＿＿＿，
接着＿＿＿＿＿＿＿＿，最后＿＿＿＿＿＿＿＿。

❻ 吃晚饭前，我先＿＿＿＿＿＿＿＿，然后＿＿＿＿＿＿＿＿，接着
＿＿＿＿＿＿＿＿，最后＿＿＿＿＿＿＿＿。

❼ 去旅行以前，我首先＿＿＿＿＿＿＿＿，接着＿＿＿＿＿＿＿＿，
另外＿＿＿＿＿＿＿＿，最后＿＿＿＿＿＿＿＿。

❽ 运动以前，我首先＿＿＿＿＿＿＿＿，其次＿＿＿＿＿＿＿＿，接着
＿＿＿＿＿＿＿＿，最后＿＿＿＿＿＿＿＿。

❾ 去看奶奶以前，我先＿＿＿＿＿＿＿＿，然后＿＿＿＿＿＿＿＿，
然后＿＿＿＿＿＿＿＿，最后＿＿＿＿＿＿＿＿。

❿ 去逛街以前，我先＿＿＿＿＿＿＿＿，然后＿＿＿＿＿＿＿＿，接后
＿＿＿＿＿＿＿＿，最后＿＿＿＿＿＿＿＿。

3. Write an imaginary story or fairy tale and use the sequencing words from the language focus.

从……开始……然后……，
突然…………接着……。
最后………………………

CULTURAL HIGHLIGHTS

Seals and Seal Engraving

Seals are often stamped with red seal paste onto works of Chinese painting and calligraphy. The seal may give the name of the artist or his studio, the collector, or other private individuals.

The seal was originally used as a signature or sign of authority, but it eventually came to be used by all social classes and in much of Asia. The Seal Engravers' Society of Xiling in Zhejiang Province was founded a century ago and works to preserve the art of seal engraving.

The design of the seal is first sketched on paper, and then engraved on stone in reverse with a knife. In addition to having to master traditional calligraphy, the art of engraving requires a high degree of dexterity, since the artist works on a tiny surface area where every curve and every thickness of line counts. The very diverse motifs are the fruit of the artist's imagination and culture.

As an instrument of calligraphy and painting, the seal is a work of art in itself. Today, seals continue to be used in official documents and sometimes in private correspondence. Although the number of people who actually understand the complex characters used in seal engraving is decreasing, the art of seal engraving is still practiced by professionals and amateurs alike.

丁强：王叔叔，中国有哪些有名的书法家？

王叔叔：中国历史上有很多有名的书法家，如王羲之 (303 – 361)、颜真卿 (709 – 784) 等，他们都在书法艺术上取得很高的成就。
Wáng Xīzhī (303 – 361)、颜真卿 Yán Zhēnqīng (709 – 784)

丁强：哦，我在网上读过关于王羲之的故事。据说，为了把字练好，他每天都练习书法，即使在休息的时候，也在揣摩字体的结构、笔画的气势。

王叔叔：王羲之是东晋时期有名的书法家，有"书圣"之称。他擅长隶、草、楷、行各体，风格自成一家，影响深远。他的代表作《兰亭序》被称为"天下第一行书"，其中有二十一个"之"字，每个都各具特色，没有一个是相同的。

chuǎimó 揣摩 v.		try to figure out
jiégòu 结构 n.	結構	structure
qìshì 气势 n.	氣勢	force, energy
Dōng Jìn 东晋 n.	東晉	Eastern Jin Dynasty
shūshèng 书圣 n.	書聖	sage of calligraphy
shàncháng 擅长 v.	擅長	be good at
zì chéng yì jiā 自成一家 phr.		have a unique or original style
shēnyuǎn 深远 adj.	深遠	far-reaching
Lántíng Xù 兰亭序 n.	蘭亭序	Preface to the Poems Composed at the Orchid Pavilion

Preface to the Poems Composed at the Orchid Pavilion, by Wang Xizhi

丁强：太神奇了！我可要上网看看他的作品。那颜真卿呢？

王叔叔：颜真卿是唐代 杰出的书法家。他的书法精妙，擅长行、楷，还自创"颜体"楷书。

丁强：哇，这么厉害，还能自创字体。看来我得多练习，说不定以后可以自创"丁体"书法。

王叔叔：哈哈哈哈！

shénqí 神奇 adj.		amazing
Táng dài 唐代 n.		Tang Dynasty
jiéchū 杰出 adj.	傑出	outstanding
jīngmiào 精妙 adj.		exquisite
lìhai 厉害 adj.	厲害	formidable

LANGUAGE FOCUS

When making a statement about doing something for a specific reason or for someone, as in the expression "for the sake of," we say in Chinese 为了. Look at the following sentences and see how it is used.

- 为了学好书法，他向许多有名的书法家学习。
- 为了把马画得活灵活现，徐悲鸿花了很长的时间练习画马。
- 为了维持健康，我们应该多运动。
- 为了这个比赛，你要努力锻炼。

Try This!

1. Match the sentences.

❶ 为了把字练好，　　　　　　　• a. 你应该少吃肉。

❷ 为了降低你的血压，　　　　　• b. 丁强天天都在家里练习书法。

❸ 为了不拉伤你的肌肉，　　　　• c. 我参加了国画班。

❹ 为了学习国画，　　　　　　　• d. 你应该在运动前做拉伸运动。

⑤ 为了缓解工作的压力， •

• e. 你得让自己有充足的睡眠。

⑥ 为了考到好成绩， •

• f. 齐白石天天都练习画虾。

⑦ 为了使精神变好一些， •

• g. 你应该多练瑜伽和普拉提。

⑧ 为了把虾画好， •

• h. 子明每天都很努力地学习。

2. Research a famous Chinese painter or calligrapher. In particular, find out the efforts he/she put in that enabled him/her to master painting or calligraphy writing. Create a simple introduction of at least five sentences that describe the artist. Use 为了 in your sentences.

地书

地书, which literally means writing calligraphy on the ground or writing street calligraphy, is a popular, eco-friendly, and convenient way to learn Chinese calligraphy. It is a grassroots approach to practicing calligraphy that does not pollute the environment and has spread throughout much of China. All day long, you can see people writing on the ground in the parks in Beijing, Shanghai, Xi'an, Hangzhou, Suzhou, and other major cities.

The writers or participants are mostly retirees and children, but sometimes, older adults also join in. Because of the advances of technology, writing is becoming a lost art. However, through 地书, the older generation of Chinese is passing on a cultural skill to the younger generation.

地书 is viewed as a cultural movement to save, protect, and pass down the tradition of Chinese calligraphy. It brings people together and serves as a leisure activity while providing an interpersonal connection. So, if you go to China, be sure to find someone in the park to tutor you in calligraphy.

A Experiencing the Chinese teahouse

xiǎochī 小吃 *n.*		street snack
bǎoliú 保留 *v.*		preserve
céng 层 *m.w.*	層	level, story *(of a building)*
sìhéyuàn 四合院 *n.*		Chinese quadrangles
yǎnyì dàtīng 演艺大厅 *n.*	演藝大廳	performing arts theater
lóutī 楼梯 *n.*	樓梯	staircase
chúchuāng 橱窗 *n.*	櫥窗	display window
zìhuà 字画 *n.*	字畫	calligraphy and painting
cháhú 茶壶 *n.*	茶壺	teapot
jīngjù 京剧 *n.*	京劇	Peking opera
liǎnpǔ 脸谱 *n.*	臉譜	mask
chūfā 出发 *v.*	出發	set off

子明：丁强，今天我们要带你去一个有趣的地方。

丁强：嗯？是什么有趣的地方啊？

李阿姨：是老舍茶馆！ <small>Lǎo Shě</small>

丁强：是茶馆？那是喝茶的地方吗？

王叔叔：是的，我们不但可以喝茶，还可以吃北京小吃。老舍茶馆保留了北京丰富的民间文化，所以吸引了很多游客。

李阿姨：老舍茶馆是一个三层楼的四合院，一楼是餐厅，二楼是茶馆，三楼是演艺大厅。楼梯边挂了很多名人和明星的照片。橱窗里展示的都是些老北京特有的东西，比如字画、茶壶和京剧脸谱。

丁强：听起来很有意思。我们什么时候出发？

（老舍茶馆上演相声）

丁强：子明，这两个人在台上做什么？

子明：丁强！这就是相声，难道你没看
　　　过吗？简单来说，就是两个人的
　　　脱口秀，两个人一起讲笑话。

丁强：哇！真有趣，两个人你一句我一句
　　　很有意思呢！

王叔叔：快看，接着就是我最喜欢看的京剧
　　　表演。

xiàngsheng 相声 *n.*	相聲	crosstalk
tuōkǒuxiù 脱口秀 *n.*	脫口秀	talk show
xiàohua 笑话 *n.*	笑話	joke
jiùsuàn...yě... 就算…也…		even if...

（老舍茶馆上演京剧）

丁强：这是我第一次看京剧，他们都在唱
　　　什么？我一点也听不懂！

子明：没关系，京剧的唱法和普通的唱歌
　　　很不一样。就算是中国人，也不一
　　　定听得懂京剧。

李阿姨：好啦，都别说了，我们一起欣赏演
　　　出吧。

LANGUAGE FOCUS

就算…也… expresses the meaning of "even if." 就算 is placed in the first clause to introduce a condition. 也 is placed in the second clause to describe a situation that will take place regardless of the condition in the first clause.

Examples: ❶ 丁强平日就算课业非常繁重，也会抽出时间来练字。

❷ 就算你熬夜赶作业，也做不完。

❸ 就算你不喜欢蔬菜，也不可以完全不吃。

1. Complete the following sentences.

❶ 就算明天下雨，_____。

❷ 就算你这次考试成绩很好，_____。

❸ 就算有困难，_____。

❹ 就算他当时在这里，_____。

❺ _____，我也要把报告赶完。

❻ _____，我们也不能停止训练。

❼ _____，她也会这么做。

❽ _____，也不应该动手打人。

2. Answer the following questions based on the dialog in Step 3A.

❶ 为什么老舍茶馆吸引了很多游客？

❷ 餐厅在老舍茶馆的哪一层楼？

❸ 橱窗里展示哪些东西？

❹ 老舍茶馆是一个什么样的地方？

❺ 什么是中国相声？

❻ 要是你去北京，你想去老舍茶馆吗？为什么？

 CULTURAL HIGHLIGHTS

Lao She

Lao She (老舍, 1899–1966), whose real name was Shu Qingchun (舒庆春), is a famous Chinese novelist and dramatist. He was well known for his novel *Camel Xiangzi* (骆驼祥子), also called *Rickshaw* in the United States, and the play *Teahouse*. This is the reason why Lao She Teahouse, a teahouse with cultural displays and performances at Qianmen in Beijing, is named after him.

Lao She served as a visiting professor of Chinese in both the United States and in England. He demonstrated his linguistic talents of the Beijing dialect by employing them skillfully in his works. In addition to *Camel Xiangzi* and *Teahouse*, other famous works created by Lao She include *Dragon's Beard Ditch, Crescent Moon, City of Cats, The Yellow Storm*, and the *Drum Singers*. Unfortunately, because of the persecution during the Cultural Revolution, he committed suicide by drowning. He was posthumously rehabilitated in 1979 and his complete works are now fully available.

Blog

昨天晚上我跟王叔叔一家人在梅兰芳大剧院看了一出京剧。王叔叔告诉我，京剧是中国的戏曲艺术，是文学、诗歌、唱腔、伴奏以及服装、化妆与表演艺术的大综合，因此京剧演员除了会唱和会念独白以外，还要结合表演、舞蹈和武术各方面的才能。京剧的角色类型，主要是根据剧中人物的性别、年龄、身份、地位、性格、气质来划分的。主要的京剧角色有生（男）、旦（女）、净（男）丑（男女都有）四大角色。每一个角色，都有特定的发声方法和表演方式。

Méi Lánfāng

王叔叔最崇拜的京剧演员是中国戏曲大师梅兰芳(1894-1961)先生。梅先生擅长反串，虽然他是男性演员，却能把花旦的角色演得很好。他1930年曾经到美国表演，他美丽的装扮、

jùyuàn 剧院 n.	劇院		opera theater
chū 出 m.w.	齣		(used for plays, etc.)
xìqǔ 戏曲 n.	戲曲		opera
wénxué 文学 n.	文學		literature
chàngqiāng 唱腔 n.			singing style
huàzhuāng 化妆 n.;v.	化妝		makeup; put on makeup
zōnghé 综合 v.	綜合		integrate
yīncǐ 因此 conj.			therefore, so
dúbái 独白 n.	獨白		monolog
cáinéng 才能 n.			capability
juésè 角色 n.	頓		role
huàfēn 划分 v.	劃分		divide
tèdìng 特定 adj.			specially designated
fāshēng 发声 v.	發聲		project one's voice
fāngfǎ 方法 n.			method, way
chóngbài 崇拜 v.			adore, admire
fǎnchuàn 反串 v.			play opposite gender in a play
zhuāngbàn 装扮 n.;v.	裝扮		attire; dress up

255

温柔的声音和优雅的动作，一出场就吸引了所有观众的好奇 目光。梅兰芳的演出，让人难以相信一位男演员可以把一个女性角色扮演得这么逼真。子明说下一次要带我去看电影《梅兰芳》，我很期待，希望能对这位中国的戏曲大师有多一些了解。

wēnróu			
温柔 adj.	温柔		gentle
yōuyǎ			
优雅 adj.	優雅		graceful
dòngzuò			
动作 n.	動作		movement, action
hàoqí			
好奇 adj.			curious
mùguāng			
目光 n.			look, gaze
nán yǐ xiāngxìn			
难以相信 phr.	難以相信		unbelievable
bànyǎn			
扮演 v.			play a role, act

EXTENDED VOCABULARY

Different aspects of a person

性别 n.		xìngbié	gender
年龄 n.	年齡	niánlíng	age
身份 n.		shēnfèn	identity
地位 n.		dìwèi	status
性格 n.		xìnggé	personality
气质 n.	氣質	qìzhì	disposition, qualities

Main role categories in Peking opera

生 n.		shēng	male roles
旦 n.		dàn	female roles
净 n.	淨	jìng	painted-face role
丑 n.	醜	chǒu	painted-face role

LANGUAGE FOCUS

In order to show a type of cause and effect that is equivalent to the English "therefore, as a result of, as a consequence of something," use the conjunction 因此. It is usually placed in the second part of a sentence.

Examples:
❶ 梅兰芳能把花旦的角色演得很好，因此非常有名。
❷ 齐白石的画有很高的艺术成就，因此价格都很高。
❸ 王羲之的书法对后代影响深远，因此被称为"书圣"。

256

1. Complete the following sentences with a logical conclusion using 因此.

   ❶ 书法写得好不容易，_____。

   ❷ 他不想一个人呆在家里，_____。

   ❸ 丁强对京剧很感兴趣，_____。

   ❹ 我有点不舒服，_____。

   ❺ 国画是中国的国粹，_____。

   ❻ 徐悲鸿在巴黎学过画，_____。

   ❼ 王羲之小时候天天都练字，_____。

   ❽ 他想学好中文，_____。

2. Answer the following questions based on Ding Qiang's blog in Step 3B.

   ❶ 京剧的角色的类型是怎么划分的？

   ❷ 主要的京剧角色有哪些？

   ❸ 王叔叔最崇拜的京剧演员是谁？

   ❹ 戏曲大师梅兰芳什么时候到过美国演出？

   ❺ 为什么梅兰芳一出场就吸引了观众的好奇目光？

Step Up!

1. Imagine that you are responsible for creating a virtual tour of one wing of a new Chinese museum. You will decide if you want to showcase painting, calligraphy, or Chinese opera. You may choose another Chinese art form not studied in this chapter. Create a PowerPoint of at least 10 slides that shows some of the art that will be in the wing of this museum and explain each work of art using at least two sentences to provide information about the art work or the artist. Use the vocabulary words you have learned in this lesson and appropriate structures such as 既⋯也⋯, 凡是⋯都⋯, 为了⋯⋯, 就算⋯也⋯, and 因此⋯⋯.

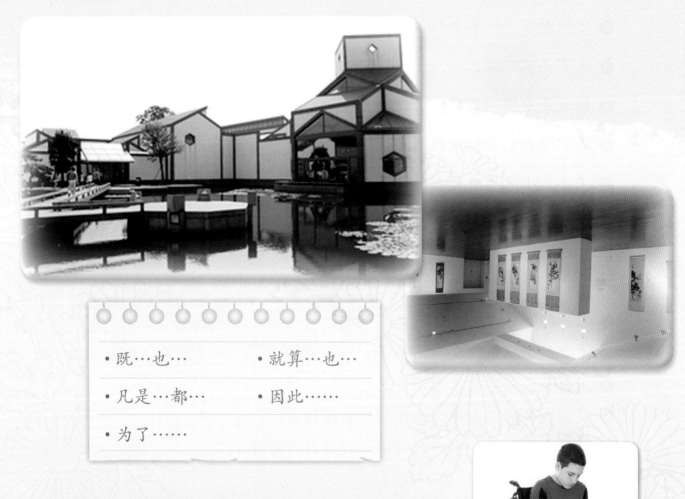

- 既⋯也⋯   - 就算⋯也⋯

- 凡是⋯都⋯   - 因此⋯⋯

- 为了⋯⋯

2. Once you have created the PowerPoint, write up a short quiz that tests some of the knowledge that students should have learned when viewing the PowerPoint. Ask students in your class to view the PowerPoint and then take the quiz.

3. With another student in the class, view both your PowerPoints and at least two other PowerPoints that students in the class have created. Then discuss with that student which of the four PowerPoints you like the best. Discuss reasons why you prefer one over the other. Come to a consensus as to which PowerPoint you like best.

Fun Time!

Along the River During the Qingming Festival (清明上河图) was painted during the Song Dynasty by the artist Zhang Zeduan (张择端, 1085–1145). The original painting is 25.5 centimeters (10 inches) in height and 5.25 meters (5.74 yards) in length. In total there are 814 people, 28 boats, 60 animals, 30 buildings, 20 vehicles, 8 sedan chairs, and 170 trees that you see in the painting. Look at a section of the painting below. How many of each item can you find in the picture?

I have learned...

Verbs

据说	據說	jùshuō	it is said	按照		ànzhào	follow
临摹	臨摹	línmó	copy from, facsimile	揣摩		chuǎimó	try to figure out
观察	觀察	guānchá	observe, watch	擅长	擅長	shàncháng	be good at
写生	寫生	xiěshēng	sketching from real life	保留		bǎoliú	preserve
展现		zhǎnxiàn	unfold before one's eyes, present	出发	出發	chūfā	set off
创作	創作	chuàngzuò	create, produce	化妆	化妝	huàzhuāng	put on makeup
篆刻		zhuànkè	carving the seal	综合	綜合	zōnghé	integrate
素描		sùmiáo	sketch	划分	劃分	huàfēn	divide
不如		bùrú	not as good as	发声	發聲	fāshēng	project one's voice
体现	體現	tǐxiàn	express, demonstrate	崇拜		chóngbài	adore, admire
通行		tōngxíng	current, general	反串		fǎnchuàn	play opposite gender in a play
抽出		chōuchū	set aside *(time)*	装扮	裝扮	zhuāngbàn	dress up
挺直		tǐngzhí	make upright	扮演		bànyǎn	play a role, act

Nouns

茶馆	茶館	cháguǎn	teahouse	虫	蟲	chóng	insect
茶具		chájù	tea set	兽	獸	shòu	animal
陈设	陳設	chénshè	set up as a display, furnish	世人		shìrén	common people
国画	國畫	guóhuà	Chinese painting	创作	創作	chuàngzuò	creative work, creation
大师	大師	dàshī	master	作品		zuòpǐn	work
竹子		zhúzi	bamboo	诗歌	詩歌	shīgē	poem, poetry
国粹	國粹	guócuì	national treasure	笔墨	筆墨	bǐmò	strokes and brushes
珍宝	珍寶	zhēnbǎo	treasure	写意	寫意	xiěyì	spontaneous expression
毛笔	毛筆	máobǐ	calligraphic brush	生命力		shēngmìnglì	vitality
山水		shānshuǐ	mountains and rivers, landscape	八骏图	八駿圖	Bā Jùn Tú	*The Eight Horses*
人物		rénwù	person, subject	字体	字體	zìtǐ	style of fonts

字帖		zìtiè	copybook for calligraphy	字画	字畫	zìhuà	calligraphy and painting
基础	基礎	jīchǔ	foundation, basis	茶壶	茶壺	cháhú	teapot
部首		bùshǒu	radical, compound of a character	京剧	京劇	jīngjù	Peking opera
姿势	姿勢	zīshì	posture	脸谱	臉譜	liǎnpǔ	mask
笔	筆	bǐ	calligraphic brush	相声	相聲	xiàngsheng	crosstalk
墨		mò	ink	脱口秀	脫口秀	tuōkǒuxiù	talk show
纸	紙	zhǐ	paper	笑话	笑話	xiàohua	joke
砚	硯	yàn	ink stone	剧院	劇院	jùyuàn	opera theater
楷书	楷書	kǎishū	standard script	戏曲	戲曲	xìqǔ	opera
篆书	篆書	zhuànshū	seal script	文学	文學	wénxué	literature
隶书	隸書	lìshū	clerical script	化妆	化妝	huàzhuāng	makeup
行书	行書	xíngshú	semi-cursive script	唱腔		chàngqiāng	singing style
草书	草書	cǎoshū	cursive script	独白	獨白	dúbái	monolog
横	橫	héng	horizontal stroke	才能		cáinéng	capability
竖	豎	shù	vertical stroke	角色		juésè	role
撇		piě	left-falling stroke	装扮	妝扮	zhuāngbàn	attire
捺		nà	right-falling stroke	方法		fāngfǎ	method, way
点	點	diǎn	dot	动作	動作	dòngzuò	movement, action
提		tí	upward stroke	目光		mùguāng	look, gaze
结构	結構	jiégòu	structure	性别		xìngbié	gender
气势	氣勢	qìshì	force, energy	年龄	年齡	niánlíng	age
东晋	東晉	Dōng Jìn	Eastern Jin Dynasty	身份		shēnfèn	identity
书圣	書聖	shūshèng	sage of calligraphy	地位		dìwèi	status
兰亭序	蘭亭序	Lántíng Xù	*Preface to the Poems Composed at the Orchid Pavilion*	性格		xìnggé	personality
唐代		Táng dài	Tang Dynasty	气质	氣質	qìzhì	disposition, qualities
小吃		xiǎochī	street snack	生		shēng	male roles
四合院		sìhéyuàn	Chinese quadrangles	旦		dàn	female roles
演艺大厅	演藝大廳	yǎnyì dàtīng	performing arts theater	净	淨	jìng	painted-face role
楼梯	樓梯	lóutī	staircase	丑	醜	chǒu	painted-face role
橱窗	櫥窗	chúchuāng	display window				

Adjectives

写实	寫實	xiěshí	*(of art style)* realistic	到位		dàowèi	satisfactory
具体	具體	jùtǐ	specific	逼真		bīzhēn	life-like

规范	規範	guīfàn	standardized	精妙		jīngmiào	exquisite
基本		jīběn	basic	厉害		lìhai	formidable
心急		xīnjí	anxious, impatient	特定		tèdìng	specially designated
自然		zìrán	natural	温柔	溫柔	wēnróu	gentle
深远	深遠	shēnyuǎn	far-reaching	优雅	優雅	yōuyǎ	graceful
神奇		shénqí	amazing	好奇		hàoqí	curious
杰出	傑出	jiéchū	outstanding				

Phrases

栩栩如生		xǔ xǔ rú shēng	have a life-like resemblance	文房四宝	文房四寶	wén fáng sì bǎo	four treasures of the study
活灵活现	活靈活現	huó líng huó xiàn	vivid, lively	自成一家		zì chéng yì jiā	have a unique or original style
大名鼎鼎		dà míng dǐng dǐng	renowned, well-known	难以相信	難以相信	nán yǐ xiāngxìn	unbelievable

Adverbs

尤其		yóuqí	especially	凡是		fánshì	every, any, all
光		guāng	just	至少	頓	zhìshào	at least

Conjunctions

接着	接著	jiēzhe	next, thereafter
总的来说	總的來說	zǒng de lái shuō	in summary
因此		yīncǐ	therefore, so

Constructions

既…也…	jì...yě...	both...and, as well as
就算…也…	jiùsuàn...yě...	even if...

Preposition

根据	根據	gēnjù	according to, based on

Measure words

层	層	céng	level, story *(of a building)*
出	齣	chū	*(used for plays, etc.)*

◇ SENTENCE PATTERNS ◇

国画<u>既</u>是中国的国粹，<u>也</u>是世界的珍宝。

徐悲鸿的马虽然细节上<u>不如</u>素描那么具体，但是马的生命力却体现得非常到位。

<u>凡是</u>学书法的人，<u>都</u>要有"文房四宝"。

<u>为了</u>把字练好，王羲之每天都练习书法。

<u>就算</u>是中国人，<u>也</u>不一定听得懂京剧。

梅兰芳能把花旦的角色演得很好，<u>因此</u>非常有名。

I can do!

Interpretive Communication

❏ I can read about Chinese cultural treasures and decipher meaning.

❏ I can understand when someone tells me about events in a sequence.

❏ I can understand when I read about works of art.

Interpersonal Communication

❏ I can express opinions of various Chinese works of art.

❏ I can converse about Chinese performing arts.

❏ I can communicate about sequential events.

Presentational Communication

❏ I can prepare a presentation on Chinese works of art.

❏ I can compare and contrast different artists and their works.

❏ I can speak about the Chinese art scene.

❏ I can sequence events in an oral and written presentation.

❏ I can write paragraphs with cohesive ideas.

Cultural Knowledge

❏ I can describe the Beijing 798 Art Zone.

❏ I can talk about the uses of seals and how a seal is engraved.

❏ I can state some of the major works of Lao She.

❏ I can expand on information about various Chinese cultural treasures.

❏ I can explain different forms of Chinese performing arts.

The changing society in China

变化中的中国社会

COMMUNICATIVE GOALS

- Discussing changing lifestyles because of new technology

- Stating and analyzing opinions on solutions to problems in urban life

- Describing one's past and current experiences

- Expressing and explaining one's current decisions and aspirations for the future

Cultural Knowledge

- China's digital natives
- The Chinese government's response to pollution
- Public telephones in China
- The Chinese subway system
- China's future developments

Get ready...

Do you know how many digital citizens there are in China now? Take a look at the table below which shows the number of digital citizens in various major Chinese cities and provinces and other related information. Think about two reasons for the increase of digital citizens in China from 2013 - 2014. Write your reasons and then turn to your partner to see if you both have the same opinions. Share your answers with the class and survey the class to find the top three reasons.

City / Province	Digital citizens (millions)	Percentage of citizens	Rate of increase 2013-2014	Ranking in terms of percentage
Beijing	15.93	75.3%	2.4%	①
Shanghai	17.16	71.1%	2.0%	②
Guangdong	72.86	68.5%	4.2%	③
Fujian	24.71	65.5%	2.9%	④
Zhejiang	34.58	62.9%	3.9%	⑤
Tianjin	9.04	61.4%	4.4%	⑥
Liaoning	25.8	58.8%	5.2%	⑦
Jiangsu	42.74	53.8%	4.4%	⑧
Shanxi	18.38	50.6%	4.7%	⑨
Xinjiang	11.39	50.3%	4.2%	⑩

Source: http://www.phb123.com/city/renkou/3022.html

STEPS *at a glance!*

USING MODERN TECHNOLOGY

A. Changing habits and preferences

有的人宁可在家里和朋友网上聊天，也不愿意出门和朋友面对面交流。

B. Living in the digital age

面对面有面对面的优点，而微信聊天则有微信聊天的好处。

EXPERIENCING LIFESTYLE CHANGES IN CHINA

A. Protecting the environment

大家再不正视环境污染问题，我们的健康就会受到很大的影响。

B. Addressing urban issues

北京必须改变现状，要不然交通拥挤问题会更加严重。

REALIZING MY CHINESE DREAM

A. Having fond memories of China

自从来到中国，我就越来越喜欢这里的风土人情了。

B. Expressing my aspirations

我希望将来可以在北京工作。

A Changing habits and preferences

新科技改变了我们的生活方式。现在买东西、打车、叫外卖、买火车票、飞机票等都可以在手机APP上完成。同时，大家也越来越依赖互联网，互联网上的社交活动也越来越多。现在几乎每个中国人都使用微信，大家喜欢自拍，每天在朋友圈里晒自己的生活。很有趣的是，很多人吃饭的时候，宁可饿着肚子，也要先用手机把所有的菜都拍下来放上网，然后才开始吃饭。当人们晒出自己的生活后，朋友圈里的好朋友还会给自己点赞。晒朋友圈和点赞成为大家社交的一部分。有的人甚至宁可在家里和朋友网上聊天，也不愿意出门和朋友面对面 交流。

每天出门，需要打车的时候，很多人会打开打车 APP "滴滴打车"（Dīdī），要不就是 "优步"（Uber），只要在屏幕上点 "我要用车"，输入 目的地，周边 的司机

wàimài 外卖 n.	外賣	take out
yīlài 依赖 v.	依賴	depend on, rely on
shèjiāo 社交 n.		social contact
jīhū 几乎 adv.	幾乎	almost
zìpāi 自拍 v.		take a selfie
nìngkě 宁可 conj.	寧可	would rather
diǎnzàn 点赞 phr.	點讚	to "like" (on social media)
shènzhì 甚至 conj.		even to the extent that
miànduìmiàn 面对面 phr.	面對面	face to face
jiāoliú 交流 v.		interact
píngmù 屏幕 n.		screen
shūrù 输入 v.	輸入	enter, key in
mùdìdì 目的地 n.		destination
zhōubiān 周边 n.	周邊	nearby, surrounding

师傅就会接单，到乘客所在的地点接他们，把他们送到目的地。

当人们需要出去吃饭时，他们会在手机上查询"离我最近的餐馆"或者是"点评最好的餐馆"，这样的信息对他们来说非常有用！当然，如果不想出去吃饭，也不想自己在家做饭，也可以通过手机APP叫外卖，非常方便。有的人宁可天天叫外卖，也不愿意到餐馆去吃饭。

总之，新科技将人们的生活变得越来越便利了！

shīfu 师傅 *n.*	師傅	*(respectful form of address for a skilled worker)*
jiēdān 接单 *phr.*	接單	receive an order
chéngkè 乘客 *n.*		passenger
cháxún 查询 *v.*	查詢	inquire
diǎnpíng 点评 *v.*	點評	review

LANGUAGE FOCUS

1. 宁可···也不··· (would rather...than...)

   宁可···也不··· expresses one's wish or preference by comparison. It is used in situations where the speaker compares two unfavorable options and chooses the less unfavorable option over the more unfavorable one. The first clause states the preferred option with 宁可 before the verb, and the second clause indicates the alternative with 也不.

   Examples: 他宁可帮妈妈做家务，也不做今天的作业。

   我宁可饿肚子，也不吃这么难吃的菜。

2. 宁可···也要··· (would rather...in order to...)

   宁可···也要··· expresses the idea that the action indicated in the first clause is chosen in order to achieve the result indicated in the second clause. In this case, the speaker is willing to pay a price in order to complete or gain something.

   Examples: 子明宁可晚上不睡觉，也要把今天的功课做完。

   丁强宁可不看今天的足球比赛，也要准备明天的考试。

Try This!

1. Match the following sentences containing 宁可…也不… and 宁可…也要….

❶ 他宁可走路去餐馆，   •   • a. 也不想上学迟到。 chí dào be late

❷ 马克宁可每天早一点起床，   •   • b. 也不要自己准备晚餐。

❸ 她宁可叫外卖，   •   • c. 也不打电话叫车。

❹ 子明宁可用手机APP叫车，   •   • d. 也不打车去餐馆。

❺ 丁强宁可不吃饭，   •   • e. 也要把钱省下来买手机。

❻ 张健宁可花多一点时间策划， •   • f. 也要把作业做完。 cèhuà plan

❼ 他宁可每餐吃面包，   •   • g. 也要把书法学好。

❽ 我宁可天天练字，   •   • h. 也要帮朋友办一个特别的生日会。

2. Imagine your friend is addicted to the Internet or a technological gadget. Working with a partner, describe to him/her the extent of your friend's addiction. Your description should contain at least five sentences. Use 宁可…也不… and 宁可…也要… in your sentences.

Example:

> 我的朋友大卫天天都玩电脑游戏。他宁可不吃饭，也要玩电脑游戏。有时一天可以玩十多个小时。他宁可一整天呆在家里，也不愿意停止玩电脑游戏。他的家人都很为他担心。

B Living in the digital age

爷爷：哎呀，子明！别看手机了，你看你们这些年轻人，一个个都变成了低头族！

子明：嘿嘿，不这样不行啊！好多朋友回复我的朋友圈，还给我点赞，所以我需要回复他们！

爷爷：你们宁可在手机上聊一整天，也不出去和大家见面聊，现在的社交怎么这么离不开手机呀？

子明：是呀！大家现在都喜欢在朋友圈分享自己生活的点滴，也可以在微信群里讨论、沟通一些事情。爷爷，你也应该开始用微信，再不用就跟不上时代了！

爷爷：你们都喜欢用微信交流，但我却觉得面对面聊天、讨论更好。

子明：面对面有面对面的优点，而微信聊天则有微信聊天的好处。有时候，发朋友圈就像写日记一样，也是记录自己生活的一种方式。

爷爷：听起来也有点道理。

dītóuzú 低头族 *n.*	低頭族	phone addicts
huífù 回复 *v.*	回復	reply
diǎndī 点滴 *n.*	點滴	bits of information
shídài 时代 *n.*	時代	era
yōudiǎn 优点 *n.*	優點	strength, advantage
ér 而 *conj.*		but, on the other hand
zé 则 *conj.*	則	*(used to indicate contrast)*
rìjì 日记 *n.*	日記	diary
dàolǐ 道理 *n.*		sense, truth

子明：是呀，爷爷！你还记得今年过年时候大家用微信"发红包"吗？多有趣啊！<u>摇</u>一摇微信，就可以<u>抢</u>到红包！还有最近非常火的"微信运动"，走路时可以记录步数还能排名，大家都在玩呢！爷爷，你不是每天都要走一万步吗？可以通过微信记录呢！

爷爷：高科技真是越来越<u>神</u>了！好的，我就听你的，也下载一个微信！

yáo 摇 v.	摇	shake
qiǎng 抢 v.	搶	snatch
shén 神 adj.		brilliant, smart

LANGUAGE FOCUS

…而…则… can be used to indicate contrast and means "while" in English. It is placed in the second clause to introduce a situation that contrasts with the situation in the first clause. In the second clause, 而 is followed by a second subject and 则 is followed by a second verb. Look at the examples to see how it is used.

Examples: ❶ 芳芳喜欢发微信，而玛丽则喜欢网购。

❷ 他觉得快餐很好吃，而我则觉得快餐不健康。

❸ 在中国，年轻人去健身房锻炼身体，而老年人则喜欢在公园里锻炼身体。

 CULTURAL HIGHLIGHTS

China's Digital Natives

Technology has changed the lives of young people all over the world, from texting to gaming and even video sharing. Young people born in the 21st century have grown up in a digital age and use information and communication technologies (ICTs) in their daily lives. This group of networked young people is often referred to as digital natives. Digital media have changed how young people learn, play, socialize, and participate in life. Modern China is no different. Of the top 10 countries with large numbers of "digital natives," China is the country with the most, having over 75 million. The United States is the second largest country with over 42 million. Next in line come India (22+ million) and Brazil (20+ million).

Online shopping is very big with digital natives, but is especially popular in China. More than 46% of young people in China say they use online ordering and delivery services. Over 60% of Chinese use digital retailing options compared to 52% in North America. Digitization in China has affected everything from shopping to entertainment. Many young Chinese would rather watch movies or television programs online than on a movie or TV screen.

Try This!

1. Finish the second half of the sentences by using ···而···则··· to indicate contrast.

   ❶ 芳芳认为微信聊天是很好的社交方式，_____。

   ❷ 我父母喜欢在公园跑步锻炼身体，_____。

   ❸ 现在很多年轻人都不喜欢做饭，喜欢到餐馆吃饭，_____。

   ❹ 很多人相信中医的疗效，_____。

   ❺ 大部分人出门就打车，_____。

   ❻ 很多学生把大部分时间花在网上，看视频、聊天，_____。

   ❼ 很多西方人喜欢中国美食，_____。

   ❽ 张健每天坐地铁上学，_____。

2. Interview at least five of your classmates to find out their views on the role of technology, the Internet, or social media in modern life. Report your findings to the class. Use the vocabulary you have learned so far in this lesson. Where possible, contrast their views with yours using ···而···则···.

   Example:

   > 芳芳和玛丽都觉得互联网对我们很重要，我们的生活几乎离不开互联网。马克觉得现代科技让生活变得非常便利，而我则认为我们现在太依赖现代科技了……

Public Telephones in China

With the advent of cell phones, we have seen the disappearance of public telephones all over the world. Public telephones used to exist on the streets, and even in restaurants and stores. In China today, it is still possible to find some public phones, but you have to know how to identify them. Some are just sitting on a counter; in some hutongs in Beijing the phones may even be on a window sill. To use the phone, you hand the proprietor the phone number and he/she dials for you and then hands you the receiver. Often, there is a gadget fixed to the phone which times your call so that you pay according to how long you talk. There is one such center in Wangfujing in Beijing with just the word "Telephone" on the doorway. When you enter, you will see a small table on which are two phones attended usually by a young lady.

A Protecting the environment

李伟：子明，这周的生物课要做关于"如何平衡经济发展和环境保护"的课题。你有什么想法吗？

子明：我们可以讨论中国在经济发展和环境保护面临的机遇和挑战。

李伟：这个主意不错。现在中国在这方面的确面临着很多的问题和困难。

子明：我们可以从中国现在面临的环境问题入手。比如北京周边排污量很大的那些工厂是导致雾霾的罪魁祸首；江苏太湖污染，影响当地生态平衡，等等。

李伟：如果只讨论环境保护问题就太片面了。我觉得要是能再考虑到中国也需要发展经济这一方面，观点就会更加完整一些。比如，发展经济需要利用环境资源，工厂排污是发展工业初期不可避免的。毕竟，中国现在还有很多贫困地区，经济发展是必须的。

rúhé 如何 *pron.*		how
kètí 课题 *n.*	課題	topic
miànlín 面临 *v.*	面臨	be faced with, be confronted with
jīyù 机遇 *n.*	機遇	opportunity
rùshǒu 入手 *v.*		start with, proceed from
dǎozhì 导致 *v.*	導致	lead to, result in
wùmái 雾霾 *n.*	霧霾	smog
zuì kuí huò shǒu 罪魁祸首 *phr.*	罪魁禍首	culprit
shēngtài 生态 *n.*	生態	ecology
piànmiàn 片面 *adj.*		one-sided, lopsided
guāndiǎn 观点 *n.*	觀點	perspective, point of view
wánzhěng 完整 *adj.*		complete
bìjìng 毕竟 *adv.*	畢竟	after all

子明：是啊，如果我是一个穷人，我也希望自己的经济条件更好一些，环境好不好就不那么重要了。

李伟：所以我们要从两个方面入手。但是也不能只重视经济发展，而忽视了环境问题。环境污染已经对所有人的生活造成了很大的困扰。大家再不正视环境污染问题，我们的健康就会受到很大的影响。

子明：是啊，现在北京对私家车已经采取尾号限行 措施，也是为了减少汽车废气排放吧。现在也鼓励大家都坐公共交通出行，减少碳排放。

李伟：这些还不够，要想真正改变环境的现状，一定要从根本上解决环境污染和经济发展的矛盾，找一个平衡点。

子明：嗯，我们还可以采访一些人，了解一下他们的观点。

李伟：这个想法很好，我们可以采访工人、普通北京市民、学生等等。

子明：好，我们就抓紧时间开始行动吧，再不开始就做不完了。下周就要交作业了！

qióngrén 穷人 *n.*	窮人	poor people
tiáojiàn 条件 *n.*	條件	condition
hūshì 忽视 *v.*	忽視	neglect, overlook
kùnrǎo 困扰 *v.*	困擾	trouble, bother
zài 再 *adv.*		*(used to indicate the continuation of a situation or inaction)*
zhèngshì 正视 *v.*	正視	face up to *(a problem, challenge, etc.)*
sījiāchē 私家车 *n.*	私傢車	private car
cáiqǔ 采取 *v.*	採取	adopt
wěihào xiànxíng 尾号限行 *phr.*	尾號限行	limiting car usage according to license plate numbers
cuòshī 措施 *n.*		measure, step
xiànzhuàng 现状 *n.*	現狀	current state
gēnběn 根本 *n.*		foundation, base
jiějué 解决 *v.*	解決	resolve
máodùn 矛盾 *n.*		conflict
cáifǎng 采访 *v.*	採訪	interview
zhuājǐn 抓紧 *phr.*	抓緊	firmly grasp

再…就… can be used to express a warning. 再 is placed in the first clause to indicate the continuation of a situation or inaction; 就 is placed in the second clause to state the consequence if the situation or inaction persists.

Examples: ❶ 你再熬夜，身体就会吃不消了。

❷ 你再不吃药，病就会越来越难治了。

❸ 我们再不鼓励低碳生活，全球变暖的问题就会更加严重了。

❹ 我们再不保护环境，世界上的污染问题就无法解决了。

Try This!

1. Look at the following pictures of problems in the environment. Make a sentence for each picture indicating the consequence if the problem is <u>not</u> addressed. Use 再…就… to make the sentences.

Example: 我们再不解决饮用水污染的问题，就没有干净的水喝了。

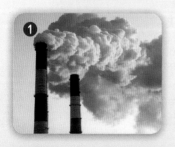

2. With reference to Exercise 2 in Step 1A about a friend who is addicted to the Internet or a technological gadget, role play a scenario with a partner in which one of you is the friend who is addicted and another of you tries to warn him/her by highlighting the consequences if he/she continues to indulge in the Internet or technological gadget. Use 再⋯就⋯ in your role play and make sure there are at least five exchanges in your role play.

Example:

A: 你不要再玩电子游戏了！

B: 别管我！我就喜欢玩！

A: 你再玩下去，健康就会受到影响。

B: 我现在人好好的，一点事都没有。

A: 你再不停止，就会让很多人为你担心。

B: 我真的没事！你别小题大做！

A: 你再这样下去，你的学习成绩就会越来越糟。

Below is an article that Ding Qiang wrote for the school magazine on his opinion on the problems of urban living and possible solutions.

天哪！机场高速又堵住了。在北京我遇到最大的困扰就是交通不便。不是因为北京的交通设施不完善，而是因为北京的车辆实在太多了，每天堵车，哪里都堵车。我觉得北京必须改变现状，要不然交通拥挤问题会更加严重。

昨天，王叔叔下班开车回家花了整整两个小时。短短几公里的路却要花这么多时间，开车还不如走路快呢！白天工作已经很累了，晚上还堵在路上。李阿姨建议王叔叔每天早点下班，要不每天都会堵在路上。

除了交通拥堵，空气污染也是一个大问题。为了尽快推动低碳生活，北京已经限制工厂的废气排放，大工厂也已经迁到外地了。希望这能够改善空气污染的情况。

解决这两个问题的一个好办法是控制车辆。首先，车辆的废气排放是空气污染的一个重要原因，控制私家车出行，比如单双号限行，或者控制车辆购买，都是可行的办法。第二，控制车辆也可以改善交通。

gāosù 高速 *n.*		highway
shèshī 设施 *n.*	設施	facilities
wánshàn 完善 *adj.*		perfect
chēliàng 车辆 *n.*	車輛	cars
yàobùrán 要不然 *conj.*		if not, or else, otherwise
zhěngzhěng 整整 *adv.*		whole, full
jìnkuài 尽快 *adv.*	儘快	as quickly as possible
xiànzhì 限制 *v.*		restrict, limit
qiān 迁 *v.*	遷	move, shift
qíngkuàng 情况 *n.*		condition, state
bànfǎ 办法 *n.*	辦法	solution
kòngzhì 控制 *v.*		control
dān 单 *adj.*	單	single, odd
shuāng 双 *adj.*	雙	even
kěxíng 可行 *adj.*		viable, feasible

The conjunction 要不(然) means "if not, or else, otherwise." It is used in the second clause to indicate a consequence, usually negative, if the condition in the first clause is not fulfilled. 然 may be omitted without changing the meaning.

Examples:

❶ 你要按时做功课，要不然你这门课的考试成绩一定会不理想。

❷ 我们必须改善地铁系统，要不交通拥挤问题会更加严重。

❸ 我们要尽快推动低碳生活，要不全球变暖就会带来更多问题。

CULTURAL HIGHLIGHTS

The Chinese Government's Response to Pollution

Because of huge industrial growth in China from the 1970s onward, there has been a large increase in air and water pollution. This is causing many Chinese people in both the public and private sectors to become concerned since studies have shown that pollution has caused an increase in lung cancer, heart attacks, and asthma.

In February 2014, the national government of China began to take action by offering over $1.65 billion to any cities and regions that make "significant progress" in controlling air pollution. They have also made it mandatory that all local governments lower the PM 2.5 index. (PM 2.5 refers to the particles, or particulate matter, that are tiny particles or droplets in the air with a width of 2 ½ microns or less.)

The national government also created a 10-year plan to curb groundwater pollution that had made tap water undrinkable and was the cause of a number of cancers. The plan calls for having monitoring systems in place and supervising the disposal of sources of pollution like garbage and industrial waste.

Although many people welcome the control measures against pollution, the enforcement has had some negative economic consequences. For example, in Sichuan's rural industrial sector, where some factories were closed, there was a loss of jobs, a decrease in tax revenue, and a decline in the city's operating budget.

1. Discuss with a partner the urban issues that you are facing in the place you live. List five of them and make a sentence for each to indicate what actions should be taken and the consequences if the actions are not taken. Use 要不 (然) in your sentences.

> *Example:* 我们应该减少汽车废气排放，要不然空气污染问题
> 会更加严重。

2. Choose the correct phrases to fill in the blanks to make the passage meaningful.

> 如果⋯就⋯   再(不)⋯就⋯   ⋯要不然⋯

昨天张健和丁强一起等地铁，没想到地铁排队的人那么多，

_____知道地铁人那么多，他们_____打车回家了。可是

已经进了地铁站，他们也没办法了。正好遇上下班高峰期，好

几趟车都满满的，他们怎么都挤不上去。丁强说："_____

挤上车，我们今天_____别想回家了！"可是人实在太多了，

_____等下一班_____太晚了，张健说："我们还是出去打

车吧！"丁强说："这个时候打车也肯定会堵，我们还是再等等

吧。下一班来的时候，我们得使劲挤上去，_____我们会很晚

才到家！"唉，_____改善交通状况，在北京生活_____不

方便了！

3. Answer questions 1–3 according to the passage on page 278 (Exercise #2) and questions 4–7 based on your own situation.

❶ 张健和丁强为什么不打车回家？　　❷ 地铁太挤，张健有什么建议？

❸ 张健和丁强最后决定采用什么交通工具回家？

❹ 如果你是张健和丁强，你会怎么做？为什么？

❺ 你住的地方有没有公共交通设施？要是有的话，请说一说你们那里的公共交通设施情况。人多不多？挤不挤？

❻ 要是你住的地方没有公共交通设施的话，你们那里的交通情况怎么样？堵车吗？

❼ 比较一下自己开车出行和采用公共交通设施出行的好处和坏处。

The Chinese Subway System

China has increased its subway system extensively over the past 15 years. The Beijing Subway opened in 1969 and is the oldest metro system in mainland China. Its ridership averages over nine million people a day. On December 28, 2014, the Beijing Subway switched from a fixed-fare to a distance-based fare system for all lines except the Airport Express. Fares start at ¥3 for a trip up to 6 km (3.7 miles); for a trip between 6 and 12km (3.7 to 7.5 miles), it costs ¥4; between 12 and 22km (7.5 to 13.7 miles), it costs ¥5; between 22 and 32km (13.7 to 20 miles), it costs ¥6. An additional ¥1 is charged for every extra 20 km (12.4 miles) if the distance exceeds 32 km (20 miles). For example, a 40 km (24.9 miles) trip would cost ¥7.

To take the Beijing Subway, passengers can purchase single-ride tickets or the *Yikatong* (一卡通) fare card, which is an integrated circuit card that stores credit for the subway, urban and suburban buses, and for other purchases. There are ticket counters or vending machines in every station for passengers to purchase tickets or add credit to the *Yikatong* card.

The Shanghai Metro System is the world's largest rapid transit system by route length and has the second largest number of stations. There are 14 lines and 337 stations totaling 548 kilometers (341 miles) of track. It is second only to Beijing in ridership with an average of eight million people using the system daily. Similar to the Beijing Subway, the Shanghai Metro uses a distance-based fare schedule. For most lines, the base fare is ¥3 for journeys under 6 km (3.7 miles), then ¥1 for each additional 10 km (6.2 miles). In addition to a single-ride ticket, fares can be paid using a Shanghai public transport card, which can be purchased at selected banks, convenience stores, and metro stations with a ¥20 deposit. This card can be loaded at ticket booths and service centers at the metro stations as well as many convenience stores and banks throughout the city.

A Having fond memories of China

子明：丁强，时间过得好快，你来中国已经一年了。你对中国的印象怎么样？

丁强：<u>自从</u>来到中国，我就越来越喜欢这里的<u>风土人情</u>了。<u>亲眼</u>看到了长城、故宫和天安门广场，和你们一起参观了国家博物馆，欣赏了著名的国画。自从去了国博，我也开始练习书法，进步很大呢！

子明：看来你在中国学到了很多！

丁强：是啊，自从来到北京，我就爱上了这里的<u>繁华</u>与活力。有时候宁可晚点儿回家吃饭，也要去前门或者后海转转。而且，在北京，我也可以继续健身。

子明：其实我从你身上也学到了很多。

丁强：是吗？哈哈，你从我身上学到了什么？

zìcóng 自从 prep.	自從	since
fēngtǔ rénqíng 风土人情 phr.	風土人情	local conditions and customs
qīnyǎn 亲眼 adv.	親眼	with one's own eyes, personally
fánhuá 繁华 adj.	繁華	flourishing, bustling

子明：自从认识你，我也开始健身了，身体
　　　健壮了不少。还有，几个月前我和
　　　妈妈有矛盾，她说我成绩退步了，不
　　　许我再唱歌。当时我听了你的建议，
　　　多和她沟通，现在她比较理解我对
　　　音乐的爱好，也慢慢接受了我想当
　　　歌手的愿望。是你让我学到了沟通的
　　　重要性。

丁强：嗯，能帮助你我也很高兴！时间过得
　　　这么快，我很舍不得离开中国。

子明：我们也舍不得让你离开。

jiànzhuàng 健壮 adj.	健壮	physically strong
lǐjiě 理解 v.		understand, comprehend
shěbude 舍不得 v.	捨不得	cannot bear to

LANGUAGE FOCUS

The preposition 自从 means "since" and is used to indicate a time or event in the past and a situation that has continued from then until now. 自从 can be used together with nouns that express the year, month, and date, or with noun phrases, verbs, and clauses to make a prepositional phrase. 自从 is normally placed at the beginning of a sentence.

Examples:　❶ 自从春节以后，我就没有再见到他。

❷ 自从我来到北京，我就爱上了炸酱面。

❸ 自从他有了微信，他天天都在朋友圈里晒照片。

❹ 自从上了中国历史课，我就一直想去中国，亲眼
　　看看长城和故宫。

❺ 自从认识了丁强，张健的英语就越说越好了。

Try This!

1. Working in pairs, tell your partner about the changes you have encountered or the progress you have made since you started learning Chinese. Create at least five sentences in your description. Use 自从 in your sentences.

   Example:

   > 自从我开始学中文，我就越来越喜欢中国文化了。中国国画和书法都非常有美感，京剧也很有意思。自从看了徐悲鸿的画，我就对国画非常感兴趣，还报名参加了国画班。学习国画不容易，但我却学得很开心。现在我的国画画得很不错呢！

2. Read the following paragraph and answer the questions in complete sentences.

   > 去年十一假期，我去了西安，亲眼领略了十三朝古都
   > $\overset{\text{lǐnglüè}}{}$ $\overset{\text{cháo}}{}$
   > appreciate dynasty
   > 西安的风土人情。西安既有大城市的繁华，也有古都的历史感。看起来，西安的市中心并不是很繁华，但是其实鼓楼中心充满了活力。如果到市中心转转就会发现有很多有特色的西安美食，非常好吃！自从我来到西安，我就一直吃个不停。当然，我也去参观了著名的历史古迹，比如
   > $\overset{\text{Qín Shǐhuáng bīngmǎyǒng}}{}$
   > 西安的秦始皇兵马俑，还去爬了华山。西安真的是一个既
   > Emperor Qin Terracotta Army
   > 有好吃的又有好玩的地方。我还真舍不得离开呢！

   ❶ 作者对西安的总体评价是什么？
   review

   ❷ 作者认为西安的特点是什么？

   ❸ 作者最喜欢西安哪一点？

   ❹ 作者去了哪些地方？

   ❺ 为什么作者舍不得离开西安？

   ❻ 要是你去西安，你会去看什么名胜古迹？

   ❼ 你知道西安有哪些有名的食品吗？

Below is an essay written by Ding Qiang during his Chinese writing class on his thoughts about the student exchange program that is coming to an end as well as his future dreams and aspirations.

很快就要离开北京回美国了。自从来到中国，我每天遇到的都是<u>新鲜</u>的<u>事物</u>，每天都能感受到中国的文化和风土人情。北京经济发展<u>迅速</u>、社会<u>繁荣</u>，又这么充满活力，我希望自己将来能在北京发展。

在北京生活的这一年对我影响非常大，也改变了我的很多想法。我决定回到美国以后，<u>报考</u>大学的经济<u>系</u>。读<u>本科</u><u>阶段</u>，除了完成学业、拿到学位，我还要继续学习中文。我打算<u>选修</u>中文课，希望能提高关于<u>商务</u>中文的沟通技巧。等拿到<u>学位</u>，希望我的中文水平能更上一层楼，这样我就可以回到北京。中国正在迅速发展，我希望将来可以在这里工作。

我的<u>志向</u>是做跟中美<u>贸易</u>有关的工作，这样的工作对<u>业务</u>能力和中文水平的要求都很高，我会继续努力，在未来四到五年内，<u>实现</u>自己的理想。

xīnxiān 新鲜 *adj.*	新鮮	fresh
shìwù 事物 *n.*		things
xùnsù 迅速 *adj.*		rapid, fast
fánróng 繁荣 *adj.*	繁榮	prosperous
bàokǎo 报考 *v.*	報考	apply for *(college)*
xì 系 *n.*	係	department, faculty
běnkē 本科 *n.*		undergraduate studies
jiēduàn 阶段 *n.*	階段	stage, phase
xuǎnxiū 选修 *v.*	選修	take an elective
shāngwù 商务 *n.*	商務	business
xuéwèi 学位 *n.*	學位	academic degree
zhìxiàng 志向 *n.*		aspiration
màoyì 贸易 *n.*	貿易	trade
yèwù 业务 *n.*	業務	profession, vocation
shíxiàn 实现 *v.*	實現	realize, fulfil

希望, 打算, and 决定 are verbs that express intent. 希望 indicates one's hopes, 打算 expresses one's plans, and 决定 states one's decisions. These verbs are often used immediately after the subject in the sentence.

Examples: ❶ 我特别喜欢学中文，我希望暑假能去中国留学。

❷ 中国正在迅速发展，我希望将来可以在这里工作。

❸ 今年暑假，我打算去北京旅行。

❹ 毕业以后，我打算在信息业工作。

❺ 我很想念父母，我决定寒假回家看他们。

❻ 我决定继续留在这里学中文。

Try This!

1. Complete the following sentences by using 打算, 决定, or 希望.

❶ 北京的经济发展迅速，有很多工作机会，_____。

❷ 最近学习太忙了，虽然我很喜欢看电影，但是，_____。

❸ 现在六点半，正是北京的下班高峰期，_____。

❹ 从现在开始我要努力学中文，_____。

❺ 虽然我很想念在美国的父母，但是_____。

❻ 他宁可对着电脑一整天，_____。

❼ _____，而我则打算去餐馆吃饭。

❽ 如果明天还是有雾霾，_____。

❾ 明年北京会举办铁人三项比赛，_____？

❿ 最近胖了很多，也老是生病，_____。

2. Read the following passage and answer the questions in complete sentences.

每个人在不同时期都要完成不同的目标，也需要做出不同的选择。大学生的目标就是完成学业、拿到学位，可是，这并不是最终的目的。本科毕业以后，有的人选择继续申请研究生项目，有的人选择出国留学，有的人选择直接就业，还有的人选择自己创业。怎么做选择也是一个需要认真考虑的事情。

<small>zuìzhōng final · shēnqǐng apply · xiàngmù project · chuàngyè set up a business</small>

以前，很多中国的家长希望自己的孩子毕业以后能做公务员，认为公务员是铁饭碗；也有家长希望孩子能去国企工作，因为国企的薪酬更高。但是，现在中国家长的观念也改变了，他们开始尊重孩子的志向和选择。所以，很多父母并不干涉孩子的选择，而是继续支持和鼓励孩子。

<small>gōngwùyuán civil servant · tiěfànwǎn iron rice bowl · guóqǐ state-owned enterprise · xīnchóu salary · zūnzhòng respect · gānshè interfere</small>

❶ 短文的第一段主要说了什么？
❷ 第一段中举出了哪几个本科毕业后的选择？
❸ 为什么过去很多中国父母希望孩子去做公务员或者去国企？
❹ 现在中国家长的观念有了什么样的改变？
❺ 你对自己未来的发展是怎样打算的？请谈谈你的理想。

China's Future Developments

As the Chinese economy has grown tremendously in the past 20 years to become the world's second largest economy, China has realized that it needs to create a new, innovative model of development to keep moving forward. In order to do so, it will need to focus on the following: addressing the problem of dwindling cheap labor supply, increasing exports to maintain economic growth, and creating new sources of energy for its industries. The government's new economic policy plans to focus on domestic consumption, equality of income, and technological innovations. Emphasis will also be placed on environmental protection and conservation. These future developments aim to improve all aspects of Chinese life.

Step Up!

Read the following five pieces of advice from the commencement speech by Wang Enge (王恩哥), president of Peking University, given in 2014 and complete the following related tasks.

建议一：
结交两个朋友

一个是运动场，一个是图书馆。

到运动场锻炼身体，强健体魄 (tǐpò, body)；到图书馆博览群书 (bólǎn, read widely)，不断地 "充电" (chōng, charge)、"放电" (fàng, discharge)、"蓄电" (xù, conserve)。

建议二：
培养两种 "功夫"

一种是本分 (běnfèn, duty)，一种是本事。

做人需本分，做事靠本事。"两本" 起家靠得住。

建议三：
乐于吃 "两样东西"

一个是吃亏 (chīkuī, suffer losses)，一个是吃苦 (chīkǔ, endure hardship)。

做人不怕吃亏，做事不怕吃苦。吃亏是福，吃苦也是福。

建议四：
插上两个 "翅膀" (chìbǎng, wings)

一个叫理想，一个叫毅力。

如果一个人有了这两个 "翅膀"，他就能飞得高，飞得远。

建议五：
追求两个 "极致" (jízhì, ultimate attainment)

一个是把自己的潜力 (qiánlì, potential) 发挥 (fāhuī, bring into play) 到极致，一个是把自己的健康寿命延长 (yáncháng, extend) 到极致。

Source: http://singjinghua.blog.163.com/blog/static/1337613612013979315882/

1. Answer the following questions based on the speech by Wang Enge.

　❶ Write one sentence in Chinese to describe the main idea of this message.

　❷ 王恩哥校长提到的要结交的两个朋友是什么？

　❸ 王恩哥校长说要"到图书馆博览群书，不断地'充电'、'放电'、
　　'蓄电'"。你认为"充电"、"放电"和"蓄电"指的是什么？

　❹ 王恩哥校长说"做人需本分，做事靠本事。"你怎么理解"本分"和
　　"本事"？

　❺ 王恩哥校长说"吃亏是福，吃苦也是福"。你觉得他说得对吗？为什么？

　❻ 王恩哥校长认为什么样的人"能飞得高，飞得远"？

　❼ 王恩哥校长要大家追求的两个"极致"是什么？你同意他的说法吗？
　　为什么？

2. In his commencement speech, President Wang Enge gave 10 pieces of advice to the 2014 graduates of Peking University. The above passage shows five of the recommendations. How would you rank the importance of those five recommendations? Compare your rankings with those of one of your classmates. You should be able to explain the reasons for your ranking and find out as much as possible about your classmate's reasons for his/her ranking. Did any of his advice surprise you? Discuss with a classmate whether he/she found any part of the speech surprising. Again, be ready to explain your reasons.

3. Conduct research into some of the famous commencement speeches that have been given at American universities. Choose one American commencement speech and look for the similarities and differences between the Chinese speech you have just read and the American speech you found. Write a blog entry or a Facebook post to explain what you have learned from the two commencement speeches, compare their similarities and differences, investigate the cultural perspectives that might have caused those similarities and differences, and reflect on how the advice from the two speeches will help to guide you in your study, work, and future life.

Fun Time!

The Chinese dream (中国梦) is a term popularized after 2013 that describes a set of personal and national ideals in China. Below are four posters that illustrate the role of the individual in fulfilling the Chinese dream. Read the text in each poster and exchange opinions with your partner about your American dream (美国梦).

I have learned...

NEW WORDS

Verbs

依赖	依賴	yīlài	depend on, rely on	困扰	困擾	kùnrǎo	trouble, bother
自拍		zìpāi	take a selfie	正视	正視	zhèngshì	face up to (a problem, challenge, etc.)
交流		jiāoliú	interact	采取	採取	cáiqǔ	adopt
输入	輸入	shūrù	enter, key in	解决	解決	jiějué	resolve
查询	查詢	cháxún	inquire	采访	採訪	cáifǎng	interview
点评	點評	diǎnpíng	review	限制		xiànzhì	restrict, limit
回复	回復	huífù	reply	迁	遷	qiān	move, shift
摇	搖	yáo	shake	控制		kòngzhì	control
抢	搶	qiǎng	snatch	理解		lǐjiě	understand, comprehend
面临	面臨	miànlín	be faced with, be confronted with	舍不得	捨不得	shěbude	cannot bear to
入手		rùshǒu	start with, proceed from	报考	報考	bàokǎo	apply for (college)
导致	導致	dǎozhì	lead to, result in	选修	選修	xuǎnxiū	take an elective
忽视	忽視	hūshì	neglect, overlook	实现	實現	shíxiàn	realize, fulfil

Nouns

外卖	外賣	wàimài	take out	优点	優點	yōudiǎn	strength, advantage
社交		shèjiāo	social contact	日记	日記	rìjì	diary
屏幕		píngmù	screen	道理		dàolǐ	sense, truth
目的地		mùdìdì	destination	课题	課題	kètí	topic
周边	周邊	zhōubiān	nearby, surrounding	机遇	機遇	jīyù	opportunity
师傅	師傅	shìfu	(respectful form of address for a skilled worker)	雾霾	霧霾	wùmái	smog
乘客		chéngkè	passenger	生态	生態	shēngtài	ecology
低头族	低頭族	dītóuzú	phone addicts	观点	觀點	guāndiǎn	perspective, point of view
点滴	點滴	diǎndī	bits of information	穷人	窮人	qióngrén	poor people
时代	時代	shídài	era	条件	條件	tiáojiàn	condition

私家车	私傢車	sījiāchē	private car	事物		shìwù	things
措施		cuòshī	measure, step	系	係	xì	department, faculty
现状	現狀	xiànzhuàng	current state	本科		běnkē	undergraduate studies
根本		gēnběn	foundation, base	阶段	階段	jiēduàn	stage, phase
矛盾		máodùn	conflict	商务	商務	shāngwù	business
高速		gāosù	highway	学位	學位	xuéwèi	academic degree
设施	設施	shèshī	facilities	志向		zhìxiàng	aspiration
车辆	車輛	chēliàng	cars	贸易	貿易	màoyì	trade
情况		qíngkuàng	condition, state	业务	業務	yèwù	profession, vocation
办法	辦法	bànfǎ	solution	贸易	貿易	màoyì	trade

Adjectives

神		shén	brilliant, smart	可行		kěxíng	viable, feasible
片面		piànmiàn	one-sided, lopsided	繁华	繁華	fánhuá	flourishing, bustling
完整		wánzhěng	complete	健壮	健壯	jiànzhuàng	physically strong
完善		wánshàn	perfect	新鲜	新鮮	xīnxiān	fresh
单	單	dān	single, odd	迅速		xùnsù	rapid, fast
双	雙	shuāng	even	繁荣	繁榮	fánróng	prosperous

Adverbs

几乎	幾乎	jīhū	almost	整整		zhěngzhěng	whole, full
毕竟	畢竟	bìjìng	after all	尽快	儘快	jìnkuài	as quickly as possible
再		zài	*(used to indicate the continuation of a situation or inaction)*	亲眼	親眼	qīnyǎn	with one's own eyes, personally

Conjunctions

宁可	寧可	nìngkě	would rather	则	則	zé	*(used to indicate contrast)*
甚至		shènzhì	even to the extent that	要不然		yàobùrán	if not, or else, otherwise
而		ér	but, on the other hand				

Preposition

自从	自從	zìcóng	since

Pronoun

如何		rúhé	how

Phrases

点赞	點讚	diǎnzàn	to "like" (on social media)
面对面	面對面	miànduìmiàn	face to face
接单	接單	jiēdān	receive an order
罪魁祸首	罪魁禍首	zuì kuí huò shǒu	culprit
尾号限行	尾號限行	wěihào xiànxíng	limiting car usage according to license plate numbers
抓紧	抓緊	zhuājǐn	firmly grasp
风土人情	風土人情	fēngtū rénqíng	local conditions and customs

  SENTENCE PATTERNS

有的人宁可在家里和朋友网上聊天，<u>也不</u>愿意出门和朋友面对面交流。

面对面有面对面的优点，<u>而</u>微信聊天<u>则</u>有微信聊天的好处。

大家<u>再</u>不正视环境污染问题，我们的健康<u>就</u>会受到很大的影响。

北京必须改变现状，<u>要不然</u>交通拥挤问题会更加严重。

<u>自从</u>来到中国，我<u>就</u>越来越喜欢这里的风土人情了。

我<u>希望</u>将来可以在北京工作。

I can do!

Interpretive Communication

❑ I can read about some environmental issues and decipher their meaning.

❑ I can infer information from blogs.

❑ I can read and understand how new technology has changed lifestyles in China.

Interpersonal Communication

❑ I can discuss how new technology has changed lifestyles.

❑ I can converse about the use of social media in daily life.

❑ I can talk with others about my past and current experiences.

Presentational Communication

❑ I can describe my past and current experiences.

❑ I can compare and contrast opportunities and challenges in China and other countries.

❑ I can speak about the use of social media in daily life.

❑ I can express and explain in oral and written forms my current decisions and aspirations for the future.

Cultural Knowledge

❑ I can describe China's digital natives.

❑ I can talk about China's future developments including opportunities and challenges.

❑ I can explain how the government is dealing with pollution.

❑ I can talk about the subway systems in Beijing and Shanghai.

292

APPENDICES

补课 n.	補課	bǔkè	make up lesson; remedial lesson	49
部 m.w.		bù	*(used for movies)*	191
步步高 phr.		bù bù gāo	progressing step by step	219
步调 n.	步調	bùdiào	pace	155
部分 n.		bùfèn	part, section	71
不管…都…		bùguǎn...dōu...	no matter what...	161
不如 v.		bùrú	not as good as	241
部首 n.		bùshǒu	radical, compound of a character	243
步数 n.	步數	bùshù	number of steps	143
部位 n.		bùwèi	section	132
不虚此行 phr.	不虛此行	bù xū cǐ xíng	did not make a wasted trip	112
布置 v.	佈置	bùzhì	assign	64
布置 v.	佈置	bùzhì	decorate	219

C

猜灯谜 phr.	猜燈謎	cāi dēngmí	guess lantern riddles	219
采访 v.	採訪	cǎifǎng	interview	273
才能 n.		cáinéng	capability	255
才艺 n.	才藝	cáiyì	talent	75
采取 v.	採取	cǎiqǔ	adopt	273
彩灯 n.	彩燈	cǎidēng	colored lantern	219
采购 v.	採購	cǎigòu	purchase	52
参与 v.	參與	cānyù	join, participate	143
残疾 n.	殘疾	cánjí	disabled	48
灿烂 adj.	燦爛	cànlàn	brilliant, splendid	225
草书 n.	草書	cǎoshū	cursive script	244
测验 n.	測驗	cèyàn	test	77
层 m.w.	層	céng	level, story *(of a building)*	252
曾经 adv.	曾經	céngjīng	once, formerly	161
差距 n.		chājù	difference	191
差异 n.	差異	chāyì	difference	163
茶馆 n.	茶館	cháguǎn	teahouse	236
茶壶 n.	茶壺	cháhú	teapot	252
茶具 n.		chájù	tea set	236
查询 v.	查詢	cháxún	inquire	267
差 adj.		chà	bad	139
差不多 adj.		chàbuduō	about the same	112

常常/经常 adv.	常常/經常	chángcháng/jīngcháng	often	64
常见 adj.	常見	chángjiàn	commonly seen	68
长寿面 n.	長壽面	chángshòumiàn	longevity noodles	211, 212
场面 n.	場面	chǎngmiàn	scene	196
唱腔 n.		chàngqiāng	singing style	255
产品 n.	產品	chǎnpǐn	product	110
超过 v.	超過	chāoguò	exceed	109
超越 v.		chāoyuè	surpass	143
朝 prep.		cháo	towards, to	16
车辆 n.	車輛	chēliàng	cars	276
陈设 n.	陳設	chénshè	set up as a display, furnish	236
趁 prep.		chèn	take advantage of *(time, opportunity, etc.)*	103
成才 v.		chéngcái	become a useful person	80
成功 v.		chénggōng	to succeed	160
成绩 n.	成績	chéngjì	grade, result	67
成就感 n.		chéngjiùgǎn	sense of achievement	74
乘客 n.		chéngkè	passenger	267
承受 v.		chéngshòu	bear, withstand	80
成为 v.	成為	chéngwéi	become	35
成长 v.	成長	chéngzhǎng	grow	168
吃不消 phr.		chībùxiāo	unable to bear	157
充满 v.	充滿	chōngmǎn	be filled with	163
充实 adj.	充實	chōngshí	fulfilling	68
充足 adj.		chōngzú	sufficient	129
虫 n.	蟲	chóng	insect	240
崇拜 v.		chóngbài	adore, admire	255
重阳节 n.	重陽節	Chóngyáng Jié	Chongyang Festival	215, 216
抽出 v.		chōuchū	set aside *(time)*	243
丑 n.	醜	chǒu	painted-face role	255, 256
出 m.w.	齣	chū	*(used for plays, etc.)*	255
初 n.		chū	first *(in order)*	215
出发 v.	出發	chūfā	set off	252
出来 v.	出來	chūlai	come out	33
出去 v.		chūqu	go out	33
出席 v.		chūxí	attend	222
橱窗 n.	櫥窗	chúchuāng	display window	252
揣摩 v.		chuǎimó	try to figure out	249

传说 n.	傳說	chuánshuō	legend	216
传统 n.	傳統	chuántǒng	tradition	52
喘不过气 phr.	喘不過氣	chuǎn bú guò qì	breathless	154
创 v.	創	chuàng	break (a record)	180
创办 v.	創辦	chuàngbàn	set up, found	160
创作 n.; v.	創作	chuàngzuò	creative work, creation; create, produce	240
吹灭 phr.	吹滅	chuīmiè	blow off	209
春节 n.	春節	Chūn Jié	Spring Festival	215, 216
春联 n.	春聯	chūnlián	spring couplets	52
凑热闹 phr.	湊熱鬧	còu rènao	join in the fun	52
促销 n.	促銷	cùxiāo	promotion	92
村镇 n.	村鎮	cūnzhèn	villages and towns	184
措施 n.		cuòshī	measure, step	273
错误 n.	錯誤	cuòwù	mistake	161

D

答案 n.		dá'àn	answer	163
达到 v.	達到	dádào	reach	109
打八折 v.		dǎ bā zhé	give 20% discount	92
打扫卫生 phr.	打掃衛生	dǎsǎo wèishēng	clean up	48
大号 n.	大號	dàhào	size L	99
大家 pron.		dàjiā	everyone, all	35
大减价 n.	大減價	dàjiǎnjià	sale	112
大名鼎鼎 phr.		dà míng dǐng dǐng	renowned, well-known	240
大师 n.	大師	dàshī	master	236
大型 adj.		dàxíng	big scale	180
大学 n.	大學	dàxué	college, university	67
带 v.	帶	dài	bring	32
代表 v.		dàibiǎo	represent	160
单 adj.	單	dān	single, odd	276
担心 v.	擔心	dānxīn	worry	35
旦 n.		dàn	female roles	255, 256
倒 v.		dǎo	fall, topple	163
导购员 n.	導購員	dǎogòuyuán	personal shopper	109
导致 v.	導致	dǎozhì	lead to, result in	272
倒 adv.		dào	(indicating contrast)	158
到达 v.	到達	dàodá	arrive, reach	4

到位 adj.		dàowèi	satisfactory	241
道理 n.		dàolǐ	sense, truth	269
登高 v.		dēnggāo	climb a hill or mountain	219
等 v.		děng	wait	137
的确 adv.	的確	díquè	really, indeed	92
低头族 n.	低頭族	dītóuzú	phone addicts	269
抵抗力 n.		dǐkànglì	resistance to disease	129
弟弟 n.		dìdi	younger brother	40
地点 n.	地點	dìdiǎn	location	21
递给 phr.	遞給	dìgěi	to pass on	32
地摊 n.	地攤	dìtān	street stall	52
地坛 p.n.	地壇	Dìtán	Temple of Earth	52
地位 n.		dìwèi	status	255, 256
弟媳 n.		dìxí	sister-in-law, younger brother's wife	40
点 n.	點	diǎn	dot	243, 245
点滴 n.	點滴	diǎndī	bits of information	269
典礼 n.	典禮	diǎnlǐ	ceremony	225
点评 v.	點評	diǎnpíng	review	267
点赞 phr.	點讚	diǎnzàn	to "like" (on social media)	266
电视台 n.	電視臺	diànshìtái	TV station	180
电子商务 n.	電子商務	diànzǐ shāngwù	e-commerce	160
东方明珠塔 p.n.	東方明珠塔	Dōngfāng Míngzhū Tǎ	Oriental Pearl TV Tower	21
东晋 n.	東晉	Dōng Jìn	Eastern Jin Dynasty	249
栋 m.w.	棟	dòng	(used for houses, buildings, etc.)	163
动作 n.	動作	dòngzuò	movement, action	256
动作片 n.	動作片	dòngzuòpiàn	action movie	191, 192
抖空竹 phr.		dǒu kōngzhú	Chinese yo-yo	52, 53
都市 n.		dūshì	city	11
独白 n.	獨白	dúbái	monolog	255
独立思想 phr.	獨立思想	dúlì sīxiǎng	independent mind	168
独特 adj.	獨特	dútè	special, unique	186
端午节 n.	端午節	Duānwǔ Jié	Dragon Boat Festival	215, 216
锻炼 v.	鍛煉	duànliàn	train	68
对……来说	對……來說	duì...lái shuō	as for (person)	14
队长 n.	隊長	duìzhǎng	team captain	157
顿 m.w.	頓	dùn	(used for meals)	112
多 adv.		duō	much, so	9

多少钱 pron.	多少錢	duōshao qián	how much (money)	92

E

饿 adj.; v.	餓	è	hungry; go hungry	112
而 conj		ér	but, on the other hand	269
儿女子孙 phr.	兒女子孫	érnǚ zǐsūn	children and grandchildren	39
儿童 n.	兒童	értóng	children	211
儿子 n.	兒子	érzi	son	40
耳环 n.	耳環	ěrhuán	earring	96
而且 conj.		ěrqiě	and	68

F

发声 v.	發聲	fāshēng	project one's voice	255
发音 n.	發音	fāyīn	pronunciation	219
发展 v.; n.	發展	fāzhǎn	develop; development	80
发夹 n.	髮夾	fàjiā	hairpin	96
繁华 adj.	繁華	fánhuá	flourishing, bustling	280
繁荣 adj.	繁榮	fánróng	prosperous	283
凡是 adv.		fánshì	every, any, all	243
繁重 adj.		fánzhòng	heavy	77
反串 v.		fǎnchuàn	play opposite gender in a play	255
反对 v.	反對	fǎnduì	object	168
反抗 v.		fǎnkàng	resist, revolt	168
犯 v.		fàn	commit, make (a mistake)	161
方法 n.		fāngfǎ	method, way	255
方式 n.		fāngshì	way, pattern	195
方向 n.		fāngxiàng	direction	16
防治 v.		fángzhì	provide prevention and cure	139
放弃 v.	放棄	fàngqì	give up	161
放松 v.	放鬆	fàngsōng	relax	65
分 m.w.		fēn	cent, fractional unit of Chinese currency, equal to 1/100 of a yuan	92
分心 v.		fēnxīn	divert one's attraction	195
粉丝 n.	粉絲	fěnsī	fan (of a pop star, etc.)	184
丰富 adj.	豐富	fēngfù	rich	225
风格 n.	風格	fēnggé	style	186
风景 n.	風景	fēngjǐng	scenery	9
丰盛 adj.	豐盛	fēngshèng	sumptuous, rich	155

风土人情 phr.	風土人情	fēngtǔ rénqíng	local conditions and customs	280
服务 n.	服務	fúwù	service	109
辅导 v.; n.	輔導	fǔdǎo	coach; coaching	71
俯卧撑 n.	俯臥撐	fǔwòchēng	push-up	133
负担 n.	負擔	fùdān	burden	191
附近 n.		fùjìn	nearby	16
父亲 n.	父親	fùqīn	father	40
复杂 adj.	複雜	fùzá	complicated	39

G

改变 v.	改變	gǎibiàn	change	143
改善 v.		gǎishàn	improve, make better	191
赶 v.	趕	gǎn	rush through	126
感动 v.	感動	gǎndòng	be moved	188
感觉 v.	感覺	gǎnjué	feel	44
感人 adj.		gǎnrén	touching	192
感受 n.; v.		gǎnshòu	feeling; to feel	160
高考 n.		gāokǎo	college entrance exam	67
高速 n.		gāosù	highway	276
告诉 v.	告訴	gàosu	tell	65
歌词 n.	歌詞	gēcí	song lyrics	188
哥哥 n.		gēge	older brother	40
各 pron.		gè	each	132
根本 n.		gēnběn	foundation, base	273
根据 prep.	根據	gēnjù	according to, based on	243
更 adv.		gèng	even more	77
工地 n.		gōngdì	construction site	163
功夫片 n.		gōngfūpiàn	kungfu movie	191, 192
公平 adj.		gōngpíng	fair	163
公司 n.		gōngsī	company	132
公文包/公事包 n.		gōngwénbāo/ gōngshìbāo	briefcase	96
功效 n.		gōngxiào	effect, efficacy	140
沟通 v.	溝通	gōutōng	communicate	80
购物单 n.	購物單	gòuwùdān	shopping list	103
辜负 v.	辜負	gūfù	let down	80
姑父 n.		gūfù	uncle, father's sister's husband	40
姑妈 n.	姑媽	gūmā	aunt, father's sister	40

小心 adj.; v.		xiǎoxīn	careful; take care, look out	126
校队 n.	校隊	xiàoduì	school team	157
效果 n.		xiàoguǒ	result, effect	154
笑话 n.	笑話	xiàohua	joke	253
效率 n.		xiàolǜ	efficiency	154
写生 v.	寫生	xiěshēng	sketching from real life	236
写实 adj.	寫實	xiěshí	(of art style) realistic	240
写意 n.	寫意	xiěyì	spontaneous expression	240
写照 n.	寫照	xiězhào	portrayal	154
心急 adj.		xīnjí	anxious, impatient	243
辛苦 adj.		xīnkǔ	strenuous, laborious	65
新款 n.		xīnkuǎn	new design	95
新郎 n.		xīnláng	bridegroom	222
心理健康 phr.		xīnlǐ jiànkāng	mental health	168
新娘 n.		xīnniáng	bride	222
辛勤 adj.		xīnqín	industrious, hardworking	225
心情 n.		xīnqíng	feelings, mood	77
新人 n.		xīnrén	newly wedded couple	222
欣赏 v.	欣賞	xīnshǎng	appreciate	155
新鲜 adj.	新鮮	xīnxiān	fresh	283
心意 n.		xīnyì	regards	32
新颖 adj.	新穎	xīnyǐng	new and original, novel	109
信心 n.		xìnxīn	confidence	77
信用卡 n.		xìnyòngkǎ	credit card	92
行动 v.	行動	xíngdòng	move	126
行李车 n.	行李車	xínglǐ chē	luggage cart	5
行李提取处 n.	行李提取處	xínglǐ tíqǔ chù	baggage claim	5
行书 n.	行書	xíngshú	semi-cursive script	244
性别 n.		xìngbié	gender	255, 256
性格 n.		xìnggé	personality	255, 256
幸亏 adv.	幸虧	xìngkuī	luckily	157
性情 n.		xìngqíng	temperament	71
雄伟 adj.	雄偉	xióngwěi	grand	9
绣花 n.	繡花	xiùhuā	embroidery	105
秀丽 adj.	秀麗	xiùlì	beautiful, pretty	9
秀水街市场 p.n.	秀水街市場	Xiùshuǐjiē Shìchǎng	Silk Market	103
虚弱 adj.	虛弱	xūruò	weak	140

许 v.	許	xǔ	allow, permit	165
栩栩如生 phr.		xǔ xǔ rú shēng	have a life-like resemblance	236
许愿 phr.	許願	xǔyuàn	make a wish	211
宣布 v.	宣佈	xuānbù	announce	222
旋律 n.		xuánlǜ	melody	186
选拔赛 n.	選拔賽	xuǎnbásài	selection	137
选手 n.	選手	xuǎnshǒu	candidate	181
选修 v.	選修	xuǎnxiū	take an elective	283
选秀 v.	選秀	xuǎnxiù	talent-spotting	180
选择 v.; n.	選擇	xuǎnzé	choose; choice	35
学位 n.	學位	xuéwèi	academic degree	283
学习 v.	學習	xuéxí	learn	49
学业 n.	學業	xuéyè	studies	68
训练 v.	訓練	xùnliàn	train	157
迅速 adj.		xùnsù	rapid, fast	283

Y

压力 n.	壓力	yālì	pressure	65
哑铃 n.	啞鈴	yǎlíng	dumbbell	133
烟火 n.	煙火	yānhuǒ	fireworks	219
严格 adj.	嚴格	yángé	strict	80
延误 v.	延誤	yánwù	delay	4
沿着 prep.	沿著	yánzhe	along	16
演唱会 n.	演唱會	yǎnchànghuì	concert	186
眼光 n.		yǎnguāng	one's taste in fashion	95
眼花缭乱 phr.	眼花繚亂	yǎnhuā liáoluàn	bedazzled	52
演讲 v.	演講	yǎnjiǎng	give a speech	161
演讲稿 n.	演講稿	yǎnjiǎnggǎo	text of a speech	225
演艺大厅 n.	演藝大廳	yǎnyì dàtīng	performing arts theater	252
砚 n.	硯	yàn	ink stone	243, 244
阳历 n.	陽曆	yánglì	the Gregorian calendar	215
养 v.	養	yǎng	develop	74
仰卧起坐 n.	仰臥起坐	yǎngwò qǐzuò	sit ups	134
邀请 v.	邀請	yāoqǐng	invite	184
要求 v.		yāoqiú	request, expect	77
摇 v.	搖	yáo	shake	270
摇滚 n.	搖滾	yáogǔn	rock (music)	165

遥远 adj.	遙遠	yáoyuǎn	faraway, distant	163
要不然 conj.		yàobùrán	if not, or else, otherwise	276
业务 n.	業務	yèwù	profession, vocation	283
夜校 n.		yèxiào	night school	160
一…就…		yī…jiù…	once…then…, as soon as	21
依赖 v.	依賴	yīlài	depend on, rely on	266
一带 n.	一帶	yídài	area	16
一定 adv.		yídìng	fixed, specified	109
姨父 n.		yífù	aunt, mother's sister's husband	40
一定 adv.		yídìng	certainly, surely	110
一共 adv.		yígòng	in total	112
一律 adv.		yílǜ	all, without exception	92
姨妈 n.	姨媽	yímā	aunt, mother's sister	40
一片成名 phr.		yí piàn chéng míng	became famous because of a film	196
一切 pron.		yíqiè	everything	163
仪式 n.	儀式	yíshì	ceremony	222
以及 conj.		yǐjí	and	35
已经 adv.	已經	yǐjīng	already	14
以免 conj.		yǐmiǎn	in order to avoid, lest	195
一般 adv.		yìbān	normally	16
意见 n.	意見	yìjiàn	opinion, view	68
意境 n.		yìjìng	the mood of a work of art	196
毅力 n.		yìlì	willpower, tenacity	65
意志 n.		yìzhì	will	75
因此 conj.		yīncǐ	therefore, so	255
饮食 n.	飲食	yǐnshí	diet	129
引体向上 n.		yǐntǐ xiàngshàng	chin up	133
印象 n.		yìnxiàng	impression	184
樱花 n.	櫻花	yīnghuā	cherry blossom	16
影响力 n.	影響力	yǐngxiǎnglì	influence, impact	186
应付 v.	應付	yìngfù	to deal with, to cope with	64
应考 v.	應考	yìngkǎo	sit for examinations	80
拥堵 adj.	擁堵	yōngdǔ	congested	11
拥挤 adj.	擁擠	yōngjǐ	crowded	11
永远 adv.	永遠	yǒngyuǎn	forever	154
用功 adj.		yònggōng	diligent, hardworking	67
优点 n.	優點	yōudiǎn	strength, advantage	269

优美 adj.	優美	yōuměi	fine, graceful, beautiful	9
幽默 adj.		yōumò	humorous	195
优势 n.	優勢	yōushì	advantage	71
悠闲 adj.	悠閒	yōuxián	leisurely and carefree	155
优雅 adj.	優雅	yōuyǎ	graceful	256
忧郁 adj.	憂鬱	yōuyù	depressed	77
邮费 n.	郵費	yóufèi	freight cost	103
游览 v.	遊覽	yóulǎn	sightsee	9
尤其 adv.		yóuqí	especially	236
由于…所以…	由於…所以…	yóuyú…suǒyǐ…	because of, (so)…	80
有关 v.	有關	yǒuguān	have something to do with, relate to	184
友好 adj.		yǒuhǎo	friendly	35
有名 adj.		yǒumíng	famous	180
有趣 adj.		yǒuqù	interesting	35
有氧健身操 n.		yǒuyǎng jiànshēncāo	aerobics	134
有氧运动 n.	有氧運動	yǒuyǎng yùndòng	cardiovascular exercise, cardio	134
有意义 adj.	有意義	yǒu yìyì	meaningful	48
有用 adj.		yǒuyòng	useful	129
瑜伽 n.		yújiā	yoga	134
与 conj.	與	yǔ	and	80
与 prep.	與	yǔ	with	155
语文 n.	語文	yǔwén	the Chinese language	64
遇到 v.		yùdào	encounter, meet with, face	44
预祝 v.	預祝	yùzhù	wish, congratulate beforehand	225
愉快 adj.		yúkuài	happy	155
郁闷 adj.	鬱悶	yùmèn	depressed	160
豫园 p.n.	豫園	Yùyuán	Yu Garden	21
玉渊潭 p.n.	玉淵潭	Yùyuāntán	Yu Yuan Tan Park	16, 17
元/块 m.w.	元/塊	yuán/kuài	yuan, dollar	92
原价 n.	原價	yuánjià	original price	92
原来 adv.	原來	yuánlái	so that's how it is	67
元素 n.		yuánsù	element	103
元宵 n.		yuánxiāo	sweet dumpling	219
元宵节 n.	元宵節	Yuánxiāo Jié	Lantern Festival	215, 216
原因 n.		yuányīn	reason	180
愿望 n.		yuànwàng	wish	166
愿意 v.	願意	yuànyì	be willing to	181

Abbreviations for Parts of Speech

n.	noun	m.w.	measure word	conj.	conjunction
v.	verb	p.n.	proper noun	num.	numeral
adj.	adjective	pron.	pronoun	part.	particle
adv.	adverb	prep.	preposition	aux.v.	auxiliary verb

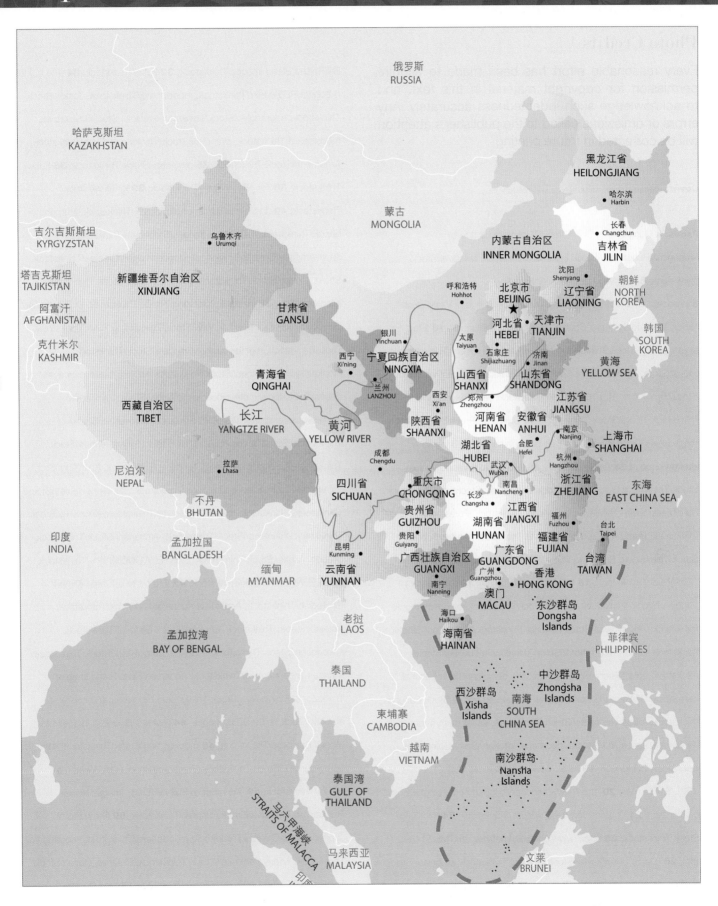

俄罗斯
RUSSIA

哈萨克斯坦
KAZAKHSTAN

黑龙江省
HEILONGJIANG

哈尔滨
Harbin

蒙古
MONGOLIA

吉尔吉斯斯坦
KYRGYZSTAN

乌鲁木齐
Urumqi

内蒙古自治区
INNER MONGOLIA

长春
Changchun

吉林省
JILIN

塔吉克斯坦
TAJIKISTAN

新疆维吾尔自治区
XINJIANG

沈阳
Shenyang

朝鲜
NORTH
KOREA

阿富汗
AFGHANISTAN

甘肃省
GANSU

呼和浩特
Hohhot

北京市
BEIJING ★

辽宁省
LIAONING

克什米尔
KASHMIR

银川
Yinchuan

河北省
HEBEI

天津市
TIANJIN

韩国
SOUTH
KOREA

太原
Taiyuan

西宁
Xi'ning

宁夏回族自治区
NINGXIA

石家庄
Shijiazhuang

济南
Jinan

黄海
YELLOW SEA

青海省
QINGHAI

兰州
LANZHOU

山西省
SHANXI

山东省
SHANDONG

西藏自治区
TIBET

长江
YANGTZE RIVER

黄河
YELLOW RIVER

西安
Xi'an

郑州
Zhengzhou

江苏省
JIANGSU

陕西省
SHAANXI

河南省
HENAN

安徽省
ANHUI

南京
Nanjing

上海市
SHANGHAI

尼泊尔
NEPAL

拉萨
Lhasa

成都
Chengdu

湖北省
HUBEI

合肥
Hefei

杭州
Hangzhou

不丹
BHUTAN

四川省
SICHUAN

重庆市
CHONGQING

武汉
Wuhan

南昌
Nancheng

浙江省
ZHEJIANG

东海
EAST CHINA SEA

印度
INDIA

孟加拉国
BANGLADESH

贵州省
GUIZHOU

长沙
Changsha

江西省
JIANGXI

福州
Fuzhou

台北
Taipei

缅甸
MYANMAR

云南省
YUNNAN

昆明
Kunming

贵阳
Guiyang

湖南省
HUNAN

广东省
GUANGDONG

福建省
FUJIAN

台湾
TAIWAN

广西壮族自治区
GUANGXI

广州
Guangzhou

香港
HONG KONG

孟加拉湾
BAY OF BENGAL

南宁
Nanning

澳门
MACAU

东沙群岛
Dongsha
Islands

菲律宾
PHILIPPINES

老挝
LAOS

海口
Haikou

海南省
HAINAN

泰国
THAILAND

西沙群岛
Xisha
Islands

中沙群岛
Zhongsha
Islands

南海
SOUTH
CHINA SEA

柬埔寨
CAMBODIA

越南
VIETNAM

南沙群岛
Nansha
Islands

泰国湾
GULF OF
THAILAND

马六甲海峡
STRAITS OF MALACCA

马来西亚
MALAYSIA

文莱
BRUNEI

Photo Credits

Every reasonable effort has been made to acquire permission for copyright material in this text, and to acknowledge such indebtedness accurately. Any errors or omissions called to the publisher's attention will be corrected in future printing.

Cover: Jupiterimages/Stockbyte/Thinkstock

Pages: 1 Hung Chung Chih/iStock/Thinkstock; **3** (t to b) KreangchaiRungfamai/iStock Editorial/Thinkstock, rasslava/iStock/Thinkstock; **5** pengyou91/iStock/Thinkstock; **6** sihasakprachum/iStock Editorial/Thinkstock; **8** (t to b) VitalyEdush/iStock/Thinkstock, Hung_Chung_Chih/iStock/Thinkstock; **10** (l to r, t to b) yangphoto/iStock/Thinkstock, Maxim Tupikov/Hemera/Thinkstock, chuyu/iStock/Thinkstock, Liufuyu/iStock/Thinkstock, Digital Vision/iStock/Thinkstock, zjpp163/iStock/Thinkstock, yangchao/iStock/Thinkstock, hxdyl/iStock/Thinkstock; **11** ChinaFotoPress/Stringer/Getty Image News/Getty Images; **14** (t to b) livechina/iStock/Thinkstock, fotokon/iStoch Editorial/Thinkstock; **15** (t to b, l to r) Vasiliki Varvaki/iStock/Thinkstock, silkwayrain/iStock/Thinkstock, Stockbyte/Thinkstock, Wavebreakmedia Ltd/Wavebreak Media/Thinkstock, Purestock/Thinkstock, Brand X Pictures/Stockbyte/Thinkstock, AndreyPopov/iStock/Thinkstock, Rudyanto Wijaya/iStock/Thinkstock, Eileen Bach/DigitalVision/Thinkstock; **16** http://map.baidu.com; **18** (l to r, t to b) bingdian/iStock/Thinkstock, axz66/iStock/Thinkstock, bingdian/iStock/Thinkstock, TkKurikawa/iStock Editorial/Thinkstock, gianliguori/iStock/Thinkstock, SeanPavonePhoto/iStock/Thinkstock, LuoJun/iStock/Thinkstock, aphotostory/iStock/Thinkstock, bingdian/iStock Editorial/Thinkstock, CQYoung/iStock Editorial/Thinkstock, axz66/iStock Editorial/Thinkstock, robert van beets/iStock/Thinkstock, VitalyEdush/iStock/Thinkstock, Jason_YU/iStock/Thinkstock, fotokon/iStock/Thinkstock, View Stock/Thinkstock; **19** http://www.onegreen.net/maps/HTML/51489.html; **20** http://www.tianciserviceapartmentshanghai.com/location.htm; **21** Thomas von Aesch/iStock/Thinkstock; **24** XiXinXing/iStock/Thinkstock; **25** http://www.onegreen.net/maps/HTML/51489.html; **26** (t to b) TkKurikawa/iStock Editorial/Thinkstock, bingdian/iStock/Thinkstock, gianliguori/iStock/Thinkstock; **30** Tetra Images - Rob Lewine/Getty Images; **31** (l to r) View Stock/Thinkstock, Plush Studios/Bill Reitzel/Blend Images/Thinkstock; **32** Fuse/Thinkstock; **34** (t to b, l to r) Zoonar RF/Zoonar/Thinkstock, moddboard/Thinkstock, JackF/iStock/Thinkstock, a-wrangler/iStock/Thinkstock, lofilolo/iStock/Thinkstock, moddboard/Thinkstock, cyano66/iStock/Thinkstock, Fuse/Thinkstock, Argument/iStock/Thinkstock; **35** ping han/iStock/Thinkstock; **36** Fuse/Thinkstock; **38** TongRo Images/Thinkstock; **39** Ignatiev/iStock/Thinkstock; **40** (t to b, l to r) imtmphoto/iStock/Thinkstock, imtmphoto/iStock/Thinkstock, Thinkstock Images/Stockbyte/Thinkstock, Jupiterimages/Creatas/Thinkstock, Jupiterimages/Creatas/Thinkstock, Stuart Jenner/iStock/Thinkstock, DragonImages/iStock/Thinkstock, XiXinXing/iStock/Thinkstock, XiXinXing/iStock/Thinkstock, Stuart Jenner/iStock/Thinkstock, Stuart Jenner/iStock/Thinkstock, Fuse/Thinkstock, Fuse/Thinkstock, monkeybusinessimages/iStock/Thinkstock, monkeybusinessimages/iStock/Thinkstock, monkeybusinessimages/iStock/Thinkstock, monkeybusinessimages/iStock/Thinkstock, monkeybusinessimages/iStock/Thinkstock, sunweitao/iStock/Thinkstock, Stuart Jenner/iStock/Thinkstock, Stuart Jenner/iStock/Thinkstock, Thinkstock Images/Stockbyte/Thinkstock, XiXinXing/iStock/Thinkstock, Catherine Yeulet/iStock/Thinkstock, Catherine Yeulet/iStock/Thinkstock, Thinkstock Images/Stockbyte/Thinkstock, XiXinXing/iStock/Thinkstock, XiXinXing/iStock/Thinkstock, vitchanan/iStock/Thinkstock, DragonImages/iStock/Thinkstock, SZE FEI WONG/iStock/Thinkstock, SZE FEI WONG/iStock/Thinkstock; **42** (l to r, t to b) Darrin Klimek/Photodisc/Thinkstock, Anastasiia Kucherenko/iStock/Thinkstock, Ablestock.com/Thinkstock, fotokon/iStock Editorial/Thinkstock, shironosov/iStock/Thinkstock, IPGGutenbergUKLtd/iStock/Thinkstock, Patrice Lange/Hemera/Thinkstock, Andersen Ross/Blend Images/Thinkstock, Kyslynskyy/iStock/Thinkstock, moddboard/Thinkstock, amoklv/iStock Editorial/Thinkstock; **44** Monkey Business Images Ltd/Money Business/Thinkstock; **45** mocker_bat/iStock/Thinkstock; **48** (t to b) mykeyruna/iStock/Thinkstock, Wavebreakmedia Ltd/Wavebreak Media/Thinkstock; **49** (l to r) Justin Sullivan/Getty Images News/Thinkstock, Photawa/iStock Editorial/Thinkstock; **50** (l to r, t to b) Jupiterimages/Creatas/Thinkstock, moodboard/Thinkstock, moodboard/Thinkstock, Andriy Petrenko/iStock/Thinkstock, Creative_Outlet/iStock/Thinkstock, Catherine Yeulet/iStock/Thinkstock, George Doyle/Stockbyte/Thinkstock, Mihajlo Maricic/iStock/Thinkstock,

Thinkstock, XiXinXing/iStock/Thinkstock, szefei/iStock/Thinkstock, Jupiterimages/Pixland/Thinkstock; **213** Jonathan Ross/Hemera/Thinkstock; **215** (t to b) Matt_Image/iStock/Thinkstock, WilliamJu/iStock/Thinkstock, Perry Svensson/iStock Editorial/Thinkstock; **216** (t to b) imtmphoto/iStock/Thinkstock, chinaview/iStock/Thinkstock, http://cn.hujiang.com/new/p538582; **219** Fuse/Thinkstock; **221** bonchan/iStock/Thinkstock; **222** (t to b) Asia Images Group/Getty images, Photowee/iStock/Thinkstock; **223** Norman Chan/iStock/Thinkstock; **224** Norman Chan/iStock/Thinkstock; **229** XiXinXing/iStock/Thinkstock; **234** 张择端/FOTOE; **235** (t to b, l to r) rasslava/iStock/Thinkstock, http://collection.sina.com.cn, Zoonar/A.Mijatovic/Zoonar/Thinkstock, La_Corivo/iStock/Thinkstock, Fuse/Thinkstock; **236** (l to r, t to b) https://en.wikipedia.org/wiki/Qi_Baishi, http://shuhua.baike.com/article-57774.html, http://arts.cultural-china.com/en/102Arts13009.html, http://qw.leshan.cn/ph/HTML/15697.html, http://www.chinesecio.com, http://qw.leshan.cn/ph/HTML/15254.html; **238** (t to b) http://www.mybeijingchina.com/beijing-attractions/798-art-district, http://www.mybeijingchina.com/beijing-attractions/798-art-district; **239** (t to b) https://en.wikipedia.org/wiki/Frederic_Remington#/media/File:Frederic_Remington.jpg, Photos.com/Thinkstock, http://www.chinesecio.com, http://qw.leshan.cn/ph/HTML/15254.html; **240** (t to b) https://en.wikipedia.org/wiki/Qi_Baishi, http://www.chinesecio.com; **241** (t to b, l to r) http://qw.leshan.cn/ph/HTML/15254.html, martateron/iStock/Thinkstock, kaewphoto/iStock/Thinkstock, kvasay/iStock/Thinkstock, yangzai/iStock/Thinkstock; **242** (l to r, t to b) ericb007/iStock/Thinkstock, cl2004lhy/iStock/Thinkstock, koosen/iStock/Thinkstock, Jupiterimages/Creatas/Thinkstock, Creatas Images/Creatas/Thinkstock, Wavebreakmedia Ltd/Wavebreak Media/Thinkstock, Medioimages/Photodisc/Photodisc/Thinkstock, TongRo Images/Thinkstock, Valentyn Volkov/Hemera/Thinkstock, Gabriel Bouvigne/iStock/Thinkstock, SZE FEI WONG/iStock/Thinkstock, Oleksiy Mark/iStock/Thinkstock, http://artsalesindex.artinfo.com/asi/lots/627897, http://qw.leshan.cn/ph/HTML/15254.html, **243** Lcc54613/iStock/Thinkstock, **246** http://www.diyad.cn/6ukufzv75ho; **248** (t to b) RyanKing999/iStock/Thinkstock, Svilen Georgiev/iStock/Thinkstock, View Stock/Thinkstock; **249** 文化传播/FOTOE; **250** http://blog.163.com/cuijing422@126/blog/static/75037500201242221012124; **251** Chunhai Cao/iStock/Thinkstock, savoia/iStock/Thinkstock;

252 (t to b) http://www.chinatourguide.com/beijing/tour_in_depth_Lao_She_Tea_house.html, https://www.google.com/search?q=lao+she+teahouse&newwindow=1&source=lnms&tbm=isch&sa=X&ved=0CAgQ_AUoAmoVChMIsrbRwYHByAIVwhY-Ch1xAAXf&biw=1366&bih=657#imgrc=bXiazB0XqDJDkM%3A; **253** (t to b) http://www.cits.net/china-guide/discover-china/crosstalk-tianjin.html, K-King Photography Media Co. Ltd/Photodisc/Thinkstock; **254** https://en.wikipedia.org/wiki/Lao_She; **255** http://www.china.org.cn/video/2009-02/18/content_17294069.htm; **258** (t to b) http://people.cs.nctu.edu.tw, http://www.szmuseum.com/default.php?mod=article&do=detail&tid=4889, Lisa F. Young/iStock/Thinkstock, omgimages/iStock/Thinkstock; **259** (t to b) 张择端/FOTOE, Fuse/Thinkstock; **264** bingdian/iStock/Thinkstock; **265** (l to r) Monkey Business Images Ltd/Monkey Business/Thinkstock, Stuart Jenner/iStock/Thinkstock, Monkey Business Images Ltd/Monkey Business/Thinkstock; **266** (t to b) XiXinXing/Thinkstock, dolgachov/iStock/Thinkstock; **267** wwwLifeonnanchangluCom; **269** (t to b) c8501089/iStock Editorial/Thinkstock, Jiann Jong Lim/iStock/Thinkstock, XiXinXing/Thinkstock; **270** szeyuen/iStock/Thinkstock; **271** http://p.gmw.cn/thread-339-1-1.html, **272** gkwt1/iStock/Thinkstock; **273** Aj_OP/iStock/Thinkstock; **274** (t to b, l to r) iStockphoto/Thinkstock, Mykhailo Shcherbyna/iStock/Thinkstock, yocamon/iStock/Thinkstock, budgetstockphoto/iStock/Thinkstock, Robin O'Connell/iStock/Thinkstock, Benjamin Goode/iStock/Thinkstock, durtyburty/iStock/Thinkstock; **275** zhang bo/iStock/Thinkstock; **276** Comstock/Stockbyte/Thinkstock; **277** (t to b) Guang Niu/Getty Images News/Thinkstock, Guang Niu/Getty Images News/Thinkstock; **279** Imran Ahmed/iStock Editorial/Thinkstock; **280** (t to b) XiXinXing/iStock/Thinkstock, luobin17/iStock/Thinkstock; **283** Ximagination/iStock/Thinkstock; **285** Sean Pavone/iStock/Thinkstock; **286** furtaev/iStock/Thinkstock; **287** (t to b) Purestock/Thinkstock, Mike Watson Images/moodboard/Thinkstock; **288** (t to b, l to r) Thammasak_Chuenchom/iStock/Thinkstock, http://www.wenming.cn/jwmsxf_294/zggygg/pml/zgmxl/index.shtml, http://www.wenming.cn/jwmsxf_294/zggygg/pml/zgmxl/index.shtml, http://www.wenming.cn/jwmsxf_294/zggygg/pml/zgmxl/index.shtml, http://www.wenming.cn/jwmsxf_294/zggygg/pml/zgmxl/index.shtml.